PATTERNS OF MARKET BEHAVIOR

BROWN UNIVERSITY BICENTENNIAL PUBLICATIONS

Studies in the Fields of General Scholarship

PATTERNS OF MARKET BEHAVIOR
Essays in Honor of Philip Taft

EDITED BY
Michael J. Brennan

BROWN UNIVERSITY PRESS
PROVIDENCE   RHODE ISLAND   1965

Designed by Willis A. Shell
Type set in Monotype 8A by The William Byrd Press, Inc.
Printed by The William Byrd Press, Inc. on Oxford English Finish.

PREFACE

In a review of his most recent book, Professor Philip Taft was described as "our most distinguished and able labor historian." For more than twenty-five years Philip Taft has enriched the lives of his students as well as the literature of economics. By the enthusiasm he communicates to students and colleagues alike, he has sparked and nourished ideas in others. The vigor of his criticism, no less than the warmth of his encouragement, has led many students to welcome the challenge of excellence.

His distinction as a scholar is reflected only in part by his outstanding books and articles in the field of labor economics. He has also served as president of the Industrial Relations Research Association and as associate editor of the journal *Labor History*. Perhaps more important, few men in this age of specialization have such broad interests and such deep knowledge of a variety of subjects—political theory, intellectual history, comparative economic systems, and philosophy.

The energy and learning of Philip Taft have benefited many outside the community of scholars. His activities include, among others, arbitration for the Federal Mediation and Conciliation Service, monitoring of labor union elections, consultation to the Department of Employment Security, testimony before the Joint Economic Committee of the United States Congress, and membership on the Labor Study Group of the Committee for Economic Development.

The thirteen essays in this volume are a tribute to Philip Taft on the occasion of his sixty-third birthday. They are contributed by his colleagues, former colleagues, and former students. Rather than attempting to prepare an essay in labor economics, each author has written in the area of his own interests and qualifications. The papers are divided into four main categories: commodity markets, resource markets, money markets, and international markets.

With a profound sense of admiration and affection, the contributors dedicate this volume to one who personifies the spirit of free inquiry.

M. J. BRENNAN

CONTENTS

PART I

COMMODITY MARKETS

On the Determination of Prices
in Futures Markets

Martin J. Beckmann[1]

THE relationship between various prices in a market with forward trading has been analyzed rather thoroughly in recent years. (See references.) But the problem of determining the level of prices is rather
less well understood.[2] The spot price in any given period will depend on
how much is carried over into the next period. This, in turn, depends on
the spot price in the next period, or on expectations concerning that
price. The problem has thus been advanced by one period. In principle,
what one would have to determine is an infinite sequence of prices and/
or expectations concerning these prices.

The thesis of this paper is that a well-determined relationship exists
between the stock of a commodity and its spot price; that this relationship can be determined recursively by considering just two periods;
and that some knowledge concerning this relationship is implicit in a
speculator's rational decision.

The problem arises whenever a commodity is storable and its supply
or demand is subject to random shocks. The classic case is that of an
agricultural crop commodity which is harvested once a year. Trading in
futures contracts does not add anything new to the problem; it is a
device to separate speculation from physical ownership of the commodity, thus reducing the capital requirements for speculation and so ex-
tending the set of persons who can be speculators. The analysis will
consider spot prices, futures prices, and expectations concerning next
year's spot prices. It will not go into institutional details or into the history of prices in the course of a crop year. Rather, we shall pretend that
the market meets once a year, when the crop is in, to determine spot
and futures prices, and that the futures contract specifies delivery after
the next harvest.

3

The first section spells out the various assumptions made. The second shows the determination of prices, when the supply of forward sales contracts by speculators is considered a given function of the "backwardation"—the difference between expected spot price and futures price. The third sketches an alternative approach in which decisions of speculators are based on maximizing the expected value of a quadratic utility function. It involves the variance as well as the expected value of the backwardation. While in principle exact solutions may be obtained by

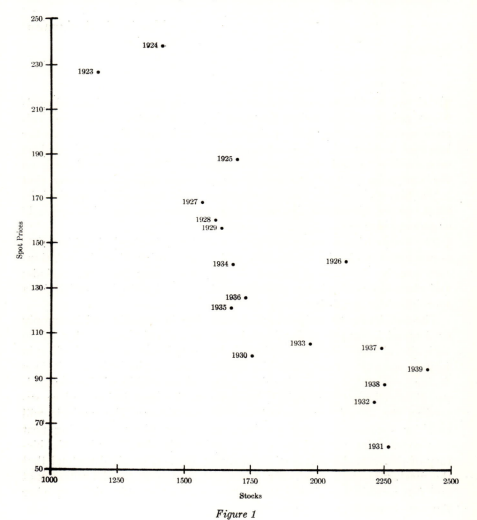

Figure 1

solving the nonlinear integral equation involved, this paper considers only approximate solutions to illustrate the determinateness of the relationships.

Figure 1 illustrates the relationship between stocks and spot prices for the case of cotton in the interwar period. No econometric analysis of the relationship, which according to this theory is nonlinear, has been attempted here.

THE MODEL

NOTATION

s = stock after harvest

$c(s)$ = marginal cost of storage for one year

p_s = spot price after harvest

p_N = spot price after the next harvest

p_F = futures price for delivery after the next harvest

$g(p_s)$ = demand for consumption

$m(p_s)$ = manufacturers' demand

$a = a[s, E(p_N - p_F)]$ = demand for hedges, or supply of forward sales contracts

$f(p_s)$ or $f(p_F)$ = planting for the next harvest

u = crop yield

$Q(u)$ = distribution of crop yield

v = utility function

w = wealth

r = rate of return on riskless assets

$p_s = \rho(s)$ = price determination function, the unknown of the problem.

(To avoid later misunderstanding, the stock s includes carryover, and the function ρ applies to stocks including carryover.)

ASSUMPTIONS

All relationships will be assumed linear unless specified otherwise.

Consumer demand is assumed to be a decreasing function of the spot price.

$$g = g(p_s) = g_0 + g_1 p_s \qquad g_1 < 0$$

Manufacturers' demand is assumed to be derived from and to be slightly in excess of consumers' demand.

$$m = m(p_s) = m_0 + m_1 p_s \qquad m_1 < 0$$

At high price levels, namely whenever carryover of other stock is zero, manufacturers' demand is assumed to be practically equal to consumers' demand. At any rate, the excess will be considered small enough in relation to average crop size to be neglected.

Marginal storage cost is an increasing function of total stocks.

$$c = c(s) = c_0 + c_1 s$$

Hedges. Owners of physical stock which is carried into the next period may hedge, i.e., sell forward part or all of their stock. To the extent that stock is not sold forward, the owner will be considered a speculator. He has concluded a fictitious futures sales contract with himself. The total volume of actual and fictitious forward sales contracts will then equal the volume of physical stock carried over into the next period. Our second approach will be in terms of this total while our first approach will be in terms of actual contracts only.

Supply of forward sales contracts. In our first approach the supply of forward sales contracts is assumed to come primarily from owners of physical stock demanding hedges. But not all stock will be hedged, the attractiveness of a hedge being dependent on the futures price and the expected value of next year's spot price; thus demand will be considered an increasing function of the amount of stock and a decreasing function of the expected value of the "backwardation"—the difference of expected spot price and futures price.

$$a = a[s, E(p_N - p_F)] = a_0 + a_1 s + a_2 E(p_N - p_F) \qquad a_1 > 0$$

$$a_2 < 0$$

In order to exclude a negative supply, the validity of this equation is restricted to:

$$|E(p_N - p_F)| < \frac{a_0 + a_1 s}{|a_2|}.$$

The demand for forward sales contracts is assumed to come from speculators who hope to gain from the backwardation. It is assumed to be an increasing function of the backwardation.

$$d = d_0 + d_1 E(p_N - p_F) \qquad d_1 > 0$$

Solving the condition that supply of forward sales contracts must equal demand, we have the statement:

(1) $$\qquad E(p_N - p_F) = b(s) = b_0 + b_1 s$$

where

$$b_0 = \frac{a_0 - d_0}{d_1 - a_2}, \qquad b_1 = \frac{a_1}{d_1 - a_2}, \qquad \text{so that} \quad b_1 > 0.$$

Supply of new crop. Plantings for next year are assumed to be an increasing function of the spot price or alternatively of the futures price. (Farmers could sell their crop forward, thus adding to the demand for forward sales contracts, but this possibility is not considered here in the determination of the backwardation.)

(2) $$f = f(p_s) = f_0 + f_1 p_s$$

or

$$f = f^*(p_F) = f_2 + f_3 p_F$$

The actual crop size is considered a random variable. It is the product of planting and yield u:

$$f(p_s) \cdot u.$$

Without restriction, let the expected value of the yield be one:

$$E(u) = 1.$$

ANALYSIS

The analysis is based on given supply and demand functions for physical stock and for forward sales contracts.

If in any year stocks are small—how small they have to be will be determined—then they will be consumed entirely in that year, or, more exactly, they will be absorbed by manufacturers. Prices are then determined by the condition that supply, the given stock, equal manufacturer's demand.

(3) $$s = m[p_s] = m[\rho(s)] = m_0 + m_1\rho(s)$$

Equation (3) should not be mistaken for a definition of ρ since it does not apply to large s when there is carryover. Hence,

$$\rho(s) = -\frac{m_0}{m_1} + \frac{1}{m_1}s$$

for sufficiently small s.

In the lower range the price determination function is then linear with slope $1/m_1 < 0$. Since no stocks are carried over into the next crop year, no hedges are demanded. The futures price plays a peculiar role now: It equilibrates the demand for bets on next year's spot price relative to the futures price.

If the actual size of next year's crop is

$$f^*(p_F) \cdot u$$

then the spot price will be

$$\rho[f^*(p_F) \cdot u]$$

provided plantings depend on the futures price. Here we have disregarded any small stocks in the hands of manufacturers that may have been carried over as excess of manufacturers' demand over consumption.

The expected value will be

(4) $$Ep_N = \int \rho[f^*(p_F) \cdot u] \, dQ(u).$$

Substituting in equation (1) which equilibrates the demand and supply of forward sales contracts, we have

(5) $$-p_F + \int \rho[f^*(p_F) \cdot u] \, dQ(u) = b_0 + b_1 s.$$

Once the function ρ is known, this equation determines the futures price. The futures price is seen to depend on current stocks and hence indirectly on the current spot price. For instance, by substituting the approximation (3) for ρ in (5) one obtains

$$p_F = \frac{m_1 b_0 + m_0 - f_2}{f_3} + \frac{b_1 m_1}{f_3} s.$$

Since $b_1 > 0$, $f_3 > 0$, $m_1 < 0$, the futures price is a decreasing function of stocks, as one would expect.

Consider next the case in which the stock is large enough that part of it will be carried over into the next crop year. Let us recall a well-known fact about the relationship of futures price and spot price in that case. Suppose the futures price exceeded the spot price plus marginal carrying cost. Then competition of extramarginal operators of storage facilities would bring the spot price up and the futures price down until at the margin storage cost just equalled the price difference.

Conversely, suppose the futures price to be less than the spot price plus marginal carrying cost. Then storage would be unprofitable for marginal operators, who would find it cheaper to sell spot and buy the same amount forward. This would cause the spot price to fall and the futures price to rise until at the margin spot price plus carrying cost equalled the futures price. Thus, whenever positive stocks are carried into the next period, the futures price must equal the spot price plus marginal carrying cost.

Returning once more to the case in which no stocks are carried over, we have the corollary statement that storage must be unprofitable, i.e, the futures price must be less than or equal to the spot price plus marginal carrying cost.

$$(6) \qquad p_F \leqq p_s + c(s)$$

The critical level of stocks at which carryover begins is the smallest s for which the "$=$" sign is assumed in (6). Call it s_0.

$$(7) \qquad p_F = p_s + c(s_0) = \rho(s_0) + c_0 + c_1 s_0$$

where p_F is still given by (5), and ρ by (3)

When stock exceeds the critical level s_0 an amount equal to

$$s - g(p_s)$$

will be carried over. The expected value of next year's spot price is

$$\int \rho[s - g(p_s) + f^*(p_F)u] \, dQ(u)$$

or

$$\int \rho[s - g(p_s) + f(p_s)u] \, dQ(u)$$

depending on which assumption is made about the planting of next year's crop.

It may be thought that this assumes implicitly that there is no carryover into the year after next. But this is not so since ρ—the relationship between stocks and prices—applies to all levels of stocks, including those with carryover. The formula (3) for ρ applies only in the range of no carryover, but will be used later as an approximation over the entire range.

Substituting in (1) we have

$$(8) \qquad -p_F + \int \rho[s - g(p_s) + f(p_s)u] \, dQ(u) = b(s).$$

Observing that futures price equals spot price plus marginal carrying cost, viz.,

$$(9) \qquad p_F = p_s + c(s),$$

we may substitute (9) and p_F in (8) and obtain an equation involving only $\rho(s)$:

$$(10) \quad -\rho(s) + \int \rho\{s - g[\rho(s)] + f[\rho(s)]u\} \, dQ(u) = b(s) + c(s), \quad s \geq s_0.$$

For values of the argument less than s_0 the function ρ under the integral is given by (3).

For $0 \leq s \leq s_0$ one may substitute the expression (3) for the first ρ under the integral and obtain an equation which involves functions ρ only in that range $s \geq s_0$ where they obey equation (10).

$$-\rho(s) + \int_0^{\frac{s_0 - s + g[\rho(s)]}{f[\rho(s)]}} \left(-\frac{m_0}{m_1} + \frac{1}{m_1}\{s - g[\rho(s)] + f[\rho(s)]u\} \right) dQ(u)$$

$$+ \int_{\frac{s_0 - s + g[\rho(s)]}{f[\rho(s)]}}^{\infty} \rho\{s - g[\rho(s)] + f[\rho(s)]u\} \, dQ(u) = b(s) + c(s),$$

While this integral equation can be solved, in principle, in terms of infinite series, it is rather unmanageable for general discussion. Instead we propose to use a linear approximation to the function ρ over its entire range. Its coefficients may then be determined by solving the integral equation (10). This will illustrate the determinateness of the price-stock relationship and allow us to check the signs involved.

Letting

$$\rho(s) = \rho_0 + \rho_1 s,$$

equation (10) assumes the form

$$-c(s) - \rho_1 g[\rho(s)] + \rho_1 f[\rho(s)] - b(s) = 0$$

or

$$-c_0 - c_1 s - \rho_1 g_0 - \rho_0 \rho_1 g_1 - \rho_1^2 g_1 s + \rho_1 f_0 + \rho_1 \rho_0 f_1 + \rho_1^2 f_1 s - b_0 - b_1 s = 0.$$

Equating coefficients of s we have

$$(11) \qquad -c_0 - g_0 \rho_1 - g_1 \rho_0 \rho_1 + f_0 \rho_1 + f_1 \rho_0 \rho_1 - b_0 = 0,$$

$$(12) \qquad -c_1 - g_1 \rho_1^2 + f_1 \rho_1^2 - b_1 = 0.$$

Solving (12) we have

$$(13) \qquad \rho_1 = -\sqrt{\frac{b_1 + c_1}{f_1 - g_1}}, \qquad \begin{matrix} b_1 > 0, & c_1 > 0, \\ f_1 > 0, & g_1 < 0. \end{matrix}$$

The correct sign for the slope of ρ is of course negative. Equation (13) states that the response of spot price to supply will be less the cheaper it is to "hedge" stocks, the cheaper it is to store stocks, the more responsive farmers are to today's price, and the more responsive consumer demand is.

The slope of ρ will be less in absolute value than the slope $1/m_1$ in the case of no carryover

$$|\rho_1| < \left|\frac{1}{m_1}\right|$$

provided

(14)
$$m_1^2 < \frac{f_1 - g_1}{b_1 + c_1}.$$

Now,

$$b_1 = \frac{a_1}{d_1 - a_2} \ll 1.$$

If the supply of forward sales contracts by commodity owners is less elastic than the demand of speculators, then

$$a_1 \ll d_1.$$

Moreover,

$$c_1 \ll 1$$

so that the right-hand side of equation (14) is large.

Alternatively, we may argue as follows. In the case of carryover,

$$E(p_N - p_F) = b_0 + c_0 + (b_1 + c_1)s$$

and this must be compared with the stock price function (in the case of no carryover).

$$p_s = \frac{m_0}{m_1} + \frac{1}{m_1}s.$$

Now, since the price is surely more sensitive than the backwardation, we have

$$\frac{1}{m_1} \gg b_1 + c_1.$$

If, however, b_1 and c_1 are large enough so that (14) may be violated, then the economics of the situation suggests that there is insufficient incentive to carry stocks into the next crop year; in this case there is no need for a futures market to make hedging possible.

From (11) one has

(15)
$$\rho_0 = \frac{c_0 + b_0 + \rho_1 g_0 - \rho_1 f_0}{f_1 \rho_1 - g_1 \rho_1}.$$

The terms c_0 and b_0 are (to a first approximation) negligibly small. If they are dropped we have

$$\rho_0 \doteq \frac{g_0 - f_0}{f_1 - g_1}.$$

Also approximately

$$-\frac{m_0}{m_1} \doteq -\frac{g_0}{g_1}.$$

Therefore

$$\rho_0 < -\frac{m_0}{m_1} \quad \text{if} \quad \frac{g_0 - f_0}{f_1 - g_1} < -\frac{g_0}{g_1}.$$

But this follows from $g_1 f_0 < 0 < g_0 f_1$.

Hence ρ has the following location:

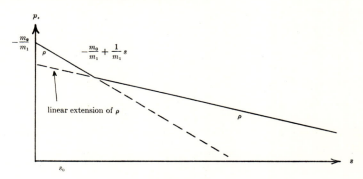

Figure 2

A similar result is obtained when the first ρ under the integral of (10) is replaced by

$$-\frac{m_0}{m_1} + \frac{1}{m_1}.$$

We remark in passing that our model covers also the degenerate case of certainty of yields. Equation (3) remains valid for $s \leqq s_0$ and equation (10) assumes the form

$$-\rho(s) - c(s) + \rho\{s - g[\rho(s)] + f[\rho(s) + c(s)]\} = 0 \quad \text{for} \quad s \geqq s_0.$$

We leave it to the reader to show that this equation has a solution which is continuous and is composed of a finite number of line segments of successively smaller slopes, the ith segment being associated with a carryover of stocks through i periods. Under certainty the market is stable, since from any initial position a steady state of no carryover and constant prices will be reached in finitely many periods.

AN ALTERNATIVE APPROACH

The discussion so far has been based on given supply and demand functions. An alternative approach may be outlined in which speculators'—and, by analogy, hedgers'—decisions are derived from maximization of expected utility, using a convenient quadratic utility function. It will be shown that the price-stock relationship is still well determined; but its derivation, which now involves also the variance of next year's crop size, is somewhat more cumbersome.

Consider a speculator with assets m who has bought forward x bushels of the commodity. Since no money changes hands until the next period, his assets may earn a safe return in a riskless investment, bringing his assets next year up to rm. After the contract has been settled his wealth will be

$$w = mr - xp_F + xp_N.$$

Let

(16) $$v = v_0 + v_1 w + v_2 w^2, \qquad v_1 > 0, \qquad v_2 < 0,$$

be his utility function.

Since we want

$$0 < \frac{dv}{dw} = v_1 + 2v_1 w,$$

this utility function is applicable only for

$$w \leqq \frac{-v_1}{2v_2}.$$

The expected value of the utility of his wealth is

$$E[v_0 + v_1(mr - xp_F + xp_N) + v_2(mr - xp_F + xp_N)^2].$$

Maximizing with respect to x (on the assumption that any budget constraint that may exist will prove ineffective) we obtain

$$2v_2xE(p_N - p_F)^2 + (v_1 + 2v_2m)E(p_N - p_F) = 0$$

or

$$x = \frac{v_1 + 2v_2m}{-v_2} \cdot \frac{E(p_N - p_F)}{E(p_N - p_F)^2}.$$

Aggregating over all speculators, we obtain the total supply of futures sales contracts, actual and fictitious,

$$a\, \frac{E(p_N - p_F)}{E(p_N - p_F)^2}$$

where a is a positive constant. By previous assumption this supply of contracts must equal demand, which in turn equals total physical stock. Thus

(17) $$s = a\, \frac{E(p_N - p_F)}{E(p_N - p_F)^2}, \qquad s > s_0.$$

Now

$$E(p_N - p_F)^2 = E(Ep_N - p_F)^2 + \text{var}\,(p_N).$$

The first term increases with increasing stocks because of the rising backwardation required to hold that stock. The second term decreases since the slope of the price function (if anything) becomes smaller, and plantings become smaller. The previous approach in terms of the backwardation alone may be justified by arguing that the denominator in (17) is approximately constant, and therefore the backwardation is approximately proportional to stock.

    Upon substitution of

(18) $$p_N = \rho\{s - g[\rho(s)] + f[\rho(s)]u\}$$

and (9) in (17) an integral equation in ρ is obtained. Substituting (3) for the first ρ under the integral, one obtains a quadratic equation in terms of ρ whose solution is of the form

(19) $$\rho = k_0 + \frac{k_1}{s} + k_2s \pm \sqrt{k_3 + \frac{k_4}{s^2} + \frac{k_5}{s} + k_6s + k_7s^2}.$$

For $s < s_0$ the approximate solution (19) is not applicable, for large values of s, it is approximately linear. A general mathematical analysis of this approximate solution would be cumbersome and would not lead to any specific conclusions, unless particular values could be assigned to the various coefficients. However, with numerical coefficients of the data functions, numerical solutions of (3) and (15)—or for that matter of (10)—can be obtained with any degree of accuracy desired, for instance by iteration. Such calculations would be justified once a firm econometric basis has been laid for the various data functions involved.

Conclusion

The operations of the futures market are surrounded by all the mysteries of decision-making under risk. Prices are not simply determined by the equilibrium of the demand for current consumption and of the total supply, since part of the stock may be carried over into the future periods. How much inevitably depends on what prices are expected to be in the future. What can be said about these expectations? According to some economists, not much, since any attempt to find a common element in expectations is up against "the fatal objection to the introduction of any aggregates or averages of expectations into economic reasoning, not merely that owning to differences in expectations of different individuals there is no one expected price, but there are gaps in the series where there is no expectation at all." On the other hand, "when everybody held the same expectation, there would be no trading at all."[3]

These statements are unassailable only when expectations are single-valued. But single-valued expectations, intuition, and hunches are more characteristic of soothsayers than of hardheaded businessmen. Prices will be affected by the outcome of next year's crop, a random variable whose distribution is, in principle, known. The question is whether this will lead to a predictable probability distribution of prices, and next, whether speculators and owners of commodities who entertain probabilistic expectations can make rational decisions. In this paper an attempt has been made to resolve these questions.

In a stationary economy where absolute time does not enter into economic relationships, all information about the future is summarized in a finite number of "state variables." These must include the stock of the commodity, but may include additional variables such as weather forecasts and information on changes in population or consumers' tastes, etc. All expectations are, therefore, also stationary, i.e., dependent only on state variables. Because of the infinite repetition of states in a stationary economy, decision-makers may be assumed to know the probabilities governing the transitions between states, e.g., the probabilities of next year's weather in relation to this year's. Of central interest for the present problem is the probability distribution of next year's prices and stocks, given the level of this year's stock. Incidentally, even when everybody has the same expectation, i.e., attaches the same probabilities to various prices in the next period, trading may still occur because of different risk preferences.

The key to the solution of these problems is that a definite relationship between stock and spot prices must exist and that this will generate a probability distribution of next year's spot prices (from the given probability distribution of crop yields), conditional on this year's stock level. It was also shown that supply and demand are sufficient to determine this postulated relationship, and that this determination does not explicitly involve infinite sequences of prices, but only relationships over two periods.

Notes

1. I am indebted to J. Stein and P. Cootner for various critical comments and helpful suggestions.
2. Consider, however, P. A. Samuelson, "Intertemporal Price Equilibrium: A Prologue to the Theory of Speculation," *Weltwirtschaftl. Archiv,* LXXIX (1957), 181–219; and J. L. Stein, "The Simultaneous Determination of Spot and Futures Prices," *American Economic Review,* LI (1961), 1012–1025.
3. R. G. Hawtrey, "Mr. Kaldor on the Forward Market," *Review of Economic Studies,* VII (1940), 202–205.

REFERENCES

J. M. Keynes, *A Treatise on Money,* The Macmillan Company (London: 1930), pp. 142–44.
N. Kaldor, "Speculation and Economic Stability," *Review of Economic Studies,* VII (1939), 1–27.
L. G. Telser, "Safety-First and Hedging," *Review of Economic Studies,* XXIII (1955), 1–16.
See also entries under 2.1322 in the AEA Index of Economic Journals.

Optimal Programs for
Sequential Investments

David Gale

INTRODUCTION

BY an *n-stage sequential investment* is meant an investment in which payments xa_n, xa_{n-1}, . . . , xa_1 are made in n successive time periods yielding a return of x in period $n + 1$. Typically, any productive activity over time leads to such an investment if one arranges to pay for the inputs to production at the times when they are needed and receives the value of the produced article when it is completed.

The study of sequential investments goes back at least to Irving Fisher, and in various ramifications it is one of the chief objects of study in texts on the mathematics of finance. Despite the fact, however, that these objects have been rather thoroughly worked over, it turns out that by using "modern methods," i.e., linear programming duality, it is still possible to say something new about them.

Before doing so let us recall in a paragraph the usual theory.

Suppose that the interest rate is i and that amounts xa_n, xa_{n-1}, . . . , xa_1 become available in n successive time periods. We may then either make use of our n-stage investment and obtain x in period $n + 1$ or we may invest each amount xa_i as it becomes available at the going rate of interest, obtaining

$$x[a_n(1 + i)^n + a_{n-1}(1 + i)^{n-1} + \cdots a_1(i + 1)]$$

in period $n + 1$. Clearly we will choose the first or second alternative according to whether the polynomial

$$p(1 + i) = a_n(1 + i)^n + \cdots + a_1(i + 1) - 1$$

is negative or positive. This suggests that we define the *internal rate of return* of the investment as the unique number ρ such that $p(1 + \rho) = 0$,

17

since this is precisely the interest rate at which our investment will just break even. The internal rate of return is therefore a natural measure of the profitability of an investment, and is a convenient number for comparing the profitability of various investments.

It should be noted that this customary analysis of a sequential investment assumes the existence of a positive external interest rate. The question we wish to examine here is the following: Suppose there were no such thing as interest or, alternatively, that the interest rate were zero; is there still some natural way to compare the "profitability" of various sequential investments? This question is intended not merely to provide an exercise in economic make-believe. In the beginning, presumably, there was no such thing as interest, and it was forced upon us among other things by the technological fact that goods can be used to produce other goods. Thus, if we find a definition of profitability independent of considerations of interest, we will have gained further insight into why interest had to be invented, as well as noting some of the reasons why the interest rate has the value it does.

Let us look at a very simple concrete example. Suppose there are two processes I_1 and I_2. In I_1 if we invest x units in period one and $2x$ units in period two we receive $4x$ units in period three. In I_2 the order is reversed; we first invest $2x$ units, then x units, and again receive $4x$. The following schematic representation should be self-explanatory.

$$I_1 : (1, 2) \to 4$$

$$I_2 : (2, 1) \to 4$$

The question is whether there is any reason to consider one of these investments more profitable than the other. In the presence of a positive rate of interest, of course, I_1 would be preferred. Our purpose here is to show that even in an interestless world I_1 is the better investment for the simplest reason imaginable; it is a better money maker. To see this, let us be very specific and assume we start out with one dollar and want to maximize the amount of money on hand five periods later, using investment I_1. At first glance we might decide to invest 1/3 dollars the first day and 2/3 the next, after which we would receive 4/3 dollars which could again be divided in parts 4/9 and 8/9 to yield finally 16/9. Table I illustrates the procedure. Here a negative number is an input to an investment sequence and a positive number is an output. The row labeled "savings" represents money brought forward from the previous period.

Now it turns out that there is a better program than the one described

TABLE I

Period	1	2		3	4		5
Savings	1	2/3		0	8/9		0
1st sequence	$-1/3$	$-2/3$	$\rightarrow$	4/3	8/9		
2nd sequence				$-4/9$	$-8/9$	$\rightarrow$	16/9

by Table 1. Instead of investing the entire dollar on the first sequence one can save out a certain amount to initiate a second sequence in period 2, and a third in period 3. The program is given by this table:

TABLE 2

Period	1	2		3		4		5
Savings	1	3/4		0		0		0
1st sequence	$-1/4$	$-1/2$	$\rightarrow$	1				
2nd sequence		$-1/4$		$-1/2$	$\rightarrow$	1		
3rd sequence				$-1/2$		-1	$\rightarrow$	2

Since $2 > 16/9$, this second program is better than the first. In fact, as we shall see, the program of Table 2 is optimal.

As a final illustration we construct a table for the optimal five-period program for the investment I_2.

TABLE 3

Period	1	2		3		4		5
Savings	1	17/35		0		0		0
1st sequence	$-18/35$	$-9/35$	$\rightarrow$	36/35				
2nd sequence		$-8/35$		$-4/35$	$\rightarrow$	16/35		
3rd sequence				$-32/35$		$-16/35$	$\rightarrow$	64/35

Note that the optimal five-period program for I_2, although not as good as the one for I_1, is still slightly better than the naive program for I_1 illustrated by Table 1, since $64/35 > 16/9$.

Our purpose here is to give the solution to the general problem of finding an optimal program for maximizing the return at the end of T periods from an n-stage investment. Those familiar with such things will recognize this as a typical dynamic linear programming problem. What is not at all typical, however, is the fact that its solution can be given by a simple explicit formula, a phenomenon which rarely occurs in such problems. Further, the solution is determined by following a natural, economically meaningful principle. Comparing the optimal programs of Tables 2 and 3 with the nonoptimal program of Table 1, we note that in the optimal cases all entries in the row labeled "savings" are zero except in the first two periods, while this is not the case in the program of Table 1. Our main result can be stated as follows:

OPTIMALITY THEOREM. In order for a program to be optimal it is only necessary to be sure that balances are held idle only during the first n periods.

We remark that it is clearly necessary to hold balances during the first n periods, since one must have funds on hand to pay the instalments of the initial sequences. The optimality principle says that one should hold idle balances only when absolutely necessary. Stated in this way, the theorem seems so natural as to be almost obvious. Perhaps so, but I know of no way to prove it without using linear programming duality theory. Furthermore, a sampling of fairly expert opinion showed that most people, myself included, when confronted with the five-period problem for I_1 or I_2 looked first at the nonoptimal method of Table 1.

The final section gives an asymptotic formula for the T-period problem for large values of T. It will be shown that the optimal output grows like ρ^T where ρ is the internal rate of return already defined. Thus we are led to the concept of internal rate of return unmotivated by interest considerations. (A somewhat weaker result of this same form but for much more general models has been obtained by Wolfe and the author.)

THE OPTIMALITY THEOREM AND FORMULA

In order to give an algebraic description of an investment program we introduce the following notation.

ξ_t represents the output of the investment in period $n + t$.

σ_t represents the savings brought forward from period $n + t - 1$ to period $n + t$.

Thus, $\xi_t + \sigma_t$ represents the amount available for inputs in period $n + t$.

Now the expenditures in period $n + t$ consist of payments of instalments on investment sequences,

$$\xi_{t+1}a_1 + \xi_{t+2}a_2 + \cdots + \xi_{t+n}a_n,$$

plus the amount σ_{t+1} to be saved and brought forward to period $t + n + 1$.

The balance equation is then

$$(1) \qquad \xi_t + \sigma_t = \sum_{i=1}^{n} \xi_{t+i} a_i + \sigma_{t+1}.$$

If we are trying the maximize capital on hand at period $n + T$, then (1) holds for $t = 1, \ldots, T$. However, it is clear that for an optimal program

$$(2) \qquad \xi_t = 0 \quad \text{for} \quad t > T,$$

since it would be wasteful to start up sequences which would not pay off until after period $n + T$.

Finally we must take account of the initial conditions. We may clearly assume that initial capital is one. This capital must be sufficient to cover all expenses of the first n periods, i.e., all instalments of the first sequence, all but the last instalment of the second, and so on. The condition is

$$\xi_1(a_1 + \cdots + a_n) + \xi_2(a_2 + \cdots + a_n) + \cdots + \xi_n a_n + \sigma_1 = 1$$

or, if we write

$$b_i = a_i + a_{i+1} + \cdots + a_n,$$

the initial condition becomes

$$(3) \qquad \sum_{i=1}^{n} \xi_i b_i + \sigma_1 = 1.$$

Subject to conditions (1), (2), and (3), we wish to maximize σ_{t+1}, and this defines our linear programming problem. It will be convenient to write out the constraints in matrix form:

$$(4)$$

$\xi_1,$	$\xi_2,$	$\cdots,$	$\xi_n,$	$\xi_{n+1},$	$\cdots,$	$\xi_T,$	$\sigma_1, \sigma_2,$	$\cdots,$	σ_T, σ_{T+1}	
$b_1,$	$b_2,$	$\cdots,$	b_n				1			$=1$
$-1,$	$a_1,$	$\cdots,$	$a_{n-1}, \; a_n$				$-1 \;\; 1$			$=0$
		$-1,$	$a_1,$	$\cdots \;\; a_{n-1} \;\; a_n$				$-1, \;\; 1$		$=0$
			$-1,$	$a_1, \;\; \cdots,$	a_{n-1}			$-1, \;\; 1$		$=0$
					$-1,$	$a_1,$		$-1, \;\; 1$		$=0$
						-1		$-1, \;\; 1$		$=0$

Now it is easy to find a feasible solution to these constraints. First set

$$\sigma_1 = \sigma_2 = \cdots \sigma_T = 0.$$

Then from the last equation

$$\sigma_{T+1} = \xi_T.$$

From the second to last equation

$$\xi_{T-1} = a_1\xi_T,$$

and continuing to work backwards we get

$$\xi_{T-2} = a_1\xi_{T-1} + a_2\xi_T$$
$$\cdots\cdots\cdots\cdots\cdots$$

and in general

(5) $$\xi_t = \sum_{i=1}^{n} a_i\xi_{t+i},$$

so that all numbers ξ_t are determined recursively from ξ_T. Finally ξ_T can be determined from the initial condition, which now becomes

$$\sum_{i=1}^{n} b_i\xi_i = 1.$$

We can give this solution explicitly by using vectors. Let

$$x_t = (\xi_t, \xi_{t+1}, \cdots, \xi_{t+n-1})$$

and let A be the matrix whose first row is $(a_1, a_2, \cdots a_n)$ and which has 1s below the diagonal and is zero elsewhere.

$$\begin{bmatrix} a_1, & a_2, & \cdots, & a_n \\ 1, & 0 & & \\ 0, & 1, & 0 & \\ \cdots\cdots\cdots\cdots\cdots \\ 0, & \cdot\cdot & 1, & 0 \end{bmatrix}$$

Then (5) is equivalent to

(6) $$x_t = Ax_{t+1}$$

and (3) becomes

(7) $$b \cdot x_1 = 1$$

where $b = (b_1, b_2, \ldots, b_n)$.

From (2) we have $x_T = (\xi_T, 0, \ldots, 0)$ and using (6) repeatedly gives

(8) $$x_1 = A^{T-1}x_T = \xi_T A^{T-1}e_1$$

where $e_1 = (1, 0, \ldots, 0)$. Substituting (8) in (7) gives

$$\xi_T b A^{T-1} e_1 = 1$$

and we have the formula

9)
$$\boxed{\xi_T = 1/b A^{T-1} e_1}.$$

Our main result asserts that ξ_T is actually the desired maximum and that the optimal program is given by

(10)
$$\boxed{x_t = A^{T-t} e_1 / b A^{T-1} e_1}$$

which follows at once from (9) and (6).

To prove optimality we return to the equations given by the matrix (4) and change it to the equivalent system of equations obtained by replacing the rth row of (4) by the sum of the first r rows. The new set of equations are:

$$
11) \quad
\begin{array}{ccccccccccc}
\xi_1, & \xi_2, \cdots, \xi_n, & \xi_{n+1}, & \cdots, & \xi_T, & \sigma_1, & \sigma_2, \cdots, \sigma_T, & \sigma_{T+1} & \\
\end{array}
$$

$$
\left[
\begin{array}{l}
b_1, \quad b_2, \cdots, b_n \qquad\qquad\qquad\qquad 1 \\
b_1 - 1, b_1, \cdots, b_{n-1}, b_n \qquad\qquad\qquad 1 \\
\cdots\cdots\cdots\cdots\cdots\cdots\cdots\cdots\cdots\cdots\cdots \\
b_1 - 1, \cdots, b_1 - 1, b_1, \quad b_2, \cdots, b_n \qquad 1 \\
b_1 - 1, \cdots\cdots\cdots b_1 - 1, b_1, \cdots, b_{n-1} \qquad 1 \\
\cdots\cdots\cdots\cdots\cdots\cdots\cdots\cdots\cdots\cdots\cdots \\
b_1 - 1, \cdots\cdots\cdots\cdots b_1 - 1, b_1 \qquad\qquad 1 \\
b_1 - 1, \cdots\cdots\cdots\cdots\cdots b_1 - 1 \qquad\qquad\quad 1
\end{array}
\right]
\begin{array}{l}
=1 \\ =1 \\ \\ =1 \\ =1 \\ \\ =1 \\ =1
\end{array}
$$

Now the $(T+1)^{st}$ equation (11) is

(12)
$$(b_1 - 1) \sum_{i=1}^{T} \xi_i + \sigma_{T+1} = 1$$

and we are assuming $b_1 < 1$ (otherwise the investment would clearly be unprofitable and the best one could do would be to hold on to his initial capital). It therefore follows from (12) that σ_{T+1} will be a maximum provided

$$\sum_{i=1}^{T} \xi_i$$

is a maximum subject to the first T equations of (11) which can finally be rewritten as inequalities in the following form by reversing the order in which the rows are written.

(13)

$$
\begin{array}{c}
\xi_1, \quad\quad \xi_2, \quad \cdots, \quad \xi_n, \xi_{n+1}, \quad\quad \cdots, \quad\quad \xi_T \\
\left[
\begin{array}{ccccccc}
b_1 - 1, & b_1 - 1, & & & b_1 - 1, & b_1 & \\
b_1 - 1, & b_1 - 1, & & b_1 - 1, & b_1, & b_2 & \\
\cdots\cdots\cdots\cdots\cdots\cdots\cdots\cdots\cdots\cdots\cdots\cdots\cdots\cdots\cdots\cdots \\
b_1 - 1, & b_1 - 1, & \cdots, & b_1 - 1, & b_1, & \cdots, & b_{n-1} \\
b_1 - 1, & b_1 - 1, & \cdots, & b_1, & b_2, & \cdots, & b_n \\
\cdots\cdots\cdots\cdots\cdots\cdots\cdots\cdots\cdots\cdots\cdots\cdots\cdots\cdots\cdots\cdots \\
b_1 - 1, & b_1, & \cdots, & b_{n-1}, & & & \\
b_1, & b_2, & \cdots, & b_n, & & &
\end{array}
\right]
\begin{array}{c}
\leq 1 \\
\leq 1 \\
\\
\leq 1 \\
\leq 1 \\
\\
\leq 1 \\
\leq 1
\end{array}
\end{array}
$$

Subject to (13) we wish to maximize

$$\sum_{i=1}^{T} \xi_i.$$

This is therefore a standard linear programming problem but it has a special form because (a) the constraint matrix is symmetric and (b) the right hand side vector is the same as the vector of the objective. This leads us to make the following

DEFINITION. By a *symmetric linear programming problem* is meant the problem of finding a vector $x \geq 0$ such that

(14) $x \cdot b$ is a maximum subject to

(15) $xA \leq b$

where A is symmetric.

LEMMA: In a symmetric linear program, if there exists $\bar{x} \geq 0$ such that $A\bar{x} = b$, then $\bar{x}$ is optimal.

Proof. Assume $\bar{x}$ exists. Then $\bar{x} \cdot b$ is a possible value of the program (14), (15). On the other hand, if x is any feasible vector (solution of (15)) then

$$x \cdot b = xA\bar{x} \leq b \cdot \bar{x} = \bar{x} \cdot b$$

so $\bar{x}$ is optimal.

THEOREM 1. The optimal program for the n-stage T-period sequential investment is given by (9) and (10).

Proof. We have seen that the sequential investment can be transformed to the symmetric linear program (13). From the lemma we know that the optimal solution is one in which all constraints are satisfied exactly (as equations) which is precisely the condition from which the solution (9) and (10) was determined.

AN ASYMPTOTIC FORMULA

We have seen the equation (9) gives an exact formula for the maximum value of the T-period investment problem. We note that the formula involves raising the matrix A to the power $T - 1$, and for large values of T this may be computationally inconvenient. For such cases there is a simple asymptotic formula for ξ_T which has theoretical as well as practical significance.

We first state a general result. Let A be a nonnegative square matrix which is irreducible and nonperiodic in the usual sense of the theory of Markov Chains. Let λ be the dominant eigen-value of A and let u and v be corresponding left and right eigen-vectors, i.e.,

$$uA = \lambda u \quad \text{and} \quad Av = \lambda v.$$

The following result appears to be well-known and is easily derived from the fundamental convergence theorem for Markov Chains:

THEOREM 2. For any $x \geqq 0$, $A^n x$ is asymptotic to $\lambda^n (u \cdot x) v / (u \cdot v)$.

Now let A be the matrix of the previous section.

$$\begin{bmatrix} a_1, & a_2, & \cdots, & a_n \\ 1, & 0 & & \\ 0, & 1, & 0 & \\ \multicolumn{4}{c}{\cdots\cdots\cdots\cdots\cdots\cdots} \\ 0, & \cdots\cdots & 1, & 0 \end{bmatrix}$$

Then A satisfies the conditions of the theorem. Let $p(x)$ be the polynomial

(16) $$p(x) = 1 - a_1 x - a_2 x^2 - \cdots - a_n x^n$$

and let ρ be the positive root of $p(x)$ which, as noted, is the "internal rate of return" of the investment. One easily verifies that the dominant eigenvalue λ and left and right eigen-vectors u and v are given by

$$\lambda = \frac{1}{\rho}, \quad u = (a_1\rho + a_2\rho^2 + \cdots + a_n\rho^n, \, a_2\rho + \cdots + a_n\rho^{n-1}, \, \cdots, \, a_n\rho)$$

$$v = (1, \, \rho, \, \cdots, \, \rho^{n-1}).$$

Then

$$u \cdot v = a_1\rho + 2a_2\rho^2 + \cdots + na^n\rho^n = \rho p'(\rho).$$

Applying Theorem 2 to $A^{T-1}e_1$ we get

$$A^{T-1}e_1 \sim \left(\frac{1}{\rho}\right)^{T-1} \frac{1}{\rho p'(\rho)} v = \frac{v}{\rho^T p'(\rho)}.$$

We wish to estimate $bA^{T-1}e_1$ and we note that

$$b \cdot v = (a_1 + \cdots + a_n) + (\rho a_2 + \cdots + \rho a_n) + \cdots + \rho^{n-1}a_n$$

$$= a_1 + (1 + \rho)a_2 + (1 + \rho + \rho^2)a_3 + \cdots + (1 + \rho + \cdots + \rho^{n-1})a_n$$

$$= \frac{1}{1 - \rho} [(1 - \rho)a_1 + (1 - \rho^2)a_2 + \cdots + (1 - \rho^n)a_n]$$

$$= \frac{1}{1 - \rho} (b_1 - \rho a_1 - \cdots - \rho^n a_n) = \frac{1 - b_1}{\rho - 1}.$$

Therefore

$$\xi_T \sim \frac{\rho - 1}{1 - b_1} p'(\rho)\rho^T$$

which is the desired asymptotic expression. Several remarks are in order.

(1) Asymptotically ξ_T grows geometrically and the growth rate is precisely the internal rate of return. This is the relation between growth rate and profitability which was mentioned in the introduction.

(2) The constant term does not depend on the individual coefficients a_i of $p(x)$ but only on the internal rate of return ρ, the total cost b_1, and the derivative of $p(x)$.

(3) Since ρ is rate of return $1 - \rho$ is (internal) interest rate. Thus output is proportional to interest rate and inversely proportional to profit rate which is $1 - b_1$.

(4) It would be interesting to give some economic interpretation to $p'(\rho)$.

Some Economic Aspects of Outdoor Recreation[1]

Edwin S. Mills

Introduction

DURING the last few years there has been rapidly growing interest in the economic study of outdoor recreation; three major studies have appeared concerning past, present, and future participation. Two have come from Resources for the Future[2] and one from the Outdoor Recreation Resources Review Commission.[3] All three studies agree that per capita participation in most forms of outdoor recreation has increased very rapidly since World War II and that this trend is likely to continue in the foreseeable future.

Although there is widespread agreement that the demand for outdoor recreation will continue to grow, there has been relatively little analysis of the major economic issues related to the industry. What major factors affect the demand for outdoor recreation? How costly will it be to provide the facilities needed to meet the growing demand? What is the appropriate mix of public and private enterprise in the supply of recreational facilities? Which recreational opportunities should be provided free and what prices should be charged for those that should be sold? The purpose of this paper is to analyze some of these questions for the special class of facilities provided by state parks.

The study of outdoor recreation, or any service industry, poses a major problem of chosing appropriate units in which to measure the product. The services provided by the Grand Canyon, a golf course, and a professional baseball team are not interchangeable for most consumers. For many purposes it is desirable to have a broad classification of recreational facilities divided into a small number of inclusive categories. The most useful classification has been proposed by Marion Clawson,[4] who distinguishes resource-oriented, intermediate, and user-

27

oriented facilities. Resource-oriented facilities are located to take advantage of major natural resources; examples are national parks and forests and seashore resorts. User-oriented facilities are located so as to be close to the users, almost without regard to the presence of natural resources. Local parks, swimming pools, playgrounds, and golf courses are examples. Intermediate facilities are located partly with regard to natural resources and partly with regard to the location of users. The resource requirements are often bodies of water, forests, or hilly terrain. State parks and federal reservoirs are the major facilities in this category.

In this paper, attention is focused on state parks, which are typical of the intermediate category in that their location depends partly on the presence of desirable natural resources and partly on proximity to users. The vast majority of visits are day outings. Visits to state parks have grown rapidly since World War II and are expected to increase at a rapid rate in the foreseeable future.

An idea of the anticipated growth in state park visits can be obtained from a brief comparison of the three projections already referred to. An exact comparison is not possible because of differences in definition and in the dates at which the forecasts were made. The comparison can, however, establish orders of magnitude. All three projections agree that the recent rate of growth in per capita visits to state parks cannot continue indefinitely.[5] Beyond that, however, there is little agreement concerning the future trend. The most rapid rate of growth is projected by Clawson, Held, and Stoddard.[6] They anticipate that per capita visits to intermediate facilities (including federal reservoirs in addition to state parks) in the year 2000 will be about 15, roughly 7.5 times the 1960 level of about 2.0. The more recent RFF projection by Landsberg, Fischmann, and Fisher[7] is somewhat more conservative. Their medium projection is that per capita state park visits will be 8.4 in 2000, 4.2 times the 1960 figure. The most conservative projection is that by ORRRC. Although they do not project state park visits, their projections of participation in activities such as picnicking, hiking, etc., which are often carried on in state parks, suggest a per capita growth of about 50 per cent by 2000.[8] Most comments I have read consider the third of these projections too low and the first too high. It is difficult to compare and evaluate these projections, and it is not the purpose of this paper to do so. The point to be made here is that even the most modest of the projections entails a rapid growth of demand for the services of state parks during the coming decades. Coupled with a plausible projection that population will double between 1960 and 2000, the three projections imply that state park visits in 2000 will be 15,[9] 8, and 3 times the 1960 number respectively.

The prospect of rapid growth in the demand for recreation suggests the need for detailed economic analysis of supply and demand in this industry. The rest of this paper discusses two related problems concerning state parks. The next section is concerned with the welfare problem of optimum pricing of state park visits. The third offers a detailed analysis of the demand for state park visits. The final section summarizes the implications of the previous sections for future trends in state park visits.

WELFARE CONSIDERATIONS[10]

Two closely related welfare questions have been widely discussed in the study of outdoor recreation. First, what is the optimum pricing policy? Specifically, should facilities be paid for by users or subsidized by taxpayers? Second, what is the appropriate mix of public and private ownership? Since different considerations are relevant to these two questions, they will be discussed separately. Furthermore, some of the considerations are peculiar to state parks, and the following discussion does not necessary apply to other kinds of recreational facilities.

Most conservationists and recreationists take the view that public subsidization of recreational amenities such as state parks is justified. The usual argument is that such recreational activities entail external benefits, so that society as a whole profits from an individual's recreational experience. The factors most commonly mentioned are health and the social value of an occasional return to nature.[11]

The health argument, as usually stated, is confused. In order to justify subsidization of state park visits on the grounds of health, it must be shown not only that these visits improve health, but also that individuals undervalue the resulting improvement in their health. It is undoubtedly true that a certain amount of recreation and outdoor activity are conducive to good health. However, given the other recreational activities in which Americans engage, and given the rather sedentary activities (such as picnicking) in which people often engage during state park visits, it is unlikely that the marginal reduction in state park visits that would result from the removal of subsidies would measurably affect the health of the population. Furthermore, Americans spend substantial amounts of money on other forms of outdoor recreation, such as boating and golf, and there is no evidence that they undervalue the kinds of improvements in health that result from these activities or from state park visits.

The second assertion, that society places a value on my occasional contact with nature in state parks, is logically consistent but factually dubious. This is an example of the slipperiest kind of external-effect argument; it asserts that one person's consumption affects another's utility. Such effects are notoriously difficult to measure. I conjecture that the rest of society places no more value on my state park visits than they do on my attendance at professional baseball games, and that the case for subsidization is equally weak in both examples.

A second kind of externality is often mentioned by recreationists, but its implications are rarely faced. This is the congestion effect. A substantial increase in the number of visitors per acre in a state park clearly lowers the value of the recreational experience. There can be little doubt of the reality of this factor, and its importance is emphasized most by those who believe most strongly in the value of the return to nature. Yet its clear implication is that a charge for the use of the facility should not only cover a part of the money cost of the facility but also help to compensate for the resulting increase in congestion. (This is the same phenomenon as road congestion, to which much attention has been paid recently. In the case of roads, estimates of the congestion effect suggest that it is very large indeed.[12])

In practical terms, the congestion effect is of major importance. Many state parks, particularly those near large urban areas, are already crowded to physical capacity on summer weekends.[13] The projections referred to in Section 1 indicate that extreme congestion of state parks will be avoided in the coming decades only if their acreage is increased substantially. I conjectured above that society receives only neglible external benefits from state park visits. If that is so, it is extremely unlikely that funds allocated by legislatures will be sufficient to acquire enough acreage to avoid congestion as the demand grows during the coming decades. If these arguments are accepted, it follows that those who value highly the recreational experience ought to favor admission fees that will make state parks self-financing.[14]

It is of interest to ask, in concluding this discussion, what fees would be necessary to cover the cost of state park operations. This question is made difficult by the substitutability of capital and land in state parks. One of the characteristics of state parks—even those that are used at relatively high density—is that large parts of them are virtually unused. Therefore, an alternative to the acquisition of more land is additional improvement of existing facilities. Roads, picnic facilities, sanitary facilities, and parking areas are the major improvements. Of course, improvements necessarily alter the nature of the recreational experience, and the optimal level of improvement is difficult to guess. Another alternative to the acquisition of additional acres is to develop state forests for recreational purposes.

I have made rough calculations of the cost per visit of maintaining state parks in Maryland and in the U.S. as a whole.[15] I have valued land at its purchase price, except that land acquired before 1945 has been valued at the cost of land acquired in 1945. I have assumed land to be indestructible and have used an interest rate of 4 per cent. Improvements have been valued at original cost, assuming a twenty-year useful life, straight line depreciation, and a 4 per cent interest rate. Operating costs present no problems. With these assumptions, cost per visitor in 1961 was $0.37 in the U.S. as a whole and $0.35 in Maryland. The similarity of the two costs is the result of two offsetting differences. Land costs are much higher in Maryland than in the U.S. as a whole, but visits per acre of state park are also much higher.

I turn now to the second welfare problem, the optimum mix of public and private facilities. One misconception must be cleared away at the start. It is sometimes claimed that intermediate facilities must be public because no private market exists to register demand. This is an exaggeration. In many parts of the country a variety of intermediate land-intensive facilities are privately owned and commercially operated. Artificial and natural lakes, quarries that have been converted to swimming pools, and other large recreational areas are examples. Furthermore, the causation is backwards. The reason that no private market exists in state park-like recreational areas is that the services are given away at the publicly owned areas.

Nevertheless, there are two reasons for thinking that the private provision of intermediate recreational facilities might be undesirable. The first is the phenomenon of natural monopoly. The natural monopoly phenomenon is present in some degree in any industry in which economies of scale and the industry demand are such that the optimum industry output is most cheaply produced by fewer firms than are necessary to make the market perfect. The optimum size for state park-like facilities is usually several thousand acres. Within a reasonable distance of any but the largest metropolitan areas, the optimum number of such facilities is necessarily small. Thus the market, if private, would necessarily be less than perfect. Whether the resulting distortion in resource allocation would be large is difficult to say. The very factors that make an area desirable for intermediate recreation (hilly, rocky, wooded terrain) make it undesirable for farming and most other purposes. This suggests that the potential pure rent in the best of such areas may be considerable. If so, the monopoly price would be quite high compared with social opportunity cost, and public ownership or regulation would be desirable. In such a case, there appears to be no advantage to public regulation of private facilities over public ownership of facilities.

Second is the "common pool" phenomenon. To be valuable, state park-like areas must be large. This means that an area must often be acquired from several previous owners. The price that a seller can obtain for a particular plot of land then depends on the sequence in which plots are acquired. Given the costs of transactions, it is much more profitable to be the last owner to sell than the first. This is the same phenomenon that arises in exploiting an oil pool or in using the water in a stream, and interference with the price mechanism is widely advocated in such cases. The problem also arises in land acquisition for other purposes. When a developer wishes to acquire a large tract of farmland for a housing development, he usually tries to acquire individual parcels quietly, often using third parties. That this procedure works tolerably well in the housing development example suggests that the common pool phenomenon is not a major obstacle in the case of state park-like areas. In principle, however, some interference in the operation of free markets, such as the use of eminent domain, is justified.[16] These considerations suggest that there would be no advantage in private operation of state park-like facilities. On the other hand, if state parks charged reasonable fees, it may be that private facilities would appear. If so, there would seem to be no reason for discouraging them.

THE DEMAND FOR STATE PARK VISITS[17]

Many people who project future participation in outdoor recreation are content to observe that increases in participation are closely related to increases in income and increases in the quantities of travel, and leisure. Some have gone farther and assumed that percentage changes in the latter three factors have a multiplicative effect on participation. There is a temptation to interpret this assumption as one of unit elasticity of demand for recreation with respect to income, amounts of travel, and amounts of leisure. However, this relationship is not a demand equation in the usual sense of the term. Among these factors, only income would appear in a demand equation. Travel and leisure are complementary goods. Normally, prices of such goods, but not their amounts, would be included in a demand equation.

A major advance in the analysis of the demand for recreation was made by Marion Clawson.[18] He observed that one of the major costs of a visit to a state or national park is the cost of getting there. This permitted him to interpret park visits by assuming that different consumers pay different prices for the service depending on the distance they travel to get to the park. Using data on the places of residence of visitors to selected national parks, he was able to estimate how the number of visits decreased as the cost of the visit increased with the distance to the park.

Unfortunately, data on places of residence of visitors to state parks are not normally available. The point of departure in this paper is the observation that the demand equation can be estimated without these data provided the relationship is assumed to be linear.

We start with the usual assumption that the demand for the product (state park visits) depends on its price, the prices of related products, and income. We assume that the basic relationship is linear and can be written

$$(1) \qquad V_{ij} = B_0 + B_1 d_{ij} + B_2 y_i + B_3 d_i^a + B_4 S_j + u_{ij}.$$

The symbols are as follows:

V_{ij} = number of visits per resident of the ith residential area to the jth state park

d_{ij} = distance from the ith residential area to the jth park

y_i = income per capita in the ith residential area

d_i^a = a measure of availability of the other state parks to the residents of the ith residential area

S_j = size of the jth park

u_{ij} = random term.

For the purpose of estimating equation (1) we need only assume that the cost of visiting a state park is a linear function of distance traveled. We do not need to know the cost per mile of travel. The income term requires no comment. The symbol d_i^a is a measure of the cost of the closest substitutes for a visit to the jth park, namely, visits to other state parks. In principle, a weighted average distance to other available state parks would be ideal. In fact, a simpler proxy was used for this variable; it is specified below. S_j is a measure of the quality of the jth park. Parks vary greatly in their natural attractiveness and degree of development. Although size is not a perfect measure of quality, it is the best of the available measures. S_j is therefore simply the number of acres in the jth state park.

Equation (1) implies that there is some maximum distance that anyone will travel to visit a particular park. In principle, this distance depends on y_i, d_i^a and S_j. As an approximation we will assume that it is independent of both i and j. We will refer to the set of residential areas that are less than this maximum distance from the jth park as the jth park's service area. The approximation just indicated implies that each park's service area is a circle centered on the park. The radius is unknown, and its estimation is discussed below. Write N_i for the number of residents in the ith residential area. For any i within the service area of park j, multiply both sides of equation (1) by N_i, sum over all values of i in the service area, and divide by $N_{.j} = \sum_i N_i$, where the sum is over all the residential areas in the jth park's service area. Thus, $N_{.j}$ is the total population within the jth park's service area. This gives

$$
(2) \quad \frac{\sum N_{ij} V_{ij}}{N_{.j}} = B_0 + B_1 \frac{\sum N_{ij} d_{ij}}{N_{.j}} + B_2 \frac{\sum N_{ij} y_i}{N_{.j}}
$$
$$
+ B_3 \frac{\sum d_i^a N_{ij}}{N_{.j}} + B_4 S_j + \frac{\sum N_{ij} u_{ij}}{N_{.j}}.
$$

All the sums in equation (2) are over the set of residential areas in j's service area.

The left-hand variable in equation (2) is simply the visits to the jth park per resident in its service area. The first three right-hand variables in (2) are weighted averages of distances, incomes, and state park availability within the jth park's service area. In each case the weights are proportions of the population in the park's service area that reside within each residential area.

It will be convenient to write equation (2) as

$$
(3) \quad \bar{V}_j = B_0 + B_1 \bar{d}_j + B_2 \bar{y}_j + B_3 \bar{d}_j^a + B_4 S_j + \bar{u}_j
$$

where the barred variables are the weighted averages just indicated.

Equation (3) was estimated from cross-sectional data from the year 1960. The averages appearing in equation (3) are burdensome to calculate and therefore the sample had to be kept relatively small. The choice of the sample was also influenced by the desire to include parks that represent a relatively homogeneous product. Since state parks tend to be somewhat different in the western part of the country than in the eastern part, the decision was made to use data from eastern states only. A further increase in homogeneity was obtained by excluding all state parks that are mainly salt-water beaches. Partly to increase the degree of homogeneity and partly to keep the sample size small, only state parks with at least 500 acres were used.

There are still a large number of state parks that satisfy all of the above criteria. Therefore, the decision was made to use only the state parks within three states that have unusually good data on attendance at individual state parks.[19] The states chosen were Connecticut, Maryland, and New York. Finally, Adirondack State Park in New York was excluded on the grounds that it is a resource-oriented area rather than an intermediate area. This park consists of fifteen forest preserve counties and contains about 40 per cent of all the state park acreage in the country. We are left with thirty-one state parks: seven in Connecticut, four in Maryland, and twenty in New York.[20]

Estimation of equation (3) requires estimation of the radius of the service areas and of the B coefficients. In principle, the following procedure could be used. For some fixed possible service area radius, calculate the barred variables as described below for each state park and estimate the coefficients in equation (3) by the usual least squares procedure. Repeat this process for several different service area radii and use as the estimate of the true radius the one that yields the largest R^2 for the least squares regression.

In fact, this procedure was not used. The number of residential areas increases with the square of the radius. Calculation of the averages therefore becomes very burdensome for large radii. Furthermore, there is some evidence that the average one-way distance traveled on a state park visit is between twenty-five and fifty miles.[21] This suggests that the radius of the service area is probably between seventy-five and 100 miles. In the calculations reported below, a radius of seventy-five miles was assumed.

The basic unit of residential area is assumed to be the county. The population center for each county was estimated from maps on the basis of the county's geographical center and the location of large cities and towns. The service area for each park was assumed to consist of all the counties whose population centers are within seventy-five miles of the park[22].

The variables in equation (3) were calculated as follows. The dependent variable requires data on the number of visits to each park and the population of the service area. The former were obtained on request from the three state governments, and the latter were obtained from the county population data in the 1960 U.S. Census. The distance variable was computed by a straight line from the park to each county population center. No account was taken of the quality, directness, or congestion of roads. Income per capita was calculated for each county from the Census.

It will be recalled from the discussion above that $\bar{d}_j^a$ is supposed to measure the availability of other state parks to the residents of j's service area. As was indicated above, an ideal measure would be an average distance to state parks available to residents of each county. However, that calculation would be extremely burdensome. Hence, as a proxy, a much simpler variable was used. For the ith county and the jth state park, the value of the proxy variable is the distance from the ith county's population center to the nearest state park other than the jth state park. Here again, only parks of at least 500 acres were used. This variable is a good proxy to the extent that the distance to the nearest other state park is the main effect of other state parks on visits to the jth state park. That this effect is likely to be important is suggested by the averages presented below which show that the average resident in the jth state park's service area is over twice as far from the jth park as he is from the nearest other state park.

The acreage data for the variables S_j were obtained on request from the state governments.

All the data used in the calculations are presented in the Appendix. The estimate of equation (3) is

(4) $\quad \hat{V}_i = 4334 - 46.789\,\bar{d}_i - 1.223\,\bar{y}_i + 45.870\,\bar{d}_i^a + 0.039\,S_i.$

$\qquad\qquad (3.082)\qquad(1.542)\qquad\quad(2.620)\qquad\quad(3.871)$

The numbers in parentheses are the t values of the coefficients. The coefficient of $\bar{y}$ is significant at the 10 per cent level, and that of $\bar{d}_i^a$ is significant at the 5 per cent level. All the others are significant at the 1 per cent level. R^2 is 0.633. The sample means of the variables are:

Variable	Mean	Units
$\bar{V}$	733.4	Visits per 10,000 pop.
$\bar{d}_i$	47.3	Miles (one way)
$\bar{y}_i$	2,082.4	Dollars per capita
$\bar{d}_i^a$	20.9	Miles (one way)
S_i	5,164.7	Acres

With the exception of the income variable, each coefficient in equation (4) has the expected sign. The coefficient of S_i is positive and highly significant, indicating that people find large parks much more attractive than small parks. The coefficient of $\bar{d}_i^a$ is positive, indicating that the greater the distance to the nearest alternative park, the more the visits to the jth park.

The income and distance variables require somewhat more extensive comment. The income coefficient is negative, suggesting that state park visits are an inferior good. However, since the coefficient is significant at only the 10 per cent level, the evidence is not very strong. Nevertheless, the result is not implausible if it is remembered that the sample is restricted to relatively high-income observations. Very poor people rarely visit state parks because there is almost no way of getting there except by private car, and very poor people cannot afford cars. In addition, the parks included in the sample lie in relatively high-income areas. People with relatively high incomes probably tend to substitute for state park visits such activities as visits to salt-water beaches, ownership or rental of summer homes, membership in country clubs, and longer trips involving visits to national parks and forests. Thus, the suggestion here is that the demand for state park visits may well have a positive income elasticity at relatively low incomes, but a negative income elasticity at relatively high incomes.

The coefficient of $\bar{d}_j$ has the expected sign and is highly significant. Provided we assume that the cost of a state park visit is proportionate to the distance traveled, we can interpret the coefficient of $\bar{d}_j$ as the slope of the demand curve. Since the elasticity of demand is independent of units, we can calculate the elasticity without knowing the cost per mile of travel. Evaluated at the sample means of the variables, the elasticity is 3.02. Although this indicates a very elastic demand, it is not unreasonable. In the first place, as will be argued below, state park visits are not necessarily very cheap. Therefore, evaluating the elasticity at the average distance traveled means evaluating it at quite a high price. Although we usually think of demand as being price-inelastic at low prices, an elasticity of this magnitude is not unreasonable at a fairly high price.

In the second place, this elasticity is relevant to the question: What would be the effect on visits to state park j of a 1 per cent change in the cost of visiting that park if the cost of visiting other state parks remained constant? It is not surprising that an increase in the cost of visiting a particular state park would lead to a large decrease in the visits to that park.

The more interesting question is: What would be the effect on the visits to state park j of a 1 per cent change in the cost of visiting every state park? An approximate answer to this question can be obtained from equation (4) by calculating the effect on visits per capita to state park j of a 1 per cent change in $\bar{d}_j$ and a 1 per cent change in $\bar{d}_j^a$ in the same direction. This provides an estimate of the effect on visits to park j of a simultaneous 1 per cent increase in the cost of all state parks. The elasticity of $\bar{V}_j$ with respect to $\bar{d}_j^a$, again evaluating at the sample means, is 1.31. The difference between the two elasticities is 1.71. Thus, we estimate that entrance fees which raised the cost per visit to all state parks by 1 per cent would reduce visits by 1.71 per cent.

In order to estimate the effect on visits of admission charges, we must estimate the cost per mile traveled to state parks. In equation (4), the coefficients of the two d variables relate visits to distance. If we know the cost per mile traveled, we can convert these coefficients into coefficients that relate visits to cost of the visit. Then we can estimate the effect of an admission charge, which increases the cost of the visit, on the number of visits.

It is difficult to estimate the cost per mile traveled in visiting state parks because we do not know the opportunity cost of time spent traveling. Therefore, the following calculations should be regarded as educated guesses. Think of the average state park visitor as traveling in a family group of four—two adults and two children—in the family car. Assume that the trip is completed in one day so that there are no overnight costs. Further, assume that a picnic lunch is taken, costing no more than a similar meal at home. The cost per mile of operating the car may be eight cents, or two cents per capita. Again evaluating at the sample means, this means that the trip costs the family $7.57, or about $1.90 per capita. To find out whether the travel itself yields utility or disutility, we must ask the family how much it would be willing to pay if, just for the purpose of this visit, the park could magically be located right next door. If the answer is less than $7.57, the travel gives them utility; if more, it gives them disutility.

Since the answer to the above question is unknown, the calculations have been done for three alternative possibilities. Alternative A assumes that the total cost of the trip for the average family is $10.00 (the travel gives disutility); alternative B assumes that the total cost is $7.50 (the travel gives zero utility); alternative C assumes that the total cost is $5.00 (the travel gives utility). These alternatives imply a cost per capita per mile of $.03, $.02, and $.01 respectively. We can now convert a distance coefficient B in equation (4) to a cost coefficient B' by use of the following formula:

$$B \cdot d = B' \cdot (2 \times \text{cost per mile}) d$$

or

$$B' = \frac{B}{2 \times \text{cost per mile}}.$$

The results are as follows:

Alternative	Cost per mile	B_1'	B_3'	$B_1' + B_3'$
A	$.03	−780	765	−15
B	.02	−1170	1148	−22
C	.01	−2340	2295	−45

These results can be interpreted as follows. If the cost per mile of travel to state parks is $.03 per capita, then we estimate that a $1.00 entrance fee for each state park visit would reduce visits to the typical state park by fifteen visits per year per 10,000 residents of the park's service area. If travel cost is $.02, then the $1.00 entrance fee would reduce visits by twenty-two visits per 10,000 residents. If travel cost is $.01, the figure is forty-five per 10,000 residents.

In the previous section, it was estimated that the cost per visitor of providing state parks is about $.35. This and other considerations discussed in the previous section suggest that an appropriate entrance fee might be about $.50 per visitor. The figures presented in the previous paragraph imply that such a charge might reduce visits by eight, eleven, or twenty-three visits per 10,000 residents, depending on which of the three alternatives is correct. This implies that visits to the average state park would fall off by 1 per cent, 1.5 per cent, or 3.0 per cent, depending on whether alternative A, B, or C is correct.

We can summarize these results as follows. The own-price elasticity of demand for visits to a particular state park is very high, about 3.02. The elasticity of demand for state park visits in response to a simultaneous change in the cost of all state park visits is much smaller, about 1.31. Furthermore, the cost of state park visits is fairly high even in the absence of entrance fees, probably between $5.00 and $10.00 for the typical family visit. Therefore, a modest entrance fee of $.50 per visitor would be a rather small percentage increase in the cost of the typical visit, and the effect would probably be to reduce the number of visits by no more than about 3 per cent.

These results suggest strongly that attendance would be little affected if entrance fees sufficient to cover costs were charged for state park visits. There is, however, a warning implied by the fact that the result follows from largely offsetting own-price and cross elasticities. If a small state, such as Connecticut or Maryland, were to charge entrance fees on its own, then, unless neighboring states followed similar policies, a large decrease in attendance should be expected in the fee-charging state. None of the calculations have recognized state boundaries and large parts of the service areas of many parks are in different states than the park itself.

CONCLUSION

The final remarks in this paper concern the relevance of the above calculations for long-term projections in state park attendance. It is not the purpose of this paper either to undertake new projections of state park visits or to evaluate existing projections. Nevertheless, the calculations presented in the preceding section have some strong implications for future trends that should be pointed out.

The first question to ask is what light is shed on the rapid postwar growth of state park visits by the estimates presented above. In particular, if increases in income have either a small or perverse effect on state park visits, how can we account for the observed historical increase? I have no systematic answer to the question. Using cross-sectional analysis for time-series prediction is a notoriously difficult business. Nevertheless, the following remarks are offered. First, it seems likely that the income elasticity of demand was positive in the early postwar period and has been falling gradually. The evidence presented above suggests that, at income levels in the vicinity of $2,000 per capita, the income elasticity is either negative or at least small. Yet it seems fairly obvious that at lower income levels, particularly around levels at which car ownership becomes widespread, the income effect must be positive. Hence, my conjecture is that increases in incomes have accounted for a substantial part of the postwar rise in visits, but that further increases in incomes will not result in substantial future increases in visits.

Second, there has clearly been a substantial decrease in the real cost of travel in the postwar period. According to the estimates presented above, a 1 per cent decrease in the cost per mile of travel will increase state park visits per capita by about 1.71 per cent. This price effect has probably been substantial in the postwar period. Whether it will continue to be important in the coming decades is questionable. As travel costs become smaller, a variety of other recreational areas become competitive with state parks for recreational trips.

Third, the other factors that have accounted for the postwar rise in demand for state park visits are probably demographic rather than economic. One obvious demographic factor is the large increase in the percentage of families that have small children. Another demographic factor is the rapid urbanization of the population. In rural areas, outdoor recreation takes place on farmland or on undeveloped woodland. In urban areas, such land is unavailable and recreation must be transferred to explicitly designated recreation areas, such as state parks. This factor will continue to be important as long as the rate of urbanization continues high.

Finally, we should not ignore the supply side. The acreage of state parks grew about 25 per cent between 1946 and 1961. In some states, at least, a large part of this growth was near large urban centers and undoubtedly accounted for a substantial part of the increase in visits.

What about the future? The first thing to note is that the rate of growth of state park visits already shows signs of slackening. The annual rate of growth of visits since 1956 has been substantially lower than it was in the first postwar decade.[23] Second, I believe that most people who have projected state park visits have attached too much importance to future income growth in increasing the demand. The price effect mentioned above, resulting from decreases in the real cost of travel, will undoubtedly continue to be of some importance. So also will the two demographic factors. It is difficult to believe that increases in leisure have had much effect on state park visits during the postwar period. Hours worked have changed very little and the increase in the number of people who take vacations has probably not been important, since most state park visits take place on weekends. A considerable decrease in hours worked would probably increase the number of weekday visits somewhat. Everything considered, it seems likely that future per capita growth in state park visits will be substantial, but probably much closer to the ORRRC projection than to the two RFF projections discussed in the introduction.

APPENDIX
Data on State Parks

Park	Distance to closest park	Average distance to park	Average income	Total visits	Visits per capita	Acres in park
CONNECTICUT						
Bigelow Hollow	11.3	50.0	$2,085	41,828	.0057	513
Devil's Hopyard	12.8	45.1	2,149	60,572	.0138	860
Gay City	12.9	42.0	2,138	43,703	.0095	1,542
Hurd	12.5	40.9	2,149	32,068	.0073	698
Macedonia Brook	14.2	58.1	2,086	42,744	.0046	1,845
Sleeping Giant	14.6	51.3	2,445	49,786	.0066	1,246
Penwood	12.6	45.3	2,115	52,118	.0104	839
MARYLAND						
Cunningham Falls	20.9	52.0	2,067	60,468	.0109	4,447
Deep Creek Lake	23.2	63.5	1,751	68,928	.0207	1,773
Gambrill	21.0	49.5	2,073	50,352	.0092	1,138
Patapsco	40.6	32.5	2,099	2,388,671	.4301	6,017
NEW YORK						
Allegany	33.0	55.4	1,797	687,000	.2803	58,420
Bethpage	13.6	29.4	2,404	478,000	.0290	1,520
Buttermilk Falls	21.9	50.9	1,927	76,853	.0326	675
Chenango Valley	19.4	52.4	1,757	242,088	.0978	928
Clarence Fahnestock	13.0	47.8	2,407	74,623	.0044	3,400
Cuba	35.8	55.4	1,976	66,000	.0233	650
Fillmore Glen	22.6	47.4	1,927	63,896	.0244	857
Gilbert Lake	25.4	54.3	1,894	113,835	.0461	1,569
Green Lakes	22.0	38.6	1,842	491,904	.2621	775
Harriman and Bear Mountain	13.0	39.3	2,383	4,547,000	.2612	45,332
Hempstead Lake	15.9	23.7	2,407	443,100	.0270	867
James Baird	13.9	60.1	2,387	186,434	.0106	583
Lake Taghkanic	19.6	54.6	2,149	87,166	.0187	1,002
Letchworth	44.4	46.2	1,964	529,000	.1778	13,355
Stony Brook	35.3	53.0	1,955	138,186	.0465	554
Taconic	19.0	51.8	2,153	48,107	.0104	6,200
Tallman Mountain	14.8	28.1	2,383	117,000	.0067	634
Taughannock Falls	21.7	51.7	1,915	324,435	.1223	535
Verona Beach	23.4	42.9	1,840	206,832	.1105	726
Watkins Glen	22.6	51.4	1,929	373,459	.1530	605

Notes

1. The research reported in this paper was undertaken under contract with the Maryland State Planning Department and was partly financed by an Urban Planning Grant from the Housing and Home Finance Agency. I am indebted to my colleague John Owen and to Marion Clawson of Resources for the Future for valuable comments on a first draft.
2. Marion Clawson, R. Burnell Held, and Charles H. Stoddard, *Land for the Future* (Baltimore: The Johns Hopkins Press, 1960). Especially Ch. III. Hans H. Landsberg, Leonard L. Fischmann, and Joseph L. Fisher, *Resources in America's Future* (Baltimore: The Johns Hopkins Press, 1963). Especially Ch. XI.
3. ORRRC, *Outdoor Recreation for America* (Washington: U.S. Government Printing Office, 1962). See also Study Reports 1–27. Numbers 19 and 20 report on two major sample surveys of participation in outdoor recreation. These surveys provide a wealth of data, as yet largely unexploited, for detailed study of the demand for outdoor recreation.
4. Clawson, Held, and Stoddard, *op. cit.*, p. 136.
5. If the observed 1950 to 1960 rate of growth of visits per capita to Maryland state parks were to continue to the year 2000, residents would average two state park visits per day in that year.
6. *Op. cit.*, p. 187.
7. *Op. cit.*, p. 225.
8. ORRRC Study Report 26, p. 22.
9. This figure assumes that visits to state parks and federal reservoirs will grow at equal rates, an assumption not necessarily made by Clawson, Held, and Stoddard.
10. Lest I be accused of being opposed to state parks, I would like to point out that my family's state park visits exceed the Maryland average by a factor of five.
11. For an articulate statement of this argument, see Harvey S. Perloff and Lowdon Wingo, Jr., "Urban Growth and the Planning of Outdoor Recreation," ORRRC Study Report 22, pp. 81–100.
12. See A. Walters, "Theory and Measurement of Private and Social Costs of Highway Congestion," *Econometrica*, XXIX, No. 4 (October, 1961), 676–699.
13. ORRRC Study Report 1, pp. 52–61.
14. Nothing has been said about the controversy over marginal cost vs. average cost pricing. The provision of state parks is a capital (and land) intensive process, and marginal cost must be below average cost per visit to a particular park. However, when the effect on congestion is included, it is unlikely that a price as high as average cost would be too high. In addition, the fact that low-cost sites are acquired first means that the cost per acre of the marginal park is greater than that of the average.
15. All the data came from U.S. Department of the Interior, National Park Service, *State Park Statistics.*
16. This statement should not be confused with a proposal to use eminent domain to acquire property at less than its true opportunity cost. The issue is how to prevent a seller from obtaining more than the opportunity cost of his land by being the last to sell.
17. The calculations reported in this section were performed by David Warheit.
18. "Methods of Measuring the Demand for and Value of Outdoor Recreation" (Resources for the Future: Reprint Number 10, February, 1959).
19. "Good data" means that attendance figures are either actual counts or are based on samples of actual counts, as reported by the National Park Service in *State Park Statistics—1960.*
20. Although these restrictions on the sample increase the plausibility of using equation (3), it must be remembered that they restrict the applicability of any findings to a particular class of state parks.
21. See Clawson, Held, and Stoddard, *op. cit.*, p. 180.
22. This makes the effective radius of the service area somewhat more than seventy-five miles. A small number of exceptions were made to this rule when an unbridged body of water, such as Long Island Sound, lay between the park and a population center. In such cases the service area was assumed to end at the water's edge.
23. National Park Service, *State Park Statistics—1962.*

PART II

RESOURCE MARKETS

A More General Theory of
Resource Migration

Michael J. Brennan

AMERICANS are a mobile people. Between 1955 and 1960 almost twenty-eight million persons five years of age or over—17 per cent of that population—migrated to a different county. About half of these moved to a different state. Migration among the nine Census divisions reveals (1) that migrants moved in both directions between each pair of divisions, and (2) that the magnitudes of these flows were typically in the hundreds of thousands. This population migration reflects a significant movement of labor of various skills and occupations.

Estimates of net capital exports among regions of the U.S. indicate that capital migration is also substantial.[1] As might be expected, casual observation of capital movements for selected industries strongly suggests that regional capital transfers move in different directions for different industries. Therefore, capital as well as labor is likely to flow in both directions for some pairs of regions.

In the published literature of economics over the past thirty years, studies of regional capital migration within the U.S. are virtually nonexistent. Somewhat more effort has been directed toward explanations of labor migration, yet these leave much to be desired. Except for relatively few empirical studies dealing with broadly defined industries (such as farm-nonfarm migration) or broadly defined regions (such as South-North migration) economists have left to others the task of explaining interregional migration. From cross-section samples demographers have correlated population out-migration with income, age, sex, etc. for the U.S. as a whole. Though informative, such studies do not grapple with the more interesting problem of explaining the magnitude and economic characteristics of migration flows among several regions for occupational and industrial classes of labor.[2]

45

Undoubtedly, one reason for the scarcity of multiregional migration studies has been a lack of adequate data. But aside from data availability there are many theoretical problems which have also contributed.

(1) For any given region, out-migration to several other regions is possible for both capital and labor. And in each of these other regions employment in several industries is possible.

(2) Migration from several industries in a given region is possible, and intraregional movement to any one of a number of other industries within the region is possible.

(3) Resource inputs which may be regarded as homogeneous in their capacity as factors of production are not homogeneous with respect to other determinants of migration.

(4) Decisions to migrate are influenced by nonpecuniary factors that are not subject to direct measurement.

(5) Migrations of capital and labor between any two regions are not independent.

An assumption that labor responds solely to differentials in average regional wage rates and unemployment, or that capital owners respond solely to differentials in regional rates of return, leads to conclusions which do not explain some facts and are at variance with others. Region-industry-occupation mixes entail more complex migration decisions. This paper proposes an analytical framework designed to explain magnitudes of two-way resource flows and to generate predictions of their characteristics: capital type, occupation, income, age, and family size. The model is not a completely general theory because it adopts simplifications necessary to permit quantitative estimation on the basis of available data.[3] Long-run equilibrium is conceived of as a static state in which migration among all regions is zero for every resource. Nonzero equilibrium rates of migration in the short run are determined by the maximization of net returns to migration. Nonpecuniary factors which influence migration decisions, though not directly observable, are taken into account in that they establish the forms of the pecuniary functions.

PECUNIARY DETERMINANTS OF MIGRATION

Nonpecuniary forces affecting migration are treated as costs of migrating out of a given region. Net pecuniary returns are defined as gross returns minus pecuniary costs. Since migration decisions are investment decisions, gross returns are construed as comparative regional expected income streams. In general, let region i $(i = 1, 2, \ldots, I)$ be a region *in which* expectations are formed, and let region j $(j = 1, 2, \ldots, I)$ be a region *about which* expectations are formed. Thus migration from i to j is being considered.

EXPECTED GROSS RETURNS FROM MIGRATION

The complexity of simultaneous multi-regional and multi-industrial migration can be reduced to manageable proportions by focusing upon a single measure of returns from migration between any two regions i and j. Gross returns are therefore defined as an income stream from employment in j as compared to an income stream from employment in i. However, when formulating an income stream in either i or j for a particular resource class, two aspects are distinguished: (1) real income from employment in industry k $(k = 1, 2, \ldots, K)$, and (2) the distribution of the K industries within a region—more specifically, the distribution of such industry income streams.

Future income from employment of a given resource in a particular industry and region is affected by the prevailing resource price in that industry and region, future changes in this price, changes in productivity over the employment life of the resource, degree of seasonality and cyclical fluctuations in the industry, the industry trend of growth or decline, etc. Their net effect upon income expectations can be summarized in the present value of an expected income stream. For inter-industry comparisons the discounting allows for differences in time patterns of earnings which are not reflected in average lifetime earnings alone. Given a present value from employment in each industry, migration decisions hinge upon the probability of employment in that industry. If the probability of being unemployed is included, if unemployment is treated as an "industry" yielding zero earned income, the effects of regional unemployment (where applicable) are also taken into account. Each region displays an array of industry present values and corresponding probabilities of employment. Expected gross return associated with migration from i to j, defined as the expectation of the distribution in j minus the expectation of the distribution in i for a particular resource class, reflects incentives to move intraregionally as well as industry mix and over-all regional growth.

Returns from Capital Migration

Capital investment decisions comprise two components: whether or not to invest and where to invest. A marginal efficiency of investment is postulated for each industry k and region j. That is, expected future incomes and capital cost yielding this rate of return are assumed common to all capital owners regardless of the region in which expectations are formed. Let the interest rate be identical for all industries and regions, so e_{jk} represents the marginal efficiency of investment minus the interest rate. If e_{jk} is positive, zero, or negative, it is assumed that the change in net investment in k and j will likewise be positive, zero, or negative respectively. Moreover, since owners of capital presently located there will not expand investment in k and j for $e_{jk} < 0$, then *a forteriori* no capital owners elsewhere will consider a transfer of capital to this industry and region. Nevertheless, this does not mean that capital will not flow into region j, for other industries in the region may well have large positive expected rates of return.

Given K rates of return, one for each industry in region j, capital migration also depends upon the possibility of employing capital in each industry. An industry with a high rate of return may not be accessible to some capital owners because of artificial restrictions on entry or excessive capital requirements. Likewise, the probability that capital would move to an industry with negative or zero e_{jk} is near or equal to zero. There may be a presumption that capital employed in a given industry would be attracted to the same industry elsewhere. But certainly there is no assurance that such a presumption will be realized, and one cannot determine precisely how capital migration will distribute itself among industries in another region.

In the absence of better knowledge, distinctions can be drawn among V capital classes, where each class v ($v = 1, 2, \ldots, V$) is defined by the nature of the industry in which it is currently employed (concentration ratio, manufacturing or service, etc.). Without entering into a discussion of the statistical methods of approximating the probability distribution for each class, it is assumed that for each there is an objective probability $p_{jk}(v)$ of employing capital in industry k and region j, and this probability is common to all members of the class regardless of the region of current location. In general, for some j and k the probability will be zero for at least one capital class. With a probability attached to each industry rate of return

$$(1) \qquad e_j(v) = \sum_{k=1}^{K} p_{jk}(v) \cdot e_{jk}, \qquad \sum_k p_{jk}(v) = 1, \qquad v = 1, 2, \cdots, V$$

is defined as the expected rate of return from location of capital class v in region j. The expected rate of return from location in region i, $e_i(v)$, is similarly defined.[4]

Given a single expected return from location in each region, the expected rate of return from migration of capital is the difference between regional rates of return. The expected gross return for migration of capital class v from region i to region j is defined as

$$(2) \qquad e_{ij}(v) = e_j(v) - e_i(v), \qquad v = 1, 2, \cdots, V.$$

Costs, net returns, and the behavior of net returns as migration proceeds will be discussed later.

Returns from Labor Migration

In the case of labor, occupations form the lines of distinction. The labor force in each region is divided into a set of defined occupations, where the members of different occupations are assumed to be non-competing groups. For a member of a given occupation located in region i, the expected gross return from migration to j is defined as the present value of the expected income stream from employment in j minus the present value of the expected income stream from employment in i. Let $y_{jk}(t)$ denote the real income in year t expected from employment in industry k located in region j, common to all members of that occupation regardless of the region of present location. The present value for a worker of age a is

$$(3) \qquad y_{jk}(a) = \sum_{t=1}^{A-a} \frac{y_{jk}(t)}{(1+d)^t},$$

where 1 represents the current year, A the terminal age of life expectancy, and $(1/1 + d)$ the appropriate discount rate. The discount rate and life expectancy are assumed identical for all individuals. If in addition the expected income at (hypothetical) age a is the same for all workers, regardless of actual age, then for a given industry the present value will differ among workers only with respect to age differences. Thus age is an important determinant of returns from migration.

It is assumed that a definite objective probability of employment, $p_{jk}(a)$, is attached to each $y_{jk}(a)$ and that this probability is identical for all potential migrants of the same age. Then

$$(4) \qquad y_j(a) = \sum_{k=1}^{K} p_{jk}(a) \cdot y_{jk}(a), \qquad \sum_k p_{jk} = 1,$$

is defined as the present value of the expected income stream from employment in region j by a member of the occupational class of age a. As in the case of capital, probabilities may be zero for some j and k

where applicable. In addition, if unemployment is considered as an "industry," some $y_{jk}(t)$ will be zero for all t.

The second component of gross returns from migration—the present value of the expected income stream from employment in i, $y_i(a)$—is similarly defined for $y_{ik}(a)$ and $p_{ik}(a)$ and takes account of incentives to move intraregionally. Finally, the expected gross return for migration of the given occupational class of age a from i to j is the difference

$$(5) \qquad\qquad g_{ij}(a) = y_j(a) - y_i(a).$$

It follows that there will be a separate expected gross return for each age group, where together these age groups comprise the occupational labor force in region i. On the basis of assumptions made about the relation between income expectations and age, it was seen that $y_{jk}(a)$ varies inversely with age for all k. Likewise, $y_i(a)$ will vary inversely with a. But $g_{ij}(a)$ need not. For a given industry with a given difference in the average expected lifetime earnings between two regions, a radical difference between the time patterns of earnings could operate to produce a positive correlation between $g_{ij}(a)$ and a. For example, income streams in j and i, such that for "many" industries expected income at higher ages is sufficiently greater in j, while expected income at lower ages is sufficiently greater in i, tend to generate this result. The same argument holds true for particular differences between regions in the probability of employment by age. As a consequence, $g_{ij}(a)$ can vary directly with a in principle. However, unless each of these two factors exerts a strong separate influence and they both operate in the proper direction, which is very unlikely, we may be assured that $g_{ij}(a)$ will be negatively, though imperfectly, correlated with a.

COSTS AND EXPECTED NET RETURNS FROM MIGRATION

The *net* pecuniary returns from migration are gross returns minus pecuniary costs. Costs of capital migration are not likely to be crucial. Funds to finance capital formation can be allocated geographically at relatively low cost. Given enough time, existing equipment can be transformed into liquid funds as it depreciates and retransformed into equipment elsewhere. Nevertheless, capital transfer does typically entail loss from sale of existing equipment if it is sold before it is fully depreciated; otherwise costs of transporting equipment are incurred. Relocation involves costs of site development for new plant, costs of rehiring and retraining a new labor force, and costs of legal advice and negotiations.

Some of these cost items are independent of the volume of capital migration by any one capital owner. Others rise with the amount of capital migration. For simplicity it will be assumed that capital migration is subject to rising cost as a percentage of the value of capital out-migration, and that this cost function is identical for all capital types. Thus

$$(6) \qquad n_{ij}(v) = e_{ij}(v) - z_{ij}, \qquad v = 1, 2, \cdots, V,$$

is defined as the net return to capital class v, where z_{ij} is identical for all v and increases with respect to capital migration from i to j.

The pecuniary costs of labor migration include:

(1) personal transportation cost of the worker,
(2) cost of transporting his dependents,
(3) cost of transporting movable personal property plus any loss from sale of nonmovable property,
(4) income forgone during the period of migration.

Needless to say, precise measurement of cost is difficult, and any estimate used must be arbitrary to more or less degree. Most of the components of cost depend upon geographic relocation of the household, whereas employment in a particular industry (either within region i or within region j) may occur at any one of several geographic points. In addition, intraregional migration may entail zero or nonzero cost, depending upon whether or not the household must relocate. This difficulty is less formidable than it appears, however. For only between regions for which $g_{ij}(a)$ is of very small positive magnitude are costs likely to play an important role as a pecuniary determinant of migration. And in these instances an "average" cost will likely suffice to predict the direction of migration. In all other cases expected gross returns will be of much greater magnitude than cost, and so will constitute the principal component of net pecuniary return.

Item (1) is determined by mode of transportation as well as the distance between two regions. Item (2) depends upon distance, mode of transportation, and the number of dependents. Item (3) consists of a fixed-cost component (loading and storage), plus a component dependent upon distance, plus a loss (or gain) from sale, which in turn depends upon the local market conditions in region i. Item (4) depends upon distance to the extent that greater distance entails a longer "search" for a new position, i.e., a longer interim between departure and beginning of new employment. Of course, it also depends upon current earnings in a potential migrant's present employment.

There are three cost comparisons that a potential migrant will consider: (1) the cost of migrating interregionally, (2) the cost of migrating intraregionally, and (3) the zero cost of not migrating (even though this entails a change in the industry of employment). For simplicity we shall assume the cost of intra-regional migration is zero, and let $c_{ij}(a)$ denote the cost of migration from i to j by a potential migrant of age a. Between any two regions this cost will be a constant for a worker of age a. While personal transportation cost may be taken as the same for all workers regardless of age, the other components of cost are likely to be correlated (though, again, not perfectly correlated) with age. To the extent that number of dependents, property holdings, and present income are related to age, so will cost between any two regions be related to age.

The net expected pecuniary return from migration, r_{ij}, is gross return minus total cost. Thus, for a worker of age a in region i, contemplating migration to region j, the net expected return is

$$(7) \qquad\qquad r_{ij}(a) = g_{ij}(a) - c_{ij}(a).$$

The entire occupational labor force in region i can be classified into a set of age groups, for each of which there exists an $r_{ij}(a)$. Because $g_{ij}(a)$ tends to vary inversely with a and $c_{ij}(a)$ is likely to vary directly with a, it is to be expected that one would find an imperfect negative correlation between $r_{ij}(a)$ and a.[5]

NONPECUNIARY DETERMINANTS OF MIGRATION

Only some resource services are separable from their owners. With few exceptions (e.g., certain professional groups and self-employed proprietors) the relocation of capital can be carried out without relocation of the capital owners. Labor, however, cannot be transferred geographically without relocation of the household. As a consequence, nonpecuniary factors are assumed to exert an influence upon labor migration only. Aside from gross returns expected in region j, the willingness to migrate is affected by nonpecuniary aspects of region j such as climate, urban versus rural living, differences in community culture, etc. On the cost side there are nonpecuniary costs connected with migration: the divorce of established social and family ties, the educational displacement of children, etc.—in general, a type of inertia factor. For this reason one cannot assume that those who do migrate will migrate to the region of highest expected net pecuniary return, or that all those with positive expected net returns will even migrate.

Certain plausible assumptions about the effects of these forces can be made, however. On the returns side, $r_{ij}(a)$ tends to vary inversely with age for all j, and age is a restraining factor in the willingness to migrate. For greater age normally implies more firmly established community ties with relatives and friends. In addition, greater age often implies seniority rights in present employment, and the greater security provided by these rights operates to discourage migration. On the cost side, personal and real property holdings are usually associated with community status; they also entail higher pecuniary costs of migration. Likewise, as a rule, the greater the number of dependent children, the more a household is involved in the activities of the community, and the greater is the pecuniary cost of transporting dependents. It follows that more advanced age, a larger number of dependents, and greater property holdings act to lower gross pecuniary returns and/or raise pecuniary costs, thus reducing net pecuniary returns to out-migration. These characteristics may be taken as proxies for the unobservable psychological and cultural factors affecting migration. Such an argument simply reflects the common-sense observation that, given the existence of any positive pecuniary returns to migration, younger persons with more adventurous spirits, fewer dependents, and fewer property holdings *tend* to migrate most readily. And it is precisely these groups in a given occupation which have the highest expected gross returns and the lowest total cost. This is, nevertheless, no more than a tendency, so allowance must be made for exceptions.

THE ORDERING OF MIGRATION UNITS

Let F_i denote the size of (the total number of laborers in) the occupational labor force in region i, and order all laborers from the largest to the smallest algebraic value of $r_{ij}(a)$. From this ordering form $H + 1$ classes $(0, 1, 2, \cdots, h, \cdots, H)$, where each class h has the single expected net pecuniary return per worker, r_{ij}^h, say the median for the class. Let f^h represent the size of (number of workers in) class h, so that

$$\sum_{h=0}^{H} f^h = F_i.$$

But define 0 and H as empty sets. It follows that $f^0 = 0$, $f^H = 0$, the remaining f's are in general of unequal size, and

$$r_{ij}^1 > r_{ij}^2 > \cdots > r_{ij}^{H-1}.$$

Also, rank the labor force into $S + 1$ migration classes $(0, 1, 2, \cdots, s, \cdots, S)$ where the size of each class s is denoted by m^s and

$$\sum_{s=0}^{S} m^s = F_i.$$

If any migration occurs, all members of class s migrate before any member of class $s + 1$.

In order to determine the size and composition of migration class s we wish to map the miragtion classes into the expected return classes as follows:

$$m^s = \sum_{h=0}^{H} \alpha_{sh} f^h, \qquad s = 0, 1, 2, \cdots, S,$$

$$0 \leq \alpha_{sh} < 1,$$

where

$$\sum_{h=0}^{H} \alpha_{sh} = 1, \qquad \sum_{s=0}^{s} \alpha_{sh} = 1.$$

The size and the composition of each migration class are determined by the f's and the α's. From empirical organization and ordering of the occupational labor force, each class h is characterized by age, dependents, and property holdings used to determine pecuniary returns and costs. Moreover, to each class h there corresponds an r_{ij}^h. As a consequence this mapping also yields an expected net return for each migration class. Once the α's are specified the expected net return per worker for migration class s is given by

$$r_{ij}^s = \sum_{h=0}^{H} \alpha_{sh} r_{ij}^h, \qquad s = 0, 1, 2, \cdots, S.$$

Specification of the α's

The α's may be construed as conditional probabilities, so that α_{sh} represents the probability that workers in a given expected-return class h are included in migration class s. Since h and s are both discrete variables, restricted to $H + 1$ equidistant values and $S + 1$ equidistant values respectively, explicit expression for the probability distribution of workers being in various migration classes can be derived from a variation of the Chapman-Kolmogarov equation.[6] If $P(s, h)$ denotes the probability that workers in expected-return class h are included in migration class s, the expression

$$P_{ij}(s, h) = \binom{S}{s} \left[e^{-\beta_{ij}\left(\frac{H-h}{h}\right)} \right]^s \left[1 - e^{-\beta_{ij}\left(\frac{H-h}{h}\right)} \right]^{S-s}, \qquad \beta_{ij} > 0,$$

is zero for the empty classes $h = 0$ and $H = h$. For all other values of h the density distribution by migration classes is a binomial

$$\binom{n}{x} p^x q^{n-x}$$

with

$$p = e^{-\beta_{ij}\left(\frac{H-h}{h}\right)} \quad \text{and} \quad n = S.$$

There are two parameters of this distribution which bear upon the non-pecuniary determinants of migration, the constant β_{ij} and the return class h. Let us first consider two given regions so that β_{ij} is specified. In the original binomial the moments $\mu_0 = np$, $\mu_2 = npq$, and $\mu_3 = npq(q - p)$, together with the above expression for p, lead to a neat pattern of changes as h is allowed to vary. Since

$$e^{-\beta_{ij}\left(\frac{H-h}{h}\right)}$$

increases from zero to unity as h increases, the mean,

$$S \cdot e^{-\beta_{ij}\left(\frac{H-h}{h}\right)},$$

also increases. The variance of the original binomial is a maximum at $p = \frac{1}{2}$, i.e., for

$$\hat{h} = \frac{\beta_{ij}}{\beta_{ij} + .69315} H.$$

The distribution is positively skewed at first with μ_3 approaching zero as h approaches $\hat{h}$; it is symmetrical with maximum variance when $h = \hat{h}$; it is negatively skewed for $h > \hat{h}$ with μ_3 becoming larger negative as h approaches H.

Given two regions i and j, for each value of h the probabilities α_{sh} can be computed from $P_{ij}(s, h)$ for all s. With the ordering of h according to r_{ij}^h the composition of migration classes will be such that the proportion of relatively high-return classes comprising m^s will vary inversely with s, and conversely for low-return classes. That is, the nonpecuniary determinants of migration will modify the response to pecuniary returns in that the first (last) groups to migrate, although not comprised totally of the higher (lower) pecuniary-return classes, will be weighted in accordance with the ordering of these pecuniary returns.

The parameter β_{ij} is assumed to vary with j in computing the probabilities for any region i. Variations in β_{ij} have the following effects upon the moments of the distribution. The larger β_{ij} is, the smaller is the mean value of s for given h, the larger is the variance, and the smaller (closer to zero) is the skewness of the density distribution. Thus β_{ij} is taken as a standardized fraction, $0 < \beta_{ij} < 1$, which might be assumed inversely proportional to the distance between i and j. Then the greater the distance the fewer migrants there will be, *ceteris paribus*: the larger the mean value of s, the narrower will be the variance about this mean, and the less symmetrical the allocation among migration classes for a given expected pecuniary return. This effect on the density function may be construed to reflect the impact of cultural change. Contiguous areas have similar cultural patterns, whereas greater distance generally entails more cultural variation, which is an added constraint upon migration. Therefore, *other things being the same*, if β_{ij} is inversely proportional to distance, East to West Coast migration, for example, will be smaller in volume than New England to Middle Atlantic migration.

A series of probability distributions of s at successive nonzero values of h for two regions i and j is depicted in Figure 1.

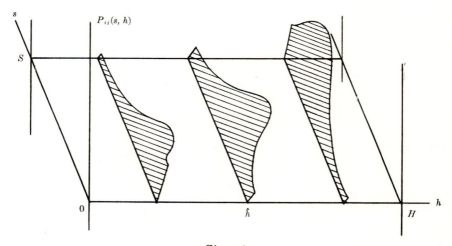

Figure 1

Of course, this method of mapping expected-return classes into migration classes also influences the behavior of returns as migration proceeds. For it follows that $r_{ij}^{s} > r_{ij}^{s+1}$ for $s = 0, 1, 2, \cdots , S-1$. Each r_{ij}^{s} is an expected return per worker in migration class s. But once the α's are specified, from the relation of r_{ij}^{s} to s the function $R_{ij}(M_{ij})$ can be formed, where M_{ij} denotes the total *ordered* migration of workers and R_{ij} represents the *cumulative* total expected returns from migration. R_{ij} is seen to be composed of a series of small linear segments, one corresponding to each class s.

In this connection a distinction must be made between two cases: that in which $r_{ij}^{s} > 0$ for $s = 0$ and $r_{ij}^{s} \leq 0$ for $s = 0$. The sign of R_{ij} will depend upon the sign of r_{ij}^{0}; it will depend upon whether any migration class has a positive expected return per worker. As migration from i to j proceeds, R_{ij} will be at first positive and increasing as M_{ij} increases. But it will increase at a decreasing rate. At some value of M_{ij} it will decrease, perhaps becoming negative eventually, because for h appropriately defined some r_{ij}^h will be negative.

In the other case, that in which no migration group has a positive expected return, $r_{ij}^0 \le 0$, the ranking of returns by migration class will be from the smallest negative to the largest negative. Because of the definition of pecuniary returns, it turns out that the smallest negative returns per worker tend to occur for the oldest worker with most dependents and property, and this contradicts the postulate of a positive correlation between pecuniary and nonpecuniary incentives to migrate. *If migration from i to j were to occur*, the first groups to migrate would be comprised most heavily of these workers. This result is of no consequence, however, for we shall define the equilibrium rate of migration from i to j as zero for $r_{ij}^0 \le 0$.

SHORT-RUN EQUILIBRIUM MIGRATION

For either resource, capital class or occupational labor class, out-migration to another given region will proceed up to the point at which expected net pecuniary returns per unit are zero. From the formulation of gross returns and costs it follows that, given any positive expected net returns, cumulative returns will increase at a decreasing rate, reach a maximum, and then decline as the resource outflow continues. If expected net returns per unit are nonpositive, cumulative returns would decrease as out-migration occurs, so out-migration to the other region for that resource class will be zero. Thus, maximization of net returns may be expressed in terms of cumulative gross returns and costs as functions of out-migration.

EQUILIBRIUM CAPITAL MIGRATION

Since the gross rate of return for a particular region is assumed given, regardless of the region in which expectations are formed, then

$$e_{ij}(v) = -e_{ji}(v), \qquad i, j = 1, 2, \cdots, I$$
$$i \ne j.$$

Moreover, the percentage cost of moving capital in one direction is the same as the cost of moving it in the opposite direction for any pair of regions:

$$z_{ij} = z_{ji}, \qquad i, j = 1, 2, \cdots, I$$
$$i \ne j.$$

It follows that if $n_{ij}(v) > 0$, then $n_{ji}(v) < 0$. Let $C_{ij}(v)$ represent the value of migration of capital class v from i to j. With an estimate of the cumulative cost function, and given the gross rate of return, cumulative expected net returns for capital class v can be approximated by a smooth continuous function

(8) $$N_{ij}(v) = [e_{ij}(v) - z_{ij}]C_{ij}(v), \qquad i, j = 1, 2, \cdots, I$$
$$i \neq j.$$

For I regions and V capital classes the general conditions of equilibrium may be written

(9) $$\frac{dN_{ij}(v)}{dC_{ij}(v)} \leq 0, \qquad \frac{dN_{ji}(v)}{dC_{ji}(v)} \leq 0, \qquad i, j = 1, 2, \cdots, I$$
$$i \neq j$$
$$v = 1, 2, \cdots, V.$$

These equations can be solved to obtain the equilibrium capital flows $\bar{C}_{ij}(v)$ and $\bar{C}_{ji}(v)$ for all i, j, and v. For $\bar{C}_{ij}(v) > 0$, the equality on the left holds and the inequality on the right holds, so that $\bar{C}_{ji}(v)$ is defined as zero. Likewise, for $\bar{C}_{ji}(v) > 0$ the inequality on the left and the equality on the right hold so $\bar{C}_{ij}(v) = 0$. When both inequalities hold, capital will not migrate in either direction.

Between any pair of regions capital of a particular class will flow in only one direction if at all. However, total capital migration may still flow in both directions simultaneously, depending primarily upon the industrial composition by region. Letting C_{ij} denote total capital migration:

$$\bar{C}_{ij} = \sum_{v} \bar{C}_{ij}(v), \qquad v = 1, 2, \cdots, V.$$

Thus, the equilibrium conditions generate total regional capital flows as well, with no presumption that gross and net capital migration must be equal. Net capital flows are given by

$$\bar{C}_{ij} - \bar{C}_{ji}, \qquad i, j = 1, 2, \cdots, I$$
$$i \neq j.$$

EQUILIBRIUM LABOR MIGRATION

For I regions let the expected return from employment in a given region be the same for a worker of age a regardless of whether he is located in that region or in any other region. Then the expected gross pecuniary return from migration differs only with respect to sign for workers of age a in region i as compared to workers of age a in region j:

$$g_{ij}(a) = -g_{ji}(a), \qquad i, j = 1, 2, \cdots, I.$$

But it does not follow that $r_{ij}(a) = -r_{ji}(a)$. In particular, it is possible that

$$r_{ij}(a_1) > 0 \quad \text{and} \quad r_{ji}(a_2) > 0$$

even if $a_1 = a_2$, so that

$$r^*_{ij} > 0 \quad \text{and} \quad r^*_{ji} > 0$$

for $s = 0$. This possibility of positive expected returns for at least one migration class in both regions may be due to unequal costs of migration. For only if workers have the same foregone income during migration, the same number of dependents, and the same property holdings will their costs of migration between two regions be identical. Or if costs are identical for each a, the time patterns of expected returns by industries could conceivably be such that for some age group in each region (not the same age group in the two regions) a positive return is not outweighed by the α weights used in determining the composition of migration classes.

Though it is possible that $r^*_{ij} > 0$ and $r^*_{ji} > 0$ for some s, such an occurrence is bound to be rare. Nevertheless, it is not to be ignored because there are some regions among which migration proceeds simultaneously from i to j and from j to i, even for the same occupation.

The ordering of migration classes was seen to yield cumulative expected net returns R_{ij} as a function of ordered migration M_{ij} for a given occupation. Over-all, the linear segments generate an R_{ij} that increases at a decreasing rate, reaches a maximum, and declines thereafter for $r^0_{ij} > 0$. For $r^0_{ij} \leq 0$, R_{ij} is negative and decreases at an increasing rate if out-migration occurs. As in the case of capital migration, out-migration of labor is zero if cumulative net pecuniary returns are nowhere positive. If cumulative returns are positive for any migration class, out-migration is positive and proceeds up to the point at which expected return per worker is zero.

For I regions, let R_{ij} be approximated by a smooth unimodal function. With $0 \leq M_{ij} \leq F_i$ for all j and $\sum_j M_{ij} \leq F_i$, the equilibrium flow of gross out-migration is represented by $\bar{M}_{ij}$. Then the general equilibrium conditions may be written

$$(10) \qquad \frac{dR_{ij}}{dM_{ij}} \leq 0; \qquad \frac{dR_{ji}}{dM_{ji}} \leq 0, \qquad i, j = 1, 2, \cdots, I,$$

$$i \neq j.$$

These equations can be solved to obtain $\bar{M}_{ij}$ and $\bar{M}_{ji}$ for all i and j, $i \neq j$; thus net migration flows are given as $\bar{M}_{ij} - \bar{M}_{ji}$. For $\bar{M}_{ij} = 0$ the inequality on the left holds, while for $\bar{M}_{ij} > 0$ the equality on the left holds. Likewise, for $\bar{M}_{ji} = 0$ the inequality on the right holds, and for $\bar{M}_{ji} > 0$ the equality on the right holds.

It should be noted that the model permits $\bar{M}_{ij} > 0$ and $\bar{M}_{ji} > 0$ simultaneously. Their magnitudes depend mostly upon regional industrial composition, distances among regions, and the distributions of regional labor forces with respect to age, property holdings, and marital status. The mapping of return classes into migration classes also yields predictions regarding these characteristics (in terms of percentages of migrants in each category) for each pair of regions. Finally, total multiregional labor migration is given by

$$\bar{L}_{ij} = \sum \bar{M}_{ij}, \qquad i, j = 1, 2, \cdots, I$$
$$i \neq j,$$

where the summation is over occupations.

LONG-RUN IMPLICATIONS

The operational value of the model is judged by its accuracy of prediction. In particular, the added complexity must be justified by greater explanatory power as compared to simpler analytical formulations, such as responses to regional unemployment levels or unweighted average rates of return on all capital as a single class. In this connection two comments are in order. First, a preliminary empirical application to population migration among nine Census divisions indicates that the model is significantly more sensitive and successful as a predictive device than are differences in average regional wage rates, incomes by occupation, or unemployment levels. Secondly, so-called simpler theories are not really simpler. The implicit assumptions about industrial composition, occupations, age, etc. are at least as numerous as those spelled out here, and often more crude.

If one accepts this essentially static formulation of short-run migration, certain implications unfold regarding dynamic long-run adjustments and their consequences for regional income differentials. Some of these effects will be sketched in brief outline.

LONG-RUN EQUILIBRIUM

Short-run equilibrium assumes a given initial population in each region, given expectations about the rate of increase in product demand by industry, and nonzero migrations of capital and labor. Long-run equilibrium will assume that the birth and death rates are constant in each region, that the demand for each product increases at the expected rate, and resource migration is zero among all regions. Whether and how the system, in a dynamic context, approaches equilibrium hinges on the satisfaction of these conditions.

In brief, the model predicts that capital flows to regions dominated by industries of greatest growth potential, and from regions characterized by industries of weakest growth potential. As short-run equilibrium capital migration continues over time, say from i to j, marginal rates of return will be affected in such a way that the flow will diminish and reach zero under the above assumptions about product demand and population. The marginal rates of return, assumed constant in the short run, depend upon total investment—which has its source in regional saving as well as capital imports. If relatively high rates attract capital from other regions, domestic investment will also be stimulated. If $e_j(v) > e_i(v)$ for "many" v and thus $\bar{C}_{ij} > 0$, total investment in j will also expand relative to total investment in i, given the change in product demand. As investment increases, $e_j(v)$ and $e_i(v)$ both fall. In final long-run equilibrium both $e_j(v)$ and $e_i(v)$ fall to zero for all v; the marginal rate of return equals the interest rate, i.e., the Keynesian equilibrium condition is satisfied. In the process $e_j(v)$ must fall relative to $e_i(v)$—there is greater investment in j—and so $e_{ij}(v)$ falls. Given the cost of migration as an increasing function of migration, $\bar{C}_{ij}$ also drops off and reaches zero when both e_j and e_i are zero.

Likewise, expected income on the part of labor assumes a given wage rate and future chages in wage rates based upon the expected rate of increase in product demand. Even allowing for the fact that different industries utilize different capital-labor ratios, the influx of labor in region j will cause wage rates to fall relative to wage rates in i as short-run migration continues. The entire expected income stream drops in j relative to i for every age group in an occupation. Therefore, given costs, net returns from migration fall for each migration class, and migration decreases to zero for each class.

Essentially, the adjustment to long-run equilibrium involves a geographic reshuffling of industries and occupations. Attainment of equilibrium does not, however, entail equalization of regional per capita incomes. Average income per worker will differ on the basis of new occupation and industry mixes by region. Moreover, since migrants in a given occupation are most likely to be those with the greatest earning potential, regional incomes for a given occupation may differ. In general, the effects upon regional income differentials are determined by the parameters of the short-run migration model, and only under special conditions will per capita incomes converge as compared to an initial distribution.

Long-Run Movements

Whether the system is stable, whether it approaches long-run equilibrium monotonically, depends upon changes in the structure of demand for output and changes in regional birth and death rates as migration flows continue over time.

Given the change in aggregate (national) demand for output, three cases can be distinguished. First, if the structure of total demand (relative demand for industry outputs) remains unchanged, capital migration will tend to approach zero as described in the previous section. Second, if the structure changes in favor of industries predominantly located in i—so that $e_i(v)$ rises relative to $e_j(v)$—zero migration will be reached more quickly. Indeed, if the change in structure continues, the direction of capital migration will be reversed between i and j. Third, with a change in the structure in favor of the currently faster-growing industries in j, shifts in the marginal return-investment schedule will prevent the fall in returns from migration and may even cause them to increase. Hence, capital migration will be constant, or rise, until zero capital stock in i or a faster population growth in i imposes a limit to out-migration of capital.

Internal rates of growth of regional populations, those due to causes other than migration, will also affect long-run behavior. Increasing population in j relative to i tends to speed the approach to zero labor migration by acting to reduce the wage rates in j relative to i. If j's growth rate is sufficiently greater, labor migration will reverse direction. On the other hand, if the residual population in i grows at a faster rate than the internal population in j, there will tend to be a slower adjustment to zero migration, constant migration, or increasing migration to j, depending upon the relative magnitudes of population increase by region.

Of course, these capital and labor migrations are not independent. For example, greater growth of population in region j will at the same time increase the demand for goods and services sold locally in j. *Ceteris paribus*, this will operate to raise the rate of return on investment in these industries as compared to the same industries in region i.

These long-run implications can be summarized in a very simple dynamic system. For simplicity we shall drop the v and a notations, interpreting this to mean that $n_{ij}(v)$ and $r_{ij}(a)$ are predominantly positive, so that $\bar{C}_{ij}$ and $\bar{L}_{ij}$ are positive for the pair of regions i and j. In addition, assume the cost functions are linear, i.e.,

$$z_{ij} = \lambda C_{ij}, \qquad c_{ij} = \pi L_{ij},$$

where λ and π are positive constants. Finally, let the changes in gross returns to capital migration and gross returns to labor migration be constant over time. Then the system appears as follows:

$$(11) \qquad e_{ij}(t) - e_{ij}(t-1) = \theta,$$

$$(12) \qquad g_{ij}(t) - g_{ij}(t-1) = \phi,$$

$$(13) \qquad \lambda C_{ij}(t) = e_{ij}(t),$$

$$(14) \qquad \pi L_{ij}(t) = g_{ij}(t),$$

$$(15) \qquad C_{ij}(0) = \bar{C}_{ij},$$

$$(16) \qquad L_{ij}(0) = \bar{L}_{ij}.$$

Equation (11) states that the change in gross returns to capital migration, θ, is constant over time, while (12) states that the change in gross returns to labor migration, ϕ, is constant over time. Under the assumptions of linear per unit costs of migration and positive capital and labor migration from i to j, equations (13) and (14) are simply restatements of the equilibrium conditions (9) and (10) respectively. By equations (15) and (16) the initial migration flows are taken to be the short-run equilibrium flows.

Substitution of (13) into (11) and (14) into (12) yields two first order linear homogeneous difference equations whose solutions are:

$$(17) \qquad C_{ij}(t) = (\theta/\lambda)^t \bar{C}_{ij},$$

$$(18) \qquad L_{ij}(t) = (\phi/\lambda)^t \bar{L}_{ij}.$$

The ratios (θ/λ) and (ϕ/π) are nothing other than the ratios of changes in gross returns to changes in cost of migration. Given $\lambda > 0$ and $\pi > 0$, the signs and magnitudes of θ and ϕ reflect the demand and population phenomena previously described.

In either equation, if the ratio is positive but less than unity, migration from i to j will decrease over time and approach zero monotonically. If the ratio equals unity, the migration flow remains constant; and if it is greater than unity, the flow from i to j increases monotonically over time. A negative ratio generates oscillatory migration movements about the zero long-run equilibrium. Consequently, the behavior of long-run migration hinges upon the way in which gross returns to migration vary over time in response to changes in the structure of aggregate demand and changes in the internal factors that affect regional populations.

Notes

1. J. T. Romans, "Capital Exports and Growth Among U.S. Regions" (Ph.D. thesis, Department of Economics, Brown University, June, 1963, unpublished).
2. Indeed, standard regression methods cannot be used to explain these phenomena.

An equation with migration as the dependent variable, regardless of the number of explanatory variables, does not tell why the coefficients are not larger or smaller, even if they all have the "right" sign. Such regression analysis does not determine to what other region out-migrants move. If the regression is restricted to one pair of regions, it does not tell why migrants did not choose some other region or why some workers did not migrate.

3. Consequently, aside from some passing references, statistical approximations to the theoretical concepts will not be discussed here. These approximations are based upon data already published or attainable by survey and special tabulations at feasible cost.

4. This formulation is dictated by the requirements of available data. More generally, owners of capital may be assumed to form a joint probability distribution of incomes at each time t, space s, and industry k. The set of distributions are ranked by a utility function, which when maximized generates the location decision. The formulation in the text is based upon the principle that the more concrete are the empirical predictions one wishes to make, the more restrictive are the assumptions that must be employed.

5. The influence of age, education, and industrial composition is reflected in the formulation of expected net return for each occupation. But certain other factors have been ignored. First, earnings from part-time work outside the industry of major employment are omitted. Second, if a worker's dependents are employed, they will be counted as potential labor migrants in that occupation in which they are presently employed. However, if they are not employed, the expectation of their employment in another region may influence migration independently of the expected return of the head of the household. Third, race and sex may influence expected income and the probability of employment (or promotion) in an industry. The direction and magnitude of these factors, and their net effect on migration, are by no means certain, especially since they may not be independent of age, occupation, and industrial composition. If they—in addition to other possible systematic determinants of migration—are independent of age, occupation and industrial composition, are independent of each other, and are individually small in their impact on total migration, their net effect will be random.

6. Cf. W. Feller, *An Introduction to Probability Theory and Its Applications* (New York: Wiley, 1950), Ch. 17; J. S. Cramer, "The Depreciation and Mortality of Motor Cars," *Journal of the Royal Statistical Society,* Series A, Vol. 121 (Part I, 1958), pp. 18–46.

Improved Allocation of Labor as a Source of Higher European Growth Rates[1]

Edward F. Denison

LARGE differences between Europe and America in postwar growth rates of gross national product per person employed can be traced in part to structural characteristics of their economies. One such characteristic is the proportion of employed persons who have been engaged in activities in which they contributed little to the value of the national product because labor was inefficiently allocated among activities. Large fractions of the agricultural labor force and of self-employed persons and unpaid family workers in nonagricultural activities have been prominent members of this group. Their transfer to more productive activities, specifically to nonfarm wage and salary employment, has helped to raise the national product.

This article examines, and attempts to quantify, the relationship between these particular changes in employment composition and the growth of national product per man in the United States and eight Western European countries from 1950 to 1962. It concludes that the United States has been as successful as any European country in curtailing excessive employment in these occupations. Despite this, reduction of these types of misallocation of labor has contributed much more to the 1950–1962 growth rate of output per man in continental Europe than in the United States. This was possible because the large continental countries started in 1950 from a position where the waste from misallocation was much greater. The rough estimates derived suggest that this factor accounts for fully half a percentage point or more of the difference between the 1950–1962 annual growth rates of output per man in the United States and in France, Germany, and Italy. The whole difference between the United States rate and the French, German, and Italian rates was respectively 1.5, 2.6, and 2.8 percentage

65

points, so this is a significant fraction of the gaps. The situation in four small countries varied widely, but all except Holland gained more from this source of growth than the United States. Mainly because it had the least to gain, the United Kingdom benefited even less than the United States, and nearly a percentage point in the growth rate less than the large continental countries.

ADJUSTMENTS FOR PART-TIME EMPLOYMENT IN THE UNITED STATES

Before the main subject of this paper is considered, allowance will be made for another labor force development that has contributed significantly to the poor showing of the United States in the postwar "international growth rate race" in output per person employed. Such comparisons generally use employment statistics from the Monthly Report on the Labor Force for the United States.[2] This source reports an extraordinary increase in part-time employment, the result of housewives in the middle and older age groups accepting, by choice, part-time jobs. As school attendance rose, teenagers working after school and on Saturday also contributed to the increase. From May, 1950, to May, 1962, the number of civilians at work part time (less than thirty-five hours) increased 38 per cent and the number at work full time only 8 per cent.[3] Almost half of the absolute increase in employment over the twelve years was in part-time work. The Commissioner of Labor Statistics states the increase in part-time work occurred among wage and salary workers in the nonfarm sector, mostly in the trade and service industries, and was among individuals desiring only part-time work. Nearly all the increase in part-time work was among persons working very few hours. Well over half the absolute increase was in the group which worked one to fourteen hours a week, and four-fifths in the groups working twenty-one hours or less.[4]

With full-time workers averaging forty-six or forty-seven hours a week throughout the period, and consisting mostly of adult males, it is reasonable to count as the equivalent of one person in the base year employment total an increase of perhaps four in the number of part-time workers. With this adjustment, the total increase in employment (including the armed forces) from 1950 to 1962 is cut from 14.6 per cent to 9.8. The growth rate of GNP per person employed is raised from 2.2 to 2.6 percent a year. This adjustment has been made in the tables given in this article. The relative position of the United States consequently appears more favorable (e.g., in the first column of Table 10) than in other such comparisons.

There is no indication from available sources of any comparable increase in part-time employment in Europe, nor has Europe experienced the large increase in the proportion of females in total employment which was primarily responsible for this development in the United States.[5]

Too Many Farmers, Nonfarm Proprietors, and Family Workers

The nine countries examined here have had too many agricultural workers. There has been concealed unemployment, not in the sense that farmers worked short hours but in the sense that a great many farms have been too small or their soil too poor to yield an output from full-time work that would, even with favorable farm prices, provide an income comparable to that obtained in nonfarm activities. Almost the same farm output could have been produced with many fewer workers by consolidating farms. In addition, devotion of too much of each country's resources to farming has lowered the income of even those farmers whose returns from their labor and investment would match what could be obtained in nonfarm activities if the total allocation of resources to agriculture were optimal. Incomes from labor, per person employed, have been much lower in farming than in nonfarm activities, and there have been many farms with very little output. It is safe to infer that the value of the total national product was smaller at any given time than it would have been had a smaller proportion of the labor force been allocated to agriculture and a larger to nonfarm activities—provided, of course, that other changes necessary to adapt to a reallocation of labor had also been made.

Labor *requirements*, as distinguished from use of labor, per unit of farm output were dropping sharply during the period for many reasons. Hence we can not tell from subsequent declines in agricultural employment in different countries the proportion by which farm employment was excessive, nor how much the proportion was reduced. But we do know that even if the percentage by which farm labor was too large had been the same in all countries, even uniform percentage reductions in agricultural employment would have had very different effects on nonagricultural employment in the different countries, depending upon the importance of agriculture in the total employment picture.

Employment of nonfarm proprietors, own account workers, and unpaid family workers also contains a great deal more concealed unemployment and highly unproductive work than does paid employment. Wages and salaries are an actual out-of-pocket expense to the employer, who is likely to pay out good money only if it contributes to his profit. The employed person, on his part, is less likely than those in the other labor force groups to weigh heavily considerations other than present and future income in selecting employment. He is more likely to change jobs to increase his earnings or to avoid a decline. When we observe persistent earnings differentials among wage and salary workers, we have some justification for supposing that these correspond in a rough and ready way to differences in the quality of labor employed. We certainly cannot suppose that the existence of differentials is evidence of misallocation, nor that merely transferring nonfarm paid employees from occupations or industries where average earnings are low to categories where they are higher would raise the national product.[6]

When employer and employee are one and the same, or the employee is an unpaid member of the family, the situation is substantially different. Large numbers of proprietors and own account workers tend to stress independence, position, and nonmonetary aspects of their work at the expense of income. They do not contract for any predetermined income, and all studies show that vast numbers of new entrants into business are ignorantly or irrationally optimistic about their future prospects. A large proportion of nonfarm proprietors in the United States at any time are in their first year or two of operation, continuing only until they have lost their capital. Those who once obtain a living, however modest, do not abandon their posts simply because they could earn more in paid employment. They are slow to change when their earnings decline in relation to those in alternative employments or even absolutely.[7] The presence of unpaid family workers enables the proprietor to continue operations when he could not afford hired labor and often yields even more extreme results. If two enterprises each yield a bare subsistence for a family, but one absorbs the work of family helpers in addition to the proprietor, income per person employed is even lower than in the other. Moreover, the real alternative open to family workers is frequently to leave the labor force rather than to accept a wage or salary job for others. Since the physical presence of proprietors and family workers is required to maintain the enterprise as a going concern, they usually remain in an "employed" status, usually with long nominal working hours, when little work is available.

The consequence of such factors is that in large numbers of trade and service "enterprises"—I use the term broadly to include own account workers without places of business—the net income per proprietor and family member falls far below the average earnings of wage and salary workers.

The proportion of the nonfarm labor force engaged in such activities has declined everywhere, so this statement is less descriptive of the situation in 1962 than in 1950. There can be no doubt that large numbers of these enterprises could and did disappear with no other effect than to increase the business (but not employment) of those remaining, or at most to require a disproportionately small increase in paid employment in larger establishments.

This situation need not imply (although in most countries it is the case) that the average income from labor of all nonfarm self-employed and family workers combined falls below that of wage and salary workers. The self-employed group also contains a large core of high-income professionals and proprietors of large business establishments, and many proprietors of successful smaller establishments, as well as some own account workers in skilled trades who do well enough operating on their own. Members of this "core" group could not, in general, improve their economic status by shifting to paid employment. Their average income is usually very high and offsets the low earnings of what I shall call the "fringe" group when the two are combined. Counts of the self-employed also pick up certain numbers of the shiftless or incompetent, who are unable to hold a paid job, and of individuals who cannot accept employment away from home and must earn what they can in their homes.

In all countries the total number of nonfarm self-employed and family workers combined has declined relative to the number of nonfarm wage and salary workers. Since the shiftless and incompetent are unable to move to paid employment and the "core" group lacks an incentive to do so, the contraction must refer mainly to the large "fringe" group of individuals who earn little and contribute little to output in a nonpaid status but are quite competent to hold wage and salary jobs.

COMPARISON OF EMPLOYMENT AGGREGATES

The nonagricultural wage and salary component provides a useful though imprecise indicator of the changes in employment that have seriously influenced output. Table 1 compares the increase in total employment from 1950 to 1962 (from which growth rates of GNP per man

TABLE 1

Indexes of Employment (including the Armed Forces) for 1962[a]
(1950 = 100)

	Total employment	Total non-agricultural employment	Nonagricultural wage and salary workers	Indexes of Differences		
				(2 ÷ 1)	(3 ÷ 2)	(3 ÷ 1)
	(1)	(2)	(3)	(4)	(5)	(6)
United States[b]	109.8	115.5	117.0	105.2	101.3	106.6
Belgium	107.0	112.0	117.1	104.7	104.6	109.4
Denmark	112.2	125.3	132.3	111.7	105.6	117.9
France	103.2	117.2	124.8	113.6	106.5	120.9
Germany[c]	127.9	147.1	152.5	115.0	103.6	119.2
Italy	115.6	137.4	146.3	118.9	106.5	126.6
Netherlands	116.8	123.0	129.4	105.3	105.1	110.8
Norway	103.4	112.4	115.6	108.7	102.8	111.8
United Kingdom	108.0	109.7	110.2	101.6	100.5	102.0

[a] Forestry and fishing are included with agriculture, except in the United States and Norway.
[b] This and subsequent tables have been adjusted, whenever relevant, for the increase in part-time employment in the United States. Alaska and Hawaii are excluded.
[c] Federal Republic, including the Saar and excluding West Berlin.

are computed) with increases in total nonfarm employment and in nonfarm wage and salary employment in the several countries.

In every country the index of nonagricultural employment in 1962 was above that for total employment, and the index of nonagricultural wage and salary employment was above the index for total nonagricultural employment. The point to be stressed, however, is the great variation among countries in the amount by which these indexes differ. The index of nonfarm wage and salary employment exceeds that for total employment by only 2 per cent in the United Kingdom and 7 in the United States as against 19 in Germany, 21 in France, and 27 in Italy, with the smaller countries ranged between the United States and Germany.

Among the large countries, the index for total nonagricultural employment exceeds that for total employment by only 2 per cent in the United Kingdom and 5 in the United States as against 14 in France, 15 in Germany, and 19 in Italy. These are the percentages by which 1962 nonfarm employment exceeded what it would have been if agriculture had absorbed the same percentage of total employment as it did in 1950.

France, Germany, and Italy did not succeed in drawing a larger proportion of their agricultural workers from the farm than did the United States. On the contrary, the agricultural employment decline of 31 per cent in the United States was as large as the declines in France and Germany, and well above the 19 per cent in Italy.[8] (See Table 2.) It was exceeded only in Belgium, and there by a small margin. Moreover, within the farm employment total the United States had the largest percentage decline in proprietors and own account workers, the next to the largest in unpaid family workers, and the next to the smallest in wage and salary workers. This pattern suggests especially great success in eliminating categories where underemployment is presumably greatest.

The intercountry variations in the difference between the total and nonfarm employment indexes reflect primarily variations in the importance of agricultural employment. By 1950 this was already down to 6 per cent of total employment in the United Kingdom and 12 per cent in the United States, whereas it was 25 per cent in Germany, 29 in France, and 39 in Italy (Table 6).

It is unlikely that with an optimum allocation of labor the difference between the percentage of workers devoted to agriculture in France, Germany, or Italy and the United States percentage would be as large as it actually was in 1950 and continues today. The United States advantage in efficiency is surely as great in agriculture as in nonagricultural activities, and probably greater. The relatively low income elasticity of demand for agricultural products would perhaps justify some differential because of the restriction imposed by transport costs on international movement of foods, but not an agricultural proportion twice as high in France as in America, and still higher in Germany and Italy. The implication is that the distribution of labor was, and is, farther from optimal in these coun-

TABLE 2

Selected Employment Indexes for 1962
(1950 = 100)

	Farm employment[a]	Nonfarm self-employed and unpaid family workers
United States	69	107
Belgium	65	92
Denmark	78	95
France	70	87
Germany	69	118
Italy	81	114
Netherlands	78	95
Norway	73	96
United Kingdom	79	101

[a] Includes forestry and fisheries except in Norway and the United States.

tries than in the United States—that is to say, agriculture is more over-manned in the major continental countries than it is in America. It seems probable that this is so even if artificial barriers to international trade are taken into account.

To transfer labor out of agriculture to correct an imbalance it is necessary to overcome the resistance to movement of the agricultural labor force, including potential replacements from among the farm population—that is, to overcome occupational and geographical immobility.[9] Success depends only partly on the availability of alternative employment opportunities. Despite the fact that labor markets have usually been tighter in France and Germany, if not Italy, than here during most of the period, the United States has been at least as successful as these countries in drawing people from agriculture—if, as seems reasonable, the percentage reduction in farm employment is used as the gauge. To provide jobs for the individuals transferred requires adequate demand for nonfarm products and the provision of additional nonfarm capital (or, in principle, more labor-intensive use of capital) to absorb them. The provision of adequate domestic demand poses no inherent problem (unless capital is a bottleneck) since, given the extra labor available, it implies no addition to inflationary pressure. The balance of payments may, however, be adversely affected if the reallocation process stimulates imports more than exports and the inflow of capital. The provision of capital for nonfarm production, either from saving or by transfer from the agricultural sector or abroad, is a requirement that may impose real difficulties. These restrictions have operated to limit the expansion of nonfarm jobs in Italy, but not significantly so during most of the period in the other European countries.

The point to be stressed now is that differences between the United States and the large continental countries in the divergence between the movements of total and nonagricultural employment reflect the amount of agricultural employment in the base period, not the rate at which farm employment has been reduced. Insofar as the shift of labor from agriculture contributed to growth by reducing the waste of labor, the differences between continental Europe and America in the growth obtained from this source reflected the amount of waste to be eliminated rather than degree of success in curtailing it.

I turn now to the difference between the indexes of total nonagricultural employment and nonagricultural wage and salary employment that were given in Table 1. These are reproduced in column (3) of Table 3, and compared with the share of self-employed and family workers in total employment. The index for wage and salary workers exceeded that for total nonfarm employment least in the United Kingdom and the United States. Because these are the countries in which self-employed and family workers are fewest and receive the least weight, this would be the case even if the differential between indexes of wage and salary workers and of the self-employed and family workers had been the same in all countries. There is a rough relationship of this type between columns (1) and (3) throughout the distribution, reflecting the difference in weights.

However, it is also true, as shown in column (4), that the number of self-employed and unpaid family workers contracted least, relative to wage and salary workers, in the Anglo-Saxon countries. But this need not imply that these countries were less successful than others in reducing the size of the "fringe" group relative to all nonagricultural employment. Rather, I suggest, it means that the "core" group was a much larger proportion of all self-employed and unpaid family workers where the total was small, and that the "core" group did not decline.

Table 4 provides a typical breakdown of nonfarm employers and own account workers, that for France in 1954. The professions together with employers in all industries make up only one-third of the total—a fraction suggestive of the size of what I have called the "core" group. Small merchants without employees alone outnumber them. Most of the remainder are "artisans" without employees, a group which includes the

TABLE 3

*Importance and Relative Movement of Self-Employed and
Family Workers Within Nonagricultural Employment*

	Self-employed and unpaid family workers as a per cent of total nonfarm employment		1962 index of nonfarm wage and salary employment (1950 = 100) divided by index of total nonfarm employment	1962 employment index (1950 = 100) for nonfarm self-employed and unpaid family workers divided by index of nonfarm wage and salary employment
	1950	1962		
	(1)	(2)	(3)	(4)
United Kingdom	6	6	100.5	.92
United States	12	11	101.3	.92
Germany	16	13	103.6	.77
Norway	17	15	102.8	.83
Netherlands	19	14	105.1	.73
Denmark	19	15	105.6	.72
Belgium	21	17	104.6	.79
France	21	16	106.5	.70
Italy	28	23	106.5	.78

TABLE 4

Distribution of Employers and Own Account Workers in France, 1954
(Data in thousands)

	Own account workers	Employers	Total employers and own account workers
Manufacturers	0	76	76
Artisans	458	198	657
Large merchants	48	93	141
Small merchants	762	190	952
Professions	68	44	112
Professors, literary and scientific personnel, teachers, medical and social services	23	2	25
Service workers not earning a wage	21	1	22
Artists	16	1	17
Total	1,397	605	2,003

Source: Jean Marchal, *La Répartition du Revenu National,* Paris, Génin, 1956, Vol. II, p. 26. Based on 1954 French Census.

proprietors of establishments in most of the service industries. Unpaid family workers, excluded from this table, presumably are even more heavily concentrated in the peripheral group. The situation is much the same in other countries where employers and own account workers comprise a large part of the nonfarm labor force.

Its size alone would give assurance that it is the peripheral group that largely determines both international differences in the importance of the self-employed and unpaid family workers in total nonagricultural employment and, within each country, the amount by which indexes of total nonfarm employment and of self-employed and family worker employment diverge. In fact, however, the "core" group makes up a larger proportion of all self-employed and family workers where the self-employed and family workers are an unimportant rather than an important part of nonfarm employment.[10] It is also likely that the "core" group was not shrinking. If so, the same decline (relative to total nonfarm employment) in the peripheral group in two countries would mean a larger relative decline in the total number of self-employed and family workers in the country where they are more numerous. This corresponds to the general pattern observed in Table 3.

In any case we can be fairly sure that the differences among countries shown in column (3) of Table 3 refer very largely to the relative gain in wage and salary employment at the expense of labor used very unproductively, rather than of the "core" group of skilled professionals and owner-managers of substantial enterprises.

Estimates of the Effect of Labor Force Shifts upon Growth Rates of Output Per Person Employed

We now attempt some calculations of the relationship between the developments just discussed and the growth rates of output per person employed. These are, of necessity, very crude, but should indicate the approximate magnitudes involved.

The object of the calculations is to approximate the amounts by which the combined contribution to European growth (of GNP per person employed, from 1950 to 1962) of the following factors exceeded their contribution to United States growth:

(1) The improved allocation of resources resulting from the transfer of farm workers and nonfarm self-employed and unpaid family workers from activities in which their contribution to the value of the national product was slight to more productive activities;

(2) The reduction in concealed unemployment among the same groups.

It is not feasible to isolate the separate effect of the two sources just listed. I shall, however, try to build up their combined effect as the total of three estimates. These refer, respectively, to the effect of the shift of labor from farm to nonfarm activities upon the value of output per man in the economy as a whole; to changes within the farm economy; and to changes within the nonfarm economy.

(1) We may first compute the statistical effect on real national product per man of the shift of employment from farm to nonfarm activities. This is a familiar calculation which has often been used in individual countries. All value terms used in it are expressed in constant prices of the year used in deflating the national product of the country. We simply multiply 1962 farm employment by 1950 GNP per person in agriculture, 1962 nonfarm employment by 1950 GNP per person in nonfarm industries, sum the products, and divide by total 1962 employment. The result is a hypothetical figure of what GNP per person would have been if output per man in each sector had been what it actually was in 1950 but employment had been distributed between the two sectors in the same proportion as in 1962. In Germany, it exceeds actual output per person employed in 1950 by 8.77 per cent, the largest figure among the nine countries. Spread over a twelve-year period (from 1950 to 1962) this "industrial shift" effect is equivalent to a contribution of 0.7 percentage points to the annual growth rate. Similar calculations for all the countries are shown in the first column of Table 5. The contribution is greater the larger the differential between GNP

TABLE 5

Contribution of the "Farm-Nonfarm Shift" to Growth Rates

	Based on full GNP per man differentials		Based on reduced GNP per man differentials	
	Amount	Excess over contribution to United States growth	Amount	Excess over contribution to United States growth
United States	.2	. . .	.2	. . .
Belgium	.1	−.1	.1	−.1
Denmark	.6	.4	.4	.2
France	.6	.4	.5	.3
Germany	.7	.5	.6	.4
Italy	.5	.3	.3	.1
Netherlands	.0	−.2	.0	−.2
Norway	.5	.3	.5	.3
United Kingdom	.0	−.2	.0	−.2

per person in farm and nonfarm activities in 1950 and the larger the absolute drop in the farm percentage of total employment. These estimates are given in Table 6.

This calculation overstates the gain from the industry shift insofar as the movement of farm workers lowered the average quality of the nonfarm labor force and consequently affected nonfarm productivity adversely. One important aspect of labor quality is education, and the farm labor force is less well educated than the nonfarm everywhere that data are available. I attempt to allow for this in column 3 of Table 5 by redoing the calculation after raising the ratio of nonfarm to farm GNP per person in 1950 by 20 per cent, implying that the average quality of the workers moving to nonfarm activities from agriculture was one-sixth below that of the nonfarm average. This may overcorrect the international differences because the quality differential undoubtedly varies from country to country and is probably greater in the United States than in Europe. But only a uniform and rather arbitrary adjustment is possible here.[11] I shall use this column to measure the contribution of the "farm-nonfarm shift" to the growth rate.[12] It attempts to measure the contribution to growth from moving resources from agriculture to industries where output is more highly valued, and from the reduction in concealed unemployment in the economy as a whole if there were no changes in the ratios of concealed unemployment to total employment in the farm and nonfarm sectors considered separately. I turn now to changes within each of the two sectors.

(2) The "industry shift" calculation just described implies that a

given percentage reduction in farm employment reduced farm GNP (from what it would otherwise have been) by the same percentage, so that the process did not affect farm GNP per man.[13] But the farms from which farm families dropped out without replacements were mostly those with little output, so that a given percentage reduction in employment meant a much smaller percentage reduction in output. Thus their elimination automatically raised output per person in agriculture. Unless this is taken into account, the gains from reducing farm employment will be understated. In addition, in all countries the reduction in the number of farms had little effect on the amount of farm land, but rather resulted in larger farms. This had the effect of raising output per man among the remaining farmers.[14]

To estimate the relationship between reductions in farm employment and farm GNP we need (a) a size distribution (ideally of employment, classified by GNP per person employed on the farms on which employed) and (b) some assumption as to the position within this distribution from which the employment that was eliminated came. The United States distribution closest to that desired—and it is not very close—is a distribution, from the MRLF sample, of males employed in agriculture classified by money income.[15] The data cover males employed in agriculture in March of the year following that to which the income data refer. Those with no money income are excluded. The numbers covered fall short of average male employment in the prior

TABLE 6

Factors Underlying the Computation of the "Farm-Nonfarm" Shift

	Agricultural employment as a per cent of total employment			GNP per man in agriculture as a per cent of GNP per man in nonagricultural activities[a]
	1950	1962	Decline	1950
United States	12.2	7.7	4.5	46
Belgium	10.4	6.7	3.7	66
Denmark	27.6	19.1	8.5	65
France	29.0	19.7	9.3	35
Germany	24.7	13.3	11.4	35
Italy	39.0	27.4	11.6	60
Netherlands	16.1	9.3	6.8	94
Norway	23.0	16.2	6.8	21
United Kingdom	5.7	4.0	1.7	82

[a] Measured in prices of the base year used in deflation of GNP.

year, by about 15 per cent on the average. This is partly because unpaid family workers without money income are omitted, partly because
of the secular decline in farm employment, and partly for seasonal
reasons. Females, who accounted for 16 per cent of total farm employment in 1950, are also omitted.[16] If the data for 1949 and 1950, and for
1959 and 1960, are averaged to reduce random and sampling fluctuations in annual data, the following cumulative distributions are obtained. The percentage change from 1949–1950 to 1959–1960 in the
male employment covered is virtually identical with that in total farm
employment.

The data show a pronounced decline in the concentration of income
at the top, corresponding to the expectation.[17]

The following experimental calculation was made to judge the effect
of reducing employment on GNP per person employed. Farm GNP in
1949–1950 was distributed among income size classes like money income. Employment was then reduced from the 1949–1950 to the 1959–
1960 level (a 25.2 per cent reduction) on three alternative assumptions.
First (the extreme assumption), that the employment decline came
from the bottom of the distribution; on this assumption, elimination of
25.2 per cent of 1949–1950 employment would have cut total farm GNP
by only 4.2 per cent. Second, that the employment decline came equally
from each of the three lower fifths of the distribution; on this assumption it would have reduced farm GNP by 8.9 per cent. Third,
that the employment decline came from each of the fifths in inverse
proportion to income (i.e., in proportion to the reciprocals of the shares

TABLE 7

Males Employed in Agriculture Classified by Money Income

	1949–1950		1959–1960	
	Number (000)	Per cent of total income	Number (000)	Per cent of total income
Upper 5 per cent	266.8	28.85	199.6	22.76
Upper fifth	1067.3	57.65	798.5	52.72
Upper two-fifths	2134.6	79.10	1597.0	76.24
Upper three-fifths	3201.9	91.60	2395.5	90.46
Upper four-fifths	4269.2	97.30	3194.0	97.83
Total	5336.5	100.00	3992.5	100.00

Source: Computed from U.S. Department of Commerce, Bureau of the
   Census, *Trends in the Income of Families and Persons in the
   United States: 1947 to 1960*, Technical Paper No. 8, Table 15.

of each fifth in total income); on this assumption it would have reduced farm GNP by 9.1 per cent.[18] The second and third assumptions seem plausible and yield almost identical results.

If we take the third assumption, the percentage reduction in 1949–1950 farm GNP that would have been caused by the reduction of farm employment to the 1959–1960 level is only .36 of the percentage reduction in farm employment (9.1 divided by 25.2). This figure might be further reduced on the grounds that the elimination of some small farm units released land for others, increasing output per man on the remaining units. However, I shall ignore this additional point. The assumption of the calculation is quite arbitrary, but the result that farm GNP was reduced 0.36 per cent for each 1 per cent employment decline (from the 1950 position) seems, intuitively, unlikely to be too low and therefore conservative from the standpoint of measuring the gains from employment shifts.[19]

Use of this ratio makes it possible to estimate how much the reduction of concealed unemployment within agriculture contributed to the growth rate. From 1950 to 1962 farm employment was reduced by 2,331,000, or 31.1 per cent. If this reduction had already been made in 1950, farm GNP would (using the .36 ratio) have been lower by 11.2 per cent or $2.2 billion (in 1954 prices). These workers would have been available for nonfarm production. The "industry shift" calculation has already counted the difference between the value of nonfarm and farm GNP per man for these workers (with an appropriate reduction for quality). What they could have added to 1950 nonfarm GNP that has not already been counted is, therefore, the product of 2,331,000

TABLE 8

Estimated Contribution of the Reduction of Concealed Unemployment Within Agriculture to the Growth Rate, 1950–1962[a]

	Amount (1)	Excess over United States (2)
United States	.1	. . .
Belgium	.1	. . .
Denmark	.2	.1
France	.2	.1
Germany	.2	.1
Italy	.3	.2
Netherlands	.1	. . .
Norway	.1	. . .
United Kingdom	.1	. . .

[a] In addition to contribution measured in Table 5.

workers and average farm GNP per person employed in 1950, which comes to $6.0 billion.[20] The net addition to total GNP would therefore have been $3.8 billion ($6.0 minus $2.2) or 1.2 per cent of GNP. Over the twelve-year period 1950–1962 the reduction of concealed unemployment in agriculture therefore contributed 0.1 per cent to the growth rate of total GNP that has not already been counted in the industry shift calculation.

In the absence of separate data for other countries, I assume that each 1 per cent reduction in farm employment meant a .36 per cent reduction in farm GNP in each of them, even though a smaller ratio is probably appropriate on the continent. With this assumption, the calculations for the United States can then be duplicated for the other countries. The results are shown in Table 8.

The calculated contribution to the growth rate is .3 in Italy, .2 in France, Germany, and Denmark, and .1 in the other countries. Thus allowance for this factor does not add very much to the explanation of differences in growth rates. We can be reasonably sure that the "true" figures for each country lie between a minimum of .0 (which would be the case if there were really no reduction at all in concealed unemployment) and a maximum about half again as large as the rates shown in column (1) of Table 8 (which would be the case if the reduction in employment had no adverse effect at all on total farm output).

(3) The final estimate concerns the gains from reducing the relative importance of nonfarm proprietors and family workers. The differences between the growth rates of nonfarm output per nonfarm wage and salary worker, and nonfarm output per nonfarm person employed, are given in the first column of Table 9. They are, of course, the same as the differences between growth rates of nonfarm wage and salary employment and total nonfarm employment.

I have in effect argued that an index of nonfarm wage and salary employment better measures the changes in necessary employment than an index of total nonfarm employment. Ideally, one would include with wage and salary workers what I have called the "core" group of proprietors and own account workers. However, their inclusion could hardly alter the index of wage and salary employment significantly since they are not very numerous and there is no general reason to suppose that their relative numbers have changed.

If no additional wage and salary employment at all had been required for work formerly performed by self-employed and family workers, the first column of Table 9 would measure the contribution to the growth rate of output per person employed in the nonfarm economy

TABLE 9

*Estimated Contribution of the Reduction of Underemployment
of Nonfarm Self-Employed and Unpaid Family
Workers to 1950–1962 Growth Rates*

| | Difference between growth rates of nonfarm wage and salary employment and total nonfarm employment | | Estimated contribution | |
	Amount (1)	Excess over United States (2)	Amount (3)	Excess over United States (4)
United States	.1	. . .	.1	. . .
Belgium	.4	.3	.3	.2
Denmark	.5	.4	.3	.2
France	.5	.4	.3	.2
Germany	.3	.2	.2	.1
Italy	.5	.4	.3	.2
Netherlands	.4	.3	.3	.2
Norway	.2	.1	.2	.1
United Kingdom	.0	− .1	.0	− .1

that resulted from the shrinking of the peripheral group of self-employed and unpaid family workers. I suspect this assumption would involve no great overestimate. Contraction of the peripheral group presumably entailed *some* loss of output that was not picked up by those remaining in the group, but it is hard to believe its value was very large.[21] Nonetheless, I shall cut column (1) of Table 9 by one-fourth. The reduced estimate is then multiplied by the ratio of nonfarm GNP to total GNP in 1950 to obtain the contribution to the growth rate of GNP per person employed in the economy as a whole. These estimates are given in column (3) of Table 9.

The following illustration describes one situation in which a one-fourth reduction would be appropriate. Assume, reasonably, that in retail trade the unincorporated firms that disappeared are drawn from the lower portion of a distribution by volume of business of firms without paid employees. Such firms could readily handle more volume without adding paid employees. Suppose their volume, per person engaged, to have been half that of firms with paid employees.[22] Let half the business they formerly handled go to other firms without paid employees who can absorb it without adding to employment. Let the other half go to firms with paid employees; their increase in employment need be only half as large as that in the discontinued firms to handle the same volume of business. Under these circumstances the

TABLE 10

*Contribution of Reduced Underemployment and Better Allocation of
Resources to the 1950–1962 Growth Rate of GNP per Man*

	Growth rate of national product per person employed		Contribution of reduced under-employment and better allocation of resources		Contribution of all other growth sources	
	Amount (1)	Excess over United States (2)	Amount (3)	Excess over United States (4)	Amount (5)	Excess over United States (6)
United States	2.6	...	.4	...	2.2	...
Belgium	2.4	− .2	.5	.1	1.9	− .3
Denmark	2.5	− .1	.9	.5	1.6	− .6
France	4.1	1.5	1.0	.6	3.1	.9
Germany	5.2	2.6	1.0	.6	4.2	2.0
Italy	5.4	2.8	.9	.5	4.5	2.3
Netherlands	3.3	.7	.4	.0	2.9	.7
Norway	3.5	.9	.7	.3	2.8	.6
United Kingdom	1.6	−1.0	.1	− .3	1.5	− .7

business handled by the discontinued firms will be taken care of by the addition of one paid employee to replace four self-employed and family helpers in the discontinued firms.

The contributions to growth shown in Tables 5, 8, and 9 are combined in the third column of Table 10.[23] These represent estimates, necessarily rough, of the gains from reducing underemployment among farm workers and among nonfarm self-employed persons and family workers, and from shifting labor from the activities in which these groups are engaged to activities in which the value of output is higher. For reasons mentioned at several points in the description, the estimate for the United States is likely to be on the high side, and the differences between the United States and the major continental countries to be conservative. The estimates exclude any gains from the elimination of supernumerary nonfarm wage and salary employees under the impetus of tight labor markets, although these gains may also have been important in some European countries.

The five countries with high growth rates of GNP per person employed (3.3 per cent a year or more) are Italy, Germany, France, Norway, and the Netherlands. The five that gained most (.7 to 1.0) from these sources are the same except that Denmark replaces the Netherlands. The three large continental countries top both lists. They gained .5 or .6 more from these growth sources than the United States. These are quite substantial fractions of the total difference in growth rates, as indicated in Table 10.

I have tried to show that Europe did not make more progress than the United States in reducing concealed unemployment and misallocation of labor. She obtained more growth from eliminating these sources of waste because she had more waste to eliminate.

The size of the estimated contribution of these sources to the growth rate is roughly related to, and averages 60 per cent of, the difference between growth rates of nonfarm wage and salary employment and of total employment, the divergence with which this analysis began. The comparison is given in Table 11. If we simply took 60 per cent of column (2), Table 11, we would arrive at an estimate in column (3) for the contribution of these sources to growth within .1 of the direct estimate except in Italy and Norway, where the difference would be .2 or .3. Deviations from the average relationship stem mainly from differences among countries in the 1950 ratios of GNP per man in agriculture to GNP per man in nonfarm industries. For example, the higher contribution to Norwegian than to Dutch growth results from an exceptionally low ratio of farm to nonfarm GNP per person in Norway and an exceptionally high ratio in Holland.

When allowance is made for the particular structural factors discussed in this article, including the increase in part-time employment in the United States which raised the United States growth rate by .4 before these calculations were begun, the relative position of the United

TABLE 11

Comparison of Employment Shift and Contribution to Growth, 1950–1962

	1962 index of nonfarm wage and salary employment (1950 = 100) divided by index of total employment		Contribution of reduced underemployment and better allocation of resources to growth rate
	Index (1)	Growth rate (2)	(3)
Italy	126.6	2.0	.9
France	120.9	1.6	1.0
Germany	119.2	1.5	1.0
Denmark	117.9	1.4	.9
Norway	111.8	.9	.7
Netherlands	110.8	.9	.4
Belgium	109.4	.8	.5
United States	106.6	.5	.4
United Kingdom	102.0	.2	.1

States in growth of output per person employed is substantially better than in raw data. Large differences remain to be explained by the host of other sources, however.

Note on Statistics

Data for total, farm, and nonfarm gross national product in constant prices were obtained from the latest available reports of the various countries. Base years vary. Most 1962 figures are preliminary. For Norway, published data in constant prices combine farm GNP with forestry and fishing, which are important, while current dollar data separate them. The division in 1950 and 1962 was assumed to be the same in constant as in current prices. In other countries forestry and fishing are relatively unimportant compared to agriculture and the farm estimates include them (except for the United States).

Employment and GNP estimates for each country are consistent with respect to classification of forestry and fisheries with agriculture or with other industries. Adjustments of GNP and employment estimates for changes in geographic coverage have been made when necessary.

Employment estimates are from *Manpower Statistics 1950–62*, published by OECD, with the incomplete Danish estimates in that source supplemented by official national data consistent with them. Military employment is included in total, total nonfarm, and nonfarm wage and salary employment (unless otherwise noted). French and Italian employment estimates in *Manpower Statistics 1950–62* begin with 1954 (and are not satisfactory prior to 1959 in the case of Italy) and it was necessary to extrapolate back to 1950 on the basis of other estimates.

The 1950 Italian figures that are comparable to those for 1962 are highly uncertain with respect to both total employment and its composition. The *Manpower Statistics* estimates of civilian employment were used only from 1959 to 1962, when they represent averages of four sample surveys each year. (For 1954–1958, when they are based on one sample survey a year or, in 1957 only, two, taken in different months, the series is highly erratic in movement). The 1959 *Manpower Statistics* estimates for farm and nonfarm civilian employment were extrapolated to 1950 by series estimated by SVIMEZ and used by Gardner Ackley (*Un Modello Econometrico dello Sviluppo Italiano nel Dopoguerra*, SVIMEZ, Rome, 1963, p. 92). The SVIMEZ estimates are also used by the Economic Commission for Europe. They show a contraction of farm employment that is smaller than that of some other estimates (e.g., those used by Stanley H. Cohn), and radically smaller than some others which have utilized the 1951 Italian Census (e.g., those of G. H. Peters).[24] Use of the latter source would raise substantially the Italian growth rate of total GNP per person employed given in this article and the estimate of the contribution to that growth rate made by the redistribution of labor out of agriculture. The Italian nonfarm employment estimates, and those for nonfarm wage and salary workers, are also rough.

Definitions of employment and estimating methods are not entirely uniform.[25] Also, differences among countries in tax and social security legislation affect the actual division between paid and unpaid employment. It is probable, however, that statistical differences among countries and estimating errors are smallest for nonfarm wage and salary employment. The result is that the last two columns of Table 10 may remove not only the real consequences of the economic changes discussed in this article but also some of the error and statistical incomparability in employment estimates.

Notes

1. The findings and conclusions are those of the author and do not purport to represent the views of the Brookings Institution, its trustees, authors, or other staff members. The author has benefited greatly from discussions of this subject with Jack Alterman. He was assisted by Jean-Pierre Poullier.

2. Whether this series, or data derived from establishment reports, is best suited for internal analysis of United States growth is a question I shall not examine here.

3. Both percentages are slightly overstated by inclusion of Alaska and Hawaii in 1962. All other United States data used here are adjusted for the change in geographical coverage. May data rather than annual averages are given (following Labor Department practice) because annual averages are affected by holidays occurring in the survey week, especially during 1950.

4. This sentence is based on the change from May, 1948, to May, 1963. See testimony of Ewan Clague in *Hours of Work*, Part 1, Hearings before the Select Subcommittee on Labor of the Committee on Education and Labor, House of Representatives (Washington: U.S. Government Printing Office, 1963).

5. The adjustment described in this section is intended only to improve the comparisons of output per person employed, not to move toward a man-hours basis. Differential changes among countries in average hours of full-time workers (or of part-time workers) is one of the many factors influencing the changes in output per person employed.

6. An exception might be made for compulsory military service. The arbitrarily determined pay of draftees is not an indication of the quality of labor, and an increase in the armed forces does depress national product per man. It has done so in the 1950–1962 period in all countries considered here, though not by equal amounts. However, this is an essentially different phenomenon from the labor force shifts considered in this article in that low earnings in the armed forces do not imply misallocation of labor.

7. As *The Economist* (February 1, 1964, p. 429) says, writing of France: ". . . small shopkeepers have the knack, like the peasants, of subsisting for a time at the margin. One of the awkward reasons why competition does not always have the effects that the textbooks say it should is the uneconomic reluctance of businesses to shut up shop; in practice elimination of the small retailer in France often takes a generation, the son refusing to follow his father's blind alley."

8. Alternative estimates for Italy would, however, yield a decline much closer to that for the other three countries. See Note on Statistics.

9. For convenience I write throughout this article as if the labor force shifts described entailed the actual movement of individuals from one activity to another. Much of the shift has in fact been accomplished by the failure of new entrants to match the number retiring or, more exactly, to exceed the number retiring from the declining activities by as much as they did in the labor force as a whole.

10. The following data for the Common Market countries, compiled on a consistent basis from a special survey for October, 1960, strongly support this statement insofar as employers can be taken as indicative of the size of the "core" group. The percentage who are professionals without employees can hardly vary greatly (in absolute terms) among these countries.

	Germany	France	Italy	Nether-lands	Belgium	Luxem-bourg
Per cent of nonfarm civilian employment:						
Employers	4.4	4.7	5.1	5.5	3.5	4.7
Own account workers and unpaid family workers	8.7	13.8	20.7	9.5	18.2	13.3
Total self-employed and family workers	13.1	18.5	25.8	15.0	21.7	18.1
Per cent of nonfarm self-employed and family workers:						
Employers	33.5	25.3	19.7	36.6	16.2	26.2

Source: Statistical Office of the European Communities, *Statistical Information*, 1963, No. 2 bis, Table 57.

This source provides data for international comparisons that probably are superior to those used in this article, but they are available only for one week. The data are not strictly comparable with those given in Table 3 for 1950 and 1962.

11. In *The Sources of Economic Growth in the United States and the Alternatives Before Us* (New York: Committee for Economic Development, 1962) I used a differential of one-third. A much larger differential ought in fact to be used in the United States than in Europe, except perhaps Italy, because so much (almost three-fifths from 1950 to 1960) of the reduction in farm employment occurred in the South (and disproportionately among southern Negroes). The educational background in the rural South is very far below the average for the nonfarm labor force. Median numbers of years of school completed by males 25 and over even in 1960 were only 7.7 in southern farm areas and 4.7 among nonwhites in this group as against 11.0 in urban areas in the United States as a whole. Differences in quality of education widen the real differences. In Europe those leaving agriculture tended to be the more ambitious among members of the younger farm population. For this and other reasons I believe the contribution to nonfarm work by those coming off the farm was particularly low in the United States. Thus I believe the calculated contribution to United States growth from this source of 0.2 percentage points in fact to be appreciably overstated, absolutely and relatively to European countries. This is reinforced in the case of Germany by the consideration that the farm labor force at the start of the period included industrial workers from the East, temporarily in agriculture, who subsequently re-entered the industrial sector.

In the *Sources of Economic Growth* I estimated that the reduced waste of labor in agriculture and the "industry shift" of fully employed resources together contributed .07 points to the United States growth rate of *national income* from 1929 to 1957. That estimate was lower than the .3 calculated here (combining Tables 5 and 8) not only because of the larger quality differential used but also because I assumed that from 1929 to 1957 the proportion of labor within agriculture that was unnecessary *increased* by half, and because rather than GNP differentials I used labor income differentials. The latter is a preferred procedure for which data are not presently available in these international comparisons.

12. The Dutch estimates show so high a ratio of farm to nonfarm GNP per man in 1950 (in constant prices) that if it is raised 20 per cent it exceeds unity and yields a negative contribution (of negligible size) of the farm-nonfarm shift. This result is obvious nonsense and I have used a figure of zero.

13. Put differently, it implies that the percentage of farm labor that represented concealed unemployment was unchanged, although the percentage declined in the economy as a whole because of the reduced importance of farm labor.

14. On the continent it helped make possible not only larger farms but some consolidation of separated plots of land. Fragmentation is an important source of inefficiency which has not been present in the United States, so its reduction presumably contributed to the greater increase in farm labor productivity in the continental European countries.

15. The Department of Agriculture has estimated the number of farms and sales for 1949 and 1959 classified by sales-size class in 1959 prices, but not corresponding employment data for these years. In any case, Department of Agriculture employment data bear no close resemblance to employment as counted in the MRLF.

16. A similar distribution of females employed in agriculture is available, but covers only a small fraction of female employment (presumably because most females are unpaid family workers without money income) and, the sample being very small, the data are highly erratic from year to year.

17. The share of the lowest fifth did not increase, however. This may be due to inclusion of unpaid family workers with small amounts of money income from outside sources.

18. In each case, I assume that *within* each fifth the reduction was proportional throughout the distribution.

19. One implication of the use of this .36 ratio is that the reduction of concealed unemployment has been responsible for about half the increase in GNP per person employed in agriculture since 1950. This is striking but should not be used as more than a suggestion of what may possibly be true. The calculation is as follows. With 1950 = 100, the index of real farm GNP in the United States in 1962 stood at 113, that of farm employment at 69, and that of GNP per person employed at 164. If in 1950 employment had been at the 1962 level, farm GNP per person employed would have been 129 per cent of the actual 1950 figure (since farm GNP would have been at 89 and employment at 69 per cent of the actual figures). This implies that all factors other than the reduction in concealed unemployment would have raised farm GNP per man to an index of only 127 in 1962 (164 divided by 129) had there been no reduction in concealed unemployment.

An additional calculation supports a figure of about this size. Real farm GNP was distributed among male farm employees in proportion to money income in both 1949–1950 and 1959–1960 (as above). With some estimation, it can then be calculated that the increase in GNP per person employed for the top 1,067,300 persons, corresponding to the top fifth in 1949–1950, was about 21 per cent in ten years. Since this group presumably contains little underemployment, this result may be compared with the 27 per cent in twelve years mentioned above.

The estimates in this paper are not sensitive to a substantial error in the .36 ratio, whereas the calculations in this footnote are very sensitive to it. The results, therefore, should not be interpreted as a serious attempt to analyze the increase in farm productivity as such.

20. It will be noted that the calculation is based on the absolute decline in farm employment (rather than the decline in the farm percentage of total employment as in the "industry shift" calculation) since the movement of nonfarm employment is irrelevant to the present calculation.

21. This is not contradicted by the observation that in some instances, particularly among repair services, the process has gone far enough to bring increased delays in obtaining service. However inconvenient to the consumer, slow service is not a characteristic that price indexes allow for, and hence delay does not impair the measured national product except to the small extent that the actual work done in the course of a year may be curtailed.

22. In the United States Census for 1948, retail sales per proprietor and unpaid

family worker in *all* stores without paid employees were 63 per cent as large as sales per employee, proprietor, and unpaid family worker in stores with paid employees. (However, the precise result depends on the count of unpaid family workers, which has always been higher in the Census of Business than in the Monthly Report on the Labor Force.) The 1954 and 1958 Censuses of Business did not tabulate unpaid family workers, so this calculation cannot be duplicated. The argument here would suggest the ratio should have risen, though less than in the continental countries.

23. Computations in Table 10 are from unrounded data. However, the sum of the three estimates happens to equal the total shown in Table 10 except in the case of Norway.

24. Stanley H. Cohn, "The Gross National Product of the Soviet Union: Comparative Growth Rates," U.S. Congress, Joint Economic Committee, *Dimensions of Soviet Economic Power*, Hearings, 87th Congress, 2nd Session (Washington: Government Printing Office, 1962), pp. 67–90; G. H. Peters, "Agriculture's Contribution to Economic Growth," *Westminster Bank Review* (November, 1963).

25. For example, the United Kingdom excludes all unpaid family workers, Denmark male unpaid family workers, and Norway unpaid family workers outside agriculture. The reason, however, is that in each case the numbers in omitted categories is believed very small. The Netherlands cuts the number of female unpaid family workers by one-third. The United States counts no unpaid family workers working less than fifteen hours a week. Estimates for the Common Market countries are described in Statistical Office of the European Communities, *Statistical Information*, 1963, No. 2 bis, p. 13 f.

Time, Work, and Welfare

James N. Morgan

INTRODUCTION

MAJOR events tend to focus our attention on new problems, and the happenings of the past forty years have led us to examine the relation of work to human welfare. First, a great depression dramatized the economic and psychological cost of unwanted leisure. Second, the vast increase in the labor force brought forth by the demands of World War II dramatized the extent of hidden unemployment before the war. And third, the subsequent continuation of a trend for more rather than fewer people to work, particularly wives, gave the lie to any notion that it was only patriotism or dire need that brought forth workers.

The continuation of poverty in the midst of plenty within this country, and the growing disparity of real incomes between countries, have forced attention to such problems as the wastage of human talents, the payoff from investment in human capital, and the method of measuring levels of welfare. The growing emphasis on government programs to deal with social problems has forced attention to quantitative economics as a supplement to economic theory. Social policy requires knowledge of magnitudes (how many poor?) and causes (why?).

The purpose of this paper is to summarize the problems of assessing levels of welfare, and then to provide some data in a few areas to illustrate the usefulness of empirical information as well as theory.

CONCEPTUAL FRAMEWORK

It should be stated at the beginning that our data do not measure up to our concepts. To speak of the welfare of a family implies a measure of "well-offness" in a broad sense. We start by narrowing it to material things—the ability to maintain a certain standard of living, that is, consumption of leisure, services, and goods. The amount of economic resources a family needs to achieve a given standard will depend, of course, on the family size and structure.

Families make economic choices between present and future consumption of goods and services, and between more command over goods and services on the one hand, or more leisure on the other. These choices are affected by many constraints and by complementarities. Enjoyment of leisure may require consumption of goods and services; work to produce income may provide direct pleasure.

In view of these constraints and complementarities, elaborate analytical discussions of the marginal rates of substitution between leisure and more income, present and future, seem out of place. But merely looking at the problems forces us to focus on time and decisions about the use of time as a basic factor in the analysis of individual behavior, and a basic determinant of levels of welfare.

The data are also deficient in providing only a snapshot at a moment in history, and not trends of change. The reason is that no comparable data exist for earlier periods, not only because of improvement in methods of sampling and interviewing, but also because attempts to secure data on use of time, imputed and other nonmoney income, and transfer payments have occurred only recently.

TIME

What is the relation between a man's use of his time and his level of welfare? Is time free from work a source of satisfaction? If leisure is important, why don't people use more of it? In the face of an income tax which takes at minimum 20 per cent of the monetary fruits of labor, but does not tax leisure at all, why do people seem to prefer almost anything to leisure?[1]

It is easy to point out that in theory the individual starts with twenty-four hours a day, some of which he trades in the form of work for money (or for real things if he engages in home production). If at the margin he makes $2.00 an hour, can we argue that he values his leisure time at that much, since he does not give up more of it at that price? If that were possible, then we might estimate people's total real incomes by what they would make if they worked most of the time not needed for sleeping, eating, and doing the necessary things.[2] But some people enjoy their work while others have unwanted leisure (unemployment) or don't like leisure anyway.[3]

One way to adjust incomes to make them a better measure of welfare is to estimate hourly earnings and multiply by, say, 4,000 hours a year, assuming that the other 4,760 hours (thirteen hours a day) are needed for other activities. But why multiply? If matters were that simple, hourly earnings would themselves be an adequate measure of welfare.

The major difficulty is not a conceptual problem of the relative valuation of work and leisure, nor of the measurement of two consumer surpluses, but the simple fact that many people still do not have all the opportunities they would like to work for money, even at existing wage rates.

In the 1963 Survey of Consumer Finances, a national sample of heads of spending units was asked the following question: Sometimes people don't work as much as they want to because of illness or unemployment or short work-week or lack of extra jobs. How about you, would you say that you worked less than you would have liked last year?" [If yes:] "What would you say are the main reasons you didn't work more?" Even within the middle age range, 35 to 65, a substantial fraction said they would have liked more work, varying from 5 per cent for the college graduates up to 43 per cent for those who did not go beyond elementary school.[4]

The implication is that even after the increases in labor force participation and a long period of relative good times, there is still underemployment, and it is probably underestimated by current measures. The definition of unemployment used in the Census studies of the labor force is, of necessity, kept rather formal in order to achieve some precision in estimates of short-run changes; but it is not adequate for an assessment of the extent to which people have a free choice between income and leisure.

There is also evidence of substantial short-run fluctuation in earnings. A three-way reinterview imbedded in the 1960, 1961, and 1962 Surveys of Consumer Finances revealed that there were substantial numbers of spending units whose income changed more than 5 per cent from one year to the next but who reported no change in the number of weeks worked. Some were self-employed, but a substantial number must have experienced differences in the amount of overtime, extra jobs, etc.[5] Four-fifths reported a change in spending unit income from one year to the next, three-fourths a change in the earnings of the head, and nearly half a change in the earnings of the head without any large change in the number of weeks worked.

HOURS OF WORK OF HEADS OF SPENDING UNITS

Without relying on what people say about how much work they would *like*, we can ask what factors are associated with shorter or longer annual hours of work. It takes extreme forces such as physical disability or old age to keep the head of a spending unit out of the labor force entirely, so the analysis is restricted to those in the labor force. A previous analysis already published indicated a number of explanatory factors that affected hours of work, most of them constraints of one sort or another: extreme age, one adult with children at home, physical disability, being nonwhite.[6] There were also some apparently positive motivating forces, such as low hourly earnings, plans to help relatives or send children to college, even having a wife with more education than the head, or having children.

The multiple regression technique used in that analysis could not answer the question whether the various forces were substitutes for one another, or acted cumulatively. Regression can only test the particular interactions (effects of combinations of factors) that are built into the analysis. A more flexible approach was used on the same data, first examining the pattern of clearly logically prior (exogenous) factors and then examining the residuals against a larger set.[7] The method of analysis specifies to the computer a strategy similar to that of a very patient investigator examining a body of data. The procedure sequentially divides the sample by a series of binary splits into a mutually exclusive set of subgroups. At each stage the computer selects the group with the largest unexplained sum of squares remaining in it, tries all feasible splits on each explanatory factor, and selects the best of the best. When no split can be found that seems worth making (in terms of error reduction), the process stops. The result is a decision tree showing the branching process, and a final set of groups which account for the population. The pedigree of the final groups can be used to interpret why they are so widely different on the dependent variable. The criteria all along are those of importance in reducing the unexplained sum of squares, not levels of significance. With large samples anything important is significant, but the reverse may not be true.

The sequential nature of the process makes highly intercorrelated explanatory factors particularly troublesome, and intensifies the need to consider basic structure. It is particularly important to distinguish clearly exogenous factors which could affect other factors (as well as the dependent variable) but could not be affected by them. Family background, age, sex, race, and such stable characteristics as religious preference and personality need to be used first, not jointly with such factors as occupation, which they can affect.

The following factors were considered logically prior, that is, mostly determined long ago and unlikely to be the result rather than the cause of long or short hours of work:

Explanatory characteristic	*Number of classes*
Composition of the spending unit (head male? married? children?)	8
Age of head of unit	7
Physical disability of head of unit	4
Where head grew up (farm or city, in or out of Deep South, abroad)	6
Education of head of unit	8
Race	2
Religious preference (Protestants divided into fundamentalist or other)	4
Index of achievement motivation[8]	4

The sample of 2,569 spending units with working heads was then sub-divided, using at each split the best combinations of the best factor, those that would make the maximum reduction in unexplained variance. The last three factors were never used since they never did so well as one of the first five.

The most important differentiation is between the married and the single, the former working 138 hours more than the average, and the latter 347 hours a year less than the average. Mixed with the married were a few men with children at home but no wife; mixed with the single were some women with children at home but no husband (widows, divorcees). No analysis is free from possible circularity, and it may be that the more energetic men work more and also get married, but it is equally possible that the responsibilities of marriage and children lead to greater needs and longer hours of work. Among the single people, more-over, there is a substantial group of people under 25 years of age, or 55 or older, who worked an average of only 1,495 hours in 1959.

Among the married spending unit heads, any one of several things appears to reduce working time: extreme age, physical disability, or lack of education. Only one subgroup is isolated because it works much more than average—a group of men who grew up on a farm elsewhere than in the Deep South. Most of these people are not currently farmers,

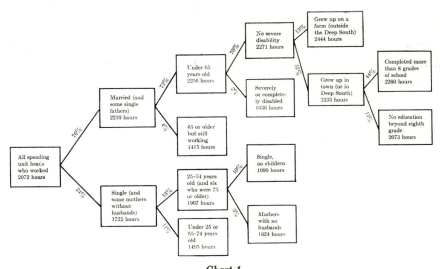

Chart 1

Hours Worked in 1959 by Heads of Spending Units of Different Types
(Background Factors Only)

Percent of all 49.4 million working spending unit heads is given on each arrow.
Standard deviation = 797 hours.

TABLE 1

*A Subdivision of Working Heads of Spending Units, To
Differentiate Those Who Work More or Less*

Hours worked in 1959	Description of subgroup	Percentage of all 49.4 million working heads of spending units
1415	Sixty-five or older, married (or single father)	4%
1495	*Single* (or mother with no husband); under 25, or sixty-five or older	11%
1624	*Mothers with no husbands*, 25–64 years old	3%
1636	Severely or completely *disabled* (married)	2%
1999	*Single*, 25–54 years old	10%
2073	*No education beyond grade school*, married, under 65, not disabled, grew up in town or on a farm in the Deep South.	13%
2280	Married, completed more than 8 grades of school, under 65, not disabled, grew up in town or on a farm in the Deep South.	44%
2444	Grew up on a farm outside the Deep South, married, under 65, not disabled.	13%
		100%

so there may well be something to the farm tradition of long hours of work.

The population tree into which the sample is divided is given in Chart 1, and a description of the eight subgroups that account for some 16 per cent of the variance is given in Table 1. A clear picture appears of a set of inhibiting forces that reduce hours of work, and only farm background and dependents to care for as possible positive forces making for longer hours of work. Actual unemployment was not used as an explanatory factor on the ground that it is intermediate rather than basic.

The population tree into which the sample is divided is given in Chart 1, and a description of the eight subgroups that account for some 16 per cent of the variance is given in Table 1. A clear picture appears of a set of inhibiting forces that reduce hours of work, and only farm background and dependents to care for as possible positive forces making for longer hours of work.

The eight subgroup means now become the standard, and we can analyze the pooled deviations from these means. A much larger set of explanatory characteristics was used in this second stage:

Explanatory characteristic	Number of classes
Hourly earning rate	9
Frequency of unemployment in past	8
Occupation	10
Whether self-employed, and whether supervises others	3
North-South migration (where grew up, where lives now)	6
Difference in education of head and wife	7
Number of states lived in	6
Stage in the family life cycle	9
Whether head or his father grew up abroad	3
Religion and frequency of attendance	7
Race	2
Urban-rural migration (where grew up, where lives now)	6
Achievement motivation and belief in work versus luck	7
Unemployment level in area	6
Plans to help relatives or send children to college	4
Size of place of residence	6
Educational difference between head and father	4
Sex of head	2

Again, at each division of the sample each of the eighteen factors had its chance. Only six were used—the first six in the list—and one of these only to discriminate between single and married, not according to educational differences.

As in the first stage of the analysis, the most important factors, which appeared first, were constraints or facilitating circumstances, rather than motivating forces proper. The self-employed work more because they can, as well as because they want to. These who report frequent unemployment work less, presumably against their will.

When these factors have been disposed of, however, more interesting forces appear. Those who earn less per hour tend to work longer hours.[9] Self-employed farmers and businessmen with low wages who grew up in the South, or moved there, work less than those with no "southern exposure".

Among the well-paid and seldom unemployed people who work for others, the single persons appear, strangely enough, to work longer hours than the married. These residual differences, however, offset a difference in the opposite direction in the initial analysis (see Chart 1). The implication is that marital status affects hours of work *except* for well-paid employees with steady jobs.

Many interesting variables, such as religion, race, past migration (South-North or rural-urban), sex of head, educational difference between head and wife, religion, or plans for the future that require money, appeared to have no great importance in affecting hours of work.

The full details are given in Chart 2, the twelve final groups of which account for 23 per cent of the variance of the residuals (an additional 19 per cent of the original variance).

The over-all implications of this analysis are that there are substantial groups in our society who work less then they would like because of some involuntary constraint. Changes over time in the severity of those constraints, or the sizes of the groups affected by them, can affect the total supply of labor as well as the welfare interpretations of the income derived from it.

Another implication is that studies of the effects of such positive motivations as rates of pay need to be confined to those who are relatively free to respond, or we may vastly underestimate their importance. We may even misinterpret the direction of their influence if it is the low-paid people who are also subject to the most involuntary idleness.

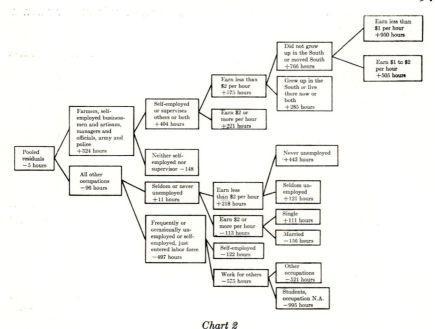

Chart 2

Hours Worked in 1959 by Spending Unit Heads, Differences from Expected Hours
(See Chart 1)

The final groups, in order by whether they worked more or less than one would have expected on the basis of the first-stage analysis, are given in Table 2.

WIVES' PARTICIPATION IN THE LABOR FORCE

For wives, the main decision is not how many hours to work, as it was for heads of units, but whether to work at all. Several studies have been made of the participation of wives in the labor force, including our own in *Income and Welfare in the United States*.[10] Again, however, aside from a few interactions built into the specifications of the dummy variables, all the analyses assumed an additive set of factors which affected all wives or none.

Applying the same procedure of analysis as before to whether the wife worked in 1959, a 1–0 variable, we first try factors which are clearly prior, determined long ago, and unlikely to be the result rather than a cause of the wife's working.

Characteristic	*Number of classes*
Stage in family life cycle	6
Age of wife	7
Education of wife	9
Where husband grew up	6
Physical condition of wife (disabled?)	4
Race	2
Religion	4
Difference in education between husband and wife	6

Only the first four were used, as can be seen in Chart 3. Young wives with no children were the most likely to work (70 per cent), and

TABLE 2

Average Deviations from Expected Annual Hours for Various Subgroups

Average deviation (hours)		Percent of working heads of spending units[a]
950	Farmers or self-employed businessmen or managers earning less than $1.00 per hour who did not grow up in the South and do not live in the South	3
505	Same as above except earning between $1.00 and $2.00 an hour	2
443	Employed by others (not managers, army or police) at a steady job (never unemployed) but earning less than $2.00 per hour	7
285	Farmers or self-employed businessmen or managers who either grew up in the South or live there now, or both, earning less than $2.00 an hour	4
221	Farmers or self-employed businessmen or managers, who earn $2.00 or more per hour	9
121	Employed (not army or police), seldom unemployed, earning less than $2.00 per hour	16
111	Employed, seldom or never unemployed, earning $2.00 or more per hour, single	6
−122	Self-employed, but not farmer, businessman, or artisan	3
−148	Neither self-employed nor supervises others, but a farmer, manager, or official, army or police	3
−156	Employed and seldom or never unemployed, earns $2.00 or more an hour, married	33
−521	Employed, but frequently or occasionally unemployed	12
−995	Employed but frequently or occasionally unemployed, gives occupation as student, housewife, or N.A.	2
		100%

[a] Of whom there were 49.4 million in 1959.

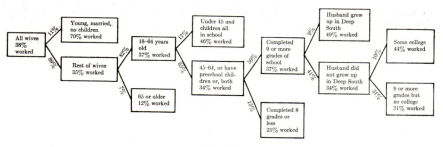

Chart 3

Percentage of Wives Who Worked in 1959, in Various Subgroups of the Population

Percentage of all 15.3 million working wives is given on the arrows.
(Sample = 2059 married couples.)

wives 65 or older the least likely (12 per cent). Among the rest, having preschool children or being 45 or older reduced participation in the labor force, as did low levels of formal education. Among wives with adequate education, having a husband who grew up in the Deep South was associated with more participation in the labor force. This is not a racial difference, or the IBM machine would have divided the sample on race at that point rather than on the husbands' backgrounds.

It is interesting to ask why race does not seem to make a difference. The main reason is that the criterion is one of importance in reducing over-all error variance, which requires that a split result in two groups which are different, but also both contain substantial fractions of the sample. A very small group may be widely different, at high levels of significance, and still its separation from the rest may not be important for prediction. In addition, when a group has as many as 70 per cent or as few as 12 per cent working, not much else *could* make any difference. As a matter of fact, the machine program provides data on the effect of each factor on each subgroup generated, and only among those 18–45 years old and with children in school did racial differences seem appreciable.[11] Apparently the demands of housekeeping keep most white women with schoolchildren from working, but not the nonwhites.

Similarly, disabilities kept a few wives from working, and having more education than the husband encouraged it, but neither of these bits of information would reduce error sufficiently to justify another subdivision of the sample.

Current factors such as unemployment of the husband, or very high earnings of the husband, or his attitude toward wives' working, were kept out of this first stage of the analysis to avoid questions of circularity or of jointness. However, the seven final groups of Chart 3, accounting for a tenth of the variance, became the norm, and deviations from their means, pooled, were analyzed using a second set of predictors:

Characteristic	*Number of classes*
Gross factor income of spending unit without the wife's earnings	10
Size of place (city size)	6
Husband's attitude toward wives' working	8
Number of states lived in (mobility)	6
Level of unemployment in the area	6
Region	4
Plans to help relatives or send children to·college	4
Unemployment experience of husband	8

As can be seen from Chart 4, only the first three of these appeared to matter. It may have been rationalization, but husbands who said that in general it was all right for wives to work were 20 per cent more likely to have working wives. On the other hand, in a substantial number of families where the husband said it was a bad thing for wives to work, the wife was 5 per cent less likely to work.

Living in a rural area also apparently makes it more difficult for a wife to work. Indeed, the details show that middle-sized cities are most conducive.

If the husband's earnings (and other earned income, not counting the wife's) were $10,000 or more, the wife was less likely to work. The detailed effect of other income on whether the wife works is almost

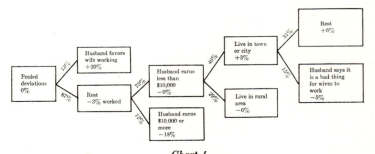

Chart 4
Deviations from Expected Proportions of Wives Working
(See Chart 3 for expectations)

Percentage of all 15.3 million working wives is given on the arrows.

identical with that derived by multiple regression in *Income and Welfare in the United States*.[12]

There were mild tendencies for wives to be more likely to work in the North Central region, or if there were plans to provide more help for relatives or to send children to college, or both, or if the husband was unemployed a great deal, but they only involved a percentage point, or two or three.

A substantial fraction of working wives work less than full time, and more than a third work less than half time. For the most part, the same factors that encouraged or discouraged working at all affected the hours of those who did work.[13]

What emerges now is a picture both of the husband's hours and the wife's working, largely dominated by circumstances rather than moved by economic motives. To determine a family's level of welfare, it is also necessary to know the rates of pay of husband and wife, and the size of the family and its needs. Analysis of the heads' hourly earnings have been published, and they tend to show that there are disadvantages, any small number of which will drive earnings down.[14] Similar studies of the earnings of wives showed that both education and experience (years in the labor force) were required for higher wages. In addition it helped to be in or near a big city, and to be a professional or self-employed businesswoman.[15] If employment and earnings are heavily affected by background factors such as education and current factors such as the stage in the family life cycle, is the economic status of the family, its level of "welfare," also partly so determined?

WELFARE AND POVERTY

How well off a family is depends on its total income and assets, its claims on the future (job stability, expectations), its protection against risks (insurance), the size and structure of the family and its needs, and the freedom it has to do what if wants with its time. There is no easy way to quantify all these on the same scale and develop a measure of "well-offness." One might value leisure (nonwork) time at the marginal wage rate of the individual, but this assumes that the leisure is wanted, that work is not enjoyed. One could convert assets into annuities, or count only the current income on them, but people persistently refuse to use their assets for current living, and the current income would be negligible for most people anyway. Similarly, people generally do not have firm enough expectations about the distant future to base their current living on it. While we have presented data elsewhere giving estimates of the proportions of people who have certain combinations of income, assets, and insurance, there is such a correlation—those with income also having assets and insurance, and vice versa—that for most purposes current income is sufficient.[16]

We can still make major improvements in estimating levels of "welfare" and explaining differences in that level, by

    (1) developing the best feasible measure of current real income,

    (2) creating some measure of need that takes account of family size and structure and location, and

    (3) taking the ratio of income to the standard budget necessary to meet minimum needs.

Briefly put, a more inclusive measure of income was developed by asking enough extra questions of a national sample so that estimates could be made of nonmoney income in the form of housing (value of free rent from living with relatives, or imputed return on net equity in an owned home), homegrown food, or do-it-yourself additions and repairs. From this, estimated federal income taxes were deducted, and the resulting measure was called gross disposable income. It included all kinds of help from relatives, government, or charities.

To avoid complex estimates of inter-unit transfers among those living together, all related people in a household were treated as a single family. This made it particularly important to take account of different family sizes. A budget standard of needs based on the age, sex, and employment status was adapted from one used by the Community Council of Greater New York. The standard is arbitrary and crude, but makes adjustment for different family structures in at least a rough way.[17]

We can now ask either what determines the level of welfare (the ratio) or what causes people to be poor (whether below .85 of the minimum budget). If we ask first not what causes poverty but what determines the level of living of families in this country, then the upper end of the scale matters too, not just whether a family is at the bottom. An analysis can be made using the actual ratio of income to budget standards as the variable to be explained.

Here, the first division is according to whether the head of the family graduated from high school. The implication is that it takes a high school diploma to make one really well off. If, in addition, one graduates from college and is mature (45 to 74), he can expect an income more than three times the minimal budget standard. Even among high-school graduates, however, a combination of extreme age (too young or too old) and being nonwhite can drive the average family income close to the mini-

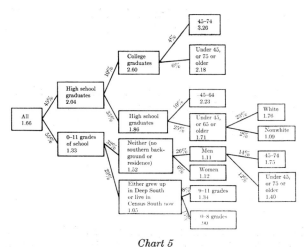

Chart 5

Average Ratio of Income to Needs, for Various Subgroups of Families

Percentages of all 53.4 million families are given on the arrows. The ten final groups account for 22% of the variance of the 2800 families in the sample.

mum standard.[18] What about those who did not graduate from high school? Combinations of disadvantages can drive their incomes to the minimum, but combinations of advantages can drive them back up, relative to their needs, to the national average. The full picture is given in Chart 5.

These are not casual findings, but the results of systematic search, and the implication of the fact that the process did not make use of the other "predictors" is that none of the following make very much difference in the over-all picture:

Marital status
Number of siblings the head has (came from large family?)
Attitude toward work and motive to achieve
Migration to or from rural area
Migration into or out of the South
Age of head at birth of first child
Religious preference
Whether doubled up (extra adults in household)

Several of these were used when the splitting process was continued, but they segregated relatively small groups. For instance, some thirty-two middle-aged college graduates who either considered luck instead of work the key to success, or had a low index of motive to achieve, or both, had an average welfare ratio of 2.15 instead of 3.26.

Who is Poor?

Averages often hide the truth, and in any case current interest and concern is less with what makes people well off than with what makes them poor. Without attaching undue significance to the ratio .85 of the budget standard, we can use the fact of falling below it as an indication of poverty, and ask what subgroups in the population have the largest proportions of poor. The results would not be changed much by a different cut-off point or a different budget standard.

The results, using a set of possible explanatory factors similar to those in the analysis of levels of welfare, are given in Chart 6. Going beyond eighth grade appears to be most important in avoiding poverty. For those who progress farther, however, various disadvantages can still produce poverty which is not removed by additional education.

If the family head not only completed less than nine grades of school but also lives in the South, the family is more likely than not to be poor

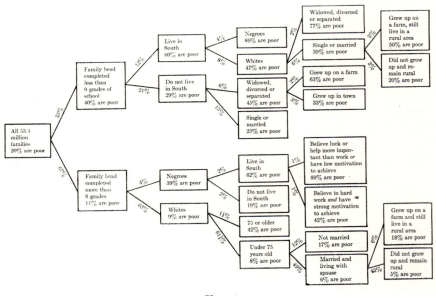

Chart 6

Incidence of Poverty Among Families of Different Types, 1959

All families given on arrows, percent of group who are poor in boxes.

—60 per cent of such families have gross disposable incomes less than .85 of the budget standard. It can be argued that needs are lower in the South, particularly in housing, but estimates of the costs of living show no great differences. If *standards* are generally lower, poverty may be less noticeable and even less irritating, but this does not make it affluence.

If, in addition to being uneducated and living in the South, the family head is nonwhite, or is widowed, divorced, or separated, or grew up on a farm and still lives in a rural area, then the family is likely to be poor. For those outside the South but with little education, broken families or farm backgrounds are again associated with poverty.

On the other hand, even with education, being a Negro in the South is likely to mean poverty. It is only among this group that attitudes and motives which we were able to measure seemed to matter. Among those who believed in hard work as the way to achieve success, *and* had a high index on our measure of motive to achieve, fewer than half were poor. This proportion was less than half that for educated southern Negroes who lacked either motive *or* the expection that success was possible.

What is new about this analysis? Everyone knows that the retired, Negroes, farmers, and uneducated people are more likely to be poor. What is new here is the focus on combinations, and the clear implication that a combination of two or three disadvantages can be crippling. Beyond that, further disadvantages can have little added effect. In other words, beyond a certain point the elimination of poverty is a complicated process, requiring that for any individual *all* the alternative causes be dealt with simultaneously. The results of tackling the causes of poverty one at a time, or working on only some of them, may be discouragingly small.

Second, it is useful to ask how large the various major subgroups are. Some 89 per cent of uneducated southern negroes are poor, but they are less than 4 per cent of all families—hence they account for only 16 per cent of the 10.9 million poor families. The largest single group of poor, in the middle of the chart, is in a group only 23 per cent of whom are poor, but the group contains 15 per cent of all families.They completed less than nine grades of school, but have no other disadvantages; they do not live in the South, and are not widowed, divorced, or separated.

Even more important, the group in the bottom right of the chart, with no disadvantages we could measure, accounted for 10 per cent of all the poor families. Only 5 per cent of such families were poor, but they are 43 per cent of all families. Hence, while we focus on multiproblem groups of which a large proportion are poor, we forget that nearly half of the poor families have only one thing working against them.

The limitations of this study need to be stated. A substantial amount of variation has not been accounted for. Some factors which we were unable to measure explain more at each stage. We have simply selected the most powerful combinations of the factors we could measure. Second, the focus on importance rather than significance means that highly significant forces which affect only very small proportions of the population are ignored. Finally, a description of who is poor at a point in time does not tell much about either past or future trends. We can guess at some things. The aged poor should decline in numbers as those not covered by Social Security die and are replaced by a new generation which is. The future of racial differences will certainly depend on the success of the tax cut and other attempts to approach full employment, and on the civil rights bill, and on the amount and quality of education of future generations of non-whites. Educational differences in earnings seem likely to persist, and have recently been getting larger.[19] In view of the changes of this decade, only a reassessment of comparable scope in 1970 will tell.

SUMMARY

How well off a family is in this country, insofar as we can measure it, depends heavily upon the hours and earnings of the adults in the family. These in turn appear to be affected more by forces beyond the current control of the individual than by the economic or other motivations we were able to measure. Formal education, even without accounting for variations in its quality, appears a powerful determinant of welfare. A minimal amount appears necessary to avoid poverty, and added amounts lead to higher earnings, easier employment for wives, less unemployment, and higher levels of well-offness.

While it may only take one or two disadvantages to produce poverty, this means that its elimination requires getting rid of *all* the problems. If we were able to assess other handicaps (emotional difficulties, lack of training, etc.), it would be even more obvious that a man must have almost everything on his side to be well off. This complementarity of advantages and substitutability of disadvantages can go a long way toward explaining a skewed distribution of income with normal distributions of talent, motive, physical condition, education, and the rest.

Notes

1. See Sebastian de Grazia, *Of Time, Work, and Leisure* (New York: Twentieth Century Fund, 1962), for an historical perspective.
2. For a still more inclusive treatment of time that treats demands on time for consumption as well as production, see Gary Becker, "On the Economics of Time," presented at the Econometric Society meetings, Boston, December 29, 1963. See also

the theoretical treatment by Leon M. Moses, "Income, Leisure, and Wage Pressure," *Economic Journal,* LXXII (June, 1962), 320–334.

3. On the need for work even without financial pressure, see Nancy Morse and Robert Weiss, "The Function and Meaning of Work and the Job," *American Sociological Review,* 20 (1955), 191–198.

4. See Lininger *et al, The 1963 Survey of Consumer Finances* (Ann Arbor: Survey Research Center, University of Michigan, 1964).

5. See Kosobud and Morgan, eds., *Consumer Behavior Over Two and Three Years,* Monograph 36 (Ann Arbor: Survey Research Center, University of Michigan, 1964).

6. See Morgan, David, Cohen, and Brazer, *Income and Welfare in the United States* (New York: McGraw Hill, 1962), pp. 73ff.

7. For details of the method see Morgan and J. Sonquist, "Problems in the Analysis of Survey Data and a Proposal, *Journal of the American Statistical Association,* LIX (June, 1963), 415–434: Morgan and Sonquist, "Some Results from a Non-Symmetrical Franching Process that Looks for Interaction Effects," *Proceedings,* Social Statistics Section, American Statistical Association, 1963, pp. 40–53; and J. Sonquist and J. Morgan *The Detection of Interaction Effects,* Survey Research Center Monograph 35 (Ann Arbor: Survey Research Center, University of Michigan, 1964).

8. The index of achievement motive was an indirect one based on laboratory evidence that achievement-oriented people tend to make strong distinctions between difficult and easy tasks, and to place high value on the difficult ones. For details see *Income and Welfare in the United States,* pp. 487–492, or Morgan, "Achievement Motivation and Economic Behavior," *Economic Development and Cultural Change,* May, 1964.

9. It is possible that some respondents exaggerated their work hours, and since hourly earnings were estimated by dividing annual earnings by annual hours, a spurious correlation between hours and hourly earnings could result. Self-employed might find it easier to exaggerate, but they might well be expected to work more too.

10. *Op cit,* Chapter 9, and references there. In addition see Elizabeth Pfeil, *Die Berufstatigkeit von Muttern* (Tubingen: J. C. B. Mohn, 1961); and Arnold Katz, "Cyclical Unemployment and Secondary Family Worker" (abstract), *Econometrica,* XXIX (July, 1961), 478; and Jacob Mincer, "Labor Force Participation of Married Women: A Study of Labor Supply," in *Aspects of Labor Economics* (Princeton: Princeton University Press, 1962).

11. For that group the proportions working were *44* for whites (N = 326) and *73* for nonwhites (N = 26).

12. P. 114.

13. See *Income and Welfare in the United States,* Chapter 11.

14. See *Income and Welfare in the United States,* Chapter 5. For a more flexible analysis like those used in this paper, see Morgan and Sonquist, "Some Results . . ." and Sonquist and Morgan, *The Detection of Interaction Effects.*

15. *Income and Welfare in the United States,* Chapter 10.

16. See *Income and Welfare in the United States,* and J. Morgan, "Measuring the Economic Status of the Aged," *Informational Economic Review,* January, 1965.

For a discussion of uncertainty in the crucial area of medical care, see Kenneth Arrow, "Uncertainty and the Economics of Medical Care," *American Economic Review,* LIII (December, 1963), 941–973.

17. The numerator can be and has been criticized for not taking account of temporarily low income of some, or of assets and insurance, and for possible understatement particularly of welfare income. The budget standard has been criticized for providing inadequately for differences in cost of living between North and South, urban and rural, and for excessive allowances for the costs of earning a living. Adjustments for any of this would have been quite arbitrary, and in most cases would have affected only very small subgroups, such as some fraction of the 6–7 per cent who are farmers.

18. The numbers are average ratios, not ratios of averages. The latter would have tended even more to hide poverty in the averages.

19. See J. Morgan and C. Lininger, "Note on Education and Income," *Quarterly Journal of Economics* (May, 1964); J. Morgan and M. David, "Education and Income," *Quarterly Journal of Economics,* LXXVII (August, 1963), 423–437; and Herman Miller, "Annual and Lifetime earnings in Relation to Education 1939–1959," *American Economic Review,* L (December, 1960), 962–986.

Changes in Occupational Structure

Mark B. Schupack

THE marginal productivity theory of wages has usually been applied to some occupational or industrial class of workers. All workers within each class have been treated as homogeneous in the sense that a single supply and demand relationship can be developed. Recent interest in the problems of older workers has, however, indicated that this assumption of homogeneity is not realistic. It prevents an adequate description of the changing pattern of the labor force. In particular, different age groups within an occupation or industry react to market forces in different ways.

Policy discussions related to structural unemployment have stressed the importance of age. Technological innovations often entail retraining and replacement of the labor force, and the willingness and ability to participate in such programs varies with age. Age is also an important determinant of industrial, occupational, and regional migration, and perhaps of firms' decisions about methods of production. For these and similar reasons, public policies designed to increase the efficiency of the economy cannot escape the consideration of age. Policy actions guided by studies that assume labor homogeneity across age groups are unlikely to be effective in achieving greater efficiency.

Taking account of the limitations of available data, this study proposes a means of measuring changes in the age structure of occupations. In the first section, a simple theoretical model is presented in which allowance is made for different reactions to market forces on the part of different age groups. In principle the parameters of the model can be estimated, but in practice the data necessary to estimate the parameters are not available at the present time. Therefore, in the second section an empirical method is outlined—a modification of the original model which permits utilization of what data are available. Finally, in the third section some preliminary results are presented. These indicate that the method holds some promise as a fruitful empirical technique.

A Simple Theoretical Model

In general, the number of workers hired in any labor market is the result of interactions of supply and demand forces. The bounds of a labor market are given by a detailed occupation.[1] To simplify the theory, it will be assumed that the demanders of labor do not distinguish among various ages of prospective employees. They set job requirements for the occupation. Then suppliers either find themselves able to do the job, and so present themselves as part of the supply curve, or cannot do the job and never enter this particular labor market. Thus age differences will show up only on the supply side of the market.

The market supply function will consist of the sum of the supply functions for each individual age group in a particular occupation. Different behavior patterns due to age are displayed in the different ways in which market changes will affect the supply curves for each individual age group. This is quite arbitrary, but simpler than assuming that demanders also distinguish among different age groups and have a different demand function for each. In the end, the two approaches may lead to the same thing, the superficial difference being a result of which side of the market is assigned certain market forces.

Little is known about the construction of a market supply curve and the individual age-group curves. Given technology and the demand for final products, development of a market demand curve for labor is straightforward. But the factors affecting supply have not been given much attention, especially from an empirical viewpoint. Ironically, the available data in this study will, in the end, force most attention and emphasis to be placed upon the supply side. Some indication of the way in which various factors affect the supply conditions may be obtained when the final empirical functions outlined in the next section are estimated.

Given a market supply curve and a market demand curve, equilibrium conditions yield a market wage and total employment. The individual age-group supply curves tell how many workers of each age are hired to make up this market total. The assumption of a single demand curve, i.e., failure to distinguish between different age groups in the production function and thus in the market demand function, means that each worker receives the same wage rate regardless of his age. If a worker cannot do the standard job at the established wage, he will not be considered part of the labor supply for this particular market. Though not strictly realistic, the assumption of a common wage for all age groups allows an easy method of distributing total employment among the different age groups. While it will be shown later that direct estimation of the parameters of this model may be impossible, the model will serve as a very useful guide for further empirical work.

On the demand side, it is assumed that a firm operates with the following production function:

$$(1) \qquad O = (a_0 + a_1L - a_2L^2 + a_3K - a_4K^2 + a_5KL)^2$$

where

O = output,
L = amount of labor used,
K = amount of capital used,
a_0 = constant,
a_i = technical coefficients.

The firm is faced with a product demand function:[2]

$$(2) \qquad O = \frac{\gamma^2}{P_0^2}$$

where

P_0 = price of the product,
γ = constant (essentially a shift parameter).

Profit maximization leads to the following first order equilibrium conditions:

$$(3) \qquad \begin{aligned} P_0 f_L - P_L &= 0 \\ P_0 f_K - P_K &= 0 \end{aligned}$$

where

P_L = price of labor input,
P_K = price of capital input,
f_L = $\partial O/\partial L$, from (1),
f_K = $\partial O/\partial K$, from (1).

It is now possible to derive an expression representing the demand for labor in terms of the other parameters of the model. Using equations (3), expressions can be found for P_L and P_K when P_0 is eliminated by using equation (2). By differentiation of equation (1), equation (3) becomes:

$$(4) \qquad \begin{aligned} P_L &= 2\gamma(a_1 - 2a_2L + a_5K), \\ P_K &= 2\gamma(a_3 - 2a_4K + a_5L). \end{aligned}$$

Since our interest is in L, K is eliminated between the equations, and the result is solved for L. Using L_d to denote the quantity of labor demanded, the resulting demand function is:

(5) $$L_d = a + bP_L$$

where

$$a = \frac{\left(\dfrac{a_1}{a_5} - \dfrac{P_K}{4\gamma a_4} - \dfrac{a_3}{2a_4}\right)}{\left(\dfrac{2a_2}{a_5} - \dfrac{a_5}{2a_4}\right)},$$

$$b = \frac{\left(-\dfrac{1}{a_5 2\gamma}\right)}{\left(\dfrac{2a_2}{a_5} - \dfrac{a_5}{2a_4}\right)}.$$

Thus, as expected, the demand for labor is a function of the price of labor, the price of capital, and the parameters of the product demand and production functions.

The supply functions rest upon less firm foundations. Of course, it is possible to start with a single worker's utility function (the utility of income, the disutility of work, the utility of leisure) and to derive a supply curve of labor which maximizes total utility. However, there is no guide as to the form which this function should take. Nor is much known about the way in which observable variables should fit into the function as affecting the various sources of utility or disutility. Instead of starting with the underlying maximization process, an a priori specification of the form of the supply functions will be given.

Let the quantity supplied for the ith age group be designated as L_i, assumed to be a function of the wage paid to labor in this occupation. Dependence upon the wage rate reflects partly the trade-off between income and leisure and partly the relative pecuniary attractiveness of alternative occupations. Further, there is a shift parameter which reflects exogenous changes in the labor force brought about by population growth or immigration. Finally, there are two other sets of forces which will be taken into account. One is the ability of workers to remain in an occupation as they age. In turn this depends upon characteristics inherent to the occupation itself: physical capacities required for the job, the type of working conditions encountered, and the amount of specific training required. The other forces are those which may induce a worker to shift to another occupation. Relative wage differences modified by the availability of alternative jobs and the ease of making the change are obviously relevant. A more detailed discussion of these factors will be given in the next section; it is sufficient at this point to note their existence.

The following supply function for the ith age group is postulated:

$$(6) \qquad L_i = e_i + \alpha_i P_L + \theta_i T_i + \sigma_i S_i,$$

where

L_i = amount of labor supplied,
e_i = shift constant,
P_L = price of labor,
T_i = trait requirements for this occupation,
S_i = attraction of substitute occupations,
α_i = constant related to price elasticity of supply,
θ_i, σ_i = trait and substitution coefficients.

Assuming three age groups, it is now possible to state the entire model in a form suitable for further work.[3] Each of the supply functions is simplified in an obvious way, and the final equation expresses market equilibrium:

$$
\begin{aligned}
L_d &= a + bP_L, \\
L_1 &= c_1 + \alpha_1 P_L, \\
L_2 &= c_2 + \alpha_2 P_L, \\
L_3 &= c_3 + \alpha_3 P_L, \\
L_d &= L_1 + L_2 + L_3.
\end{aligned}
$$

(7)

There are five equations in five unknowns: L_d, L_1, L_2, L_3, and P_L. The object is to solve for the reduced form of one of the L_i's. This expression generates the relationship between the number of workers hired in each age group and the parameters of the model. It is this relationship which provides a guide to development of an empirical function for explaining the observed changes in the L_i's.

As a first step, eliminate L_d and P_L:

$$
\begin{aligned}
L_1 &= \frac{bc_1 + \alpha_1(L_2 + L_3) - \alpha_1 a}{b - \alpha_1}, \\[2mm]
L_2 &= \frac{bc_2 + \alpha_2(L_1 + L_3) - \alpha_2 a}{b - \alpha_2}, \\[2mm]
L_3 &= \frac{bc_3 + \alpha_3(L_1 + L_2) - \alpha_3 a}{b - \alpha_3}.
\end{aligned}
$$

(8)

These three equations can then be solved for the reduced form of each age group. The resulting expression for L_1, e.g., is:

$$(9) \quad L_1 = \frac{-\alpha_1 b^3(a - c_2 - c_3) + \alpha_1 \alpha_2 b^2(a - c_2 - c_3) + b^4 c_1 - \alpha_3 b^3 c_1 - 2\alpha_2 b^3 c_1 + \alpha_2 \alpha_3 b^2 c_1 + \alpha_2^2 b^2}{-\alpha_3 \alpha_1 b^2 + b^4 - \alpha_3 b^3 - 2\alpha_2 b^3 - \alpha_1 b^3 + 2\alpha_2 \alpha_1 b^2 + \alpha_2 \alpha_3 b^2 + \alpha_2^2 b^2}$$

The model is shown geometrically in Figure 1. On the market graph the single demand curve for labor crosses the composit market supply curve of labor to determine P_L and the total amount of labor hired. P_L is then transferred to the individual age-group graphs to find the amount of each hired. The amount hired within each group will change if there is a change in any one of three supply curves or a change in the demand curve.

To insure that the model yields meaningful results, some bounds must be imposed upon the parameters. Diminishing returns in each production function and diminishing marginal utility of income and leisure require that $b < 0$ and $S_i > 0$. Nonnegative wage rates and employment require that $a > 0$. Moreover, if all c_i's are positive, then it is necessary that $a > \sum_i c_i$. If, on the other hand, some of the c_i's are negative, the conditions become somewhat more complicated.[4]

The signs of appropriate derivatives show how changes in the parameters of the model affect employment in any age group. The derivatives will be in terms of all eight parameters of equations (7). Due to the difficulty in applying the conditions in Note 4, it is not always possible to determine directly the signs of some derivatives. Appeal to the geometry of Figure 1, however, should tell what the signs would be if the proper analytical expressions were worked out.

An increase in the elasticity of supply on the part of some individual age group will increase the amount of labor hired in that age group but decrease the amount hired in all other age groups:

$$10) \qquad \frac{\partial L_i}{\partial \alpha_i} > 0, \qquad \frac{\partial L_i}{\partial \alpha_j} < 0, \qquad i \neq j.$$

Increasing the elasticity of any individual age group's supply curve will increase the elasticity of the market supply curve, which leads to an increase in the total quantity hired. But that increase comes through an increase just in the age group contributing to the increased elasticity, with an actual reduction in those age groups whose elasticity does not change.

The same general reaction is evident for shifting supply curves. A positive shift in an age group's supply curve will cause an increase in the number of workers hired in that age group and a decrease in the number hired in other age groups:

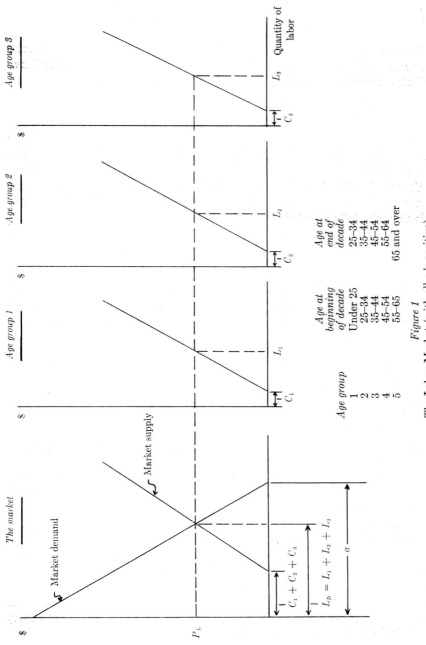

Figure 1
The Labor Market (with all c_i's positive)

$$(11) \qquad \frac{\partial L_i}{\partial c_i} > 0, \qquad \frac{\partial L_i}{\partial c_j} < 0, \qquad i \neq j.$$

On the demand side, either the slope or the intercept of the demand curve may change to increase demand. The total market quantity hired will rise, as well as the amount hired in each group:

$$(12) \qquad \frac{\partial L_i}{\partial a} > 0, \qquad \frac{\partial L_i}{\partial b} > 0.$$

The above expressions are all in terms of the parameters of the simplified model of equations (7). Except for the α_i, all the parameters have behind them some more meaningful economic terms. Of real concern is the relationship between changes in these economic terms and changes in the number of workers hired in any one age group. Taking the supply side first, the following hold:

$$(13) \qquad \frac{\partial c_i}{\partial e_i} > 0, \qquad \frac{\partial c_i}{\partial \theta_i} > 0, \qquad \frac{\partial c_i}{\partial \sigma_i} > 0.$$

An increase in the exogenous shift factor will increase the labor hired in this age group. The other two parameters, θ_i and σ_i, reflect the sensitivity of the age group supply curve to changes in trait requirements and in attractions offered by other occupations, respectively. Both of these coefficients are negative since either an increase in requirements for this occupation or an increase in the attractiveness of alternative occupations should cause a decrease in supply for this occupation. An algebraically positive change in these coefficients means less sensitivity to changes in the negative forces acting upon the supply curve. The result is a positive shift in the supply curve.

The demand side is more complicated. There are several factors in both the production and product demand functions which can affect labor demand. A curious consequence of the particular form of the functions used, however, is that neutral technological change, shifts in a_0, will not affect any of the equilibrium quantities. In more usual formulations of the production function, this result will not occur.

Three of the parameters affect only the intercept of the labor demand function. For these, the effect can be found from:

$$(14) \qquad \frac{\partial a}{\partial P_K} > 0, \qquad \frac{\partial a}{\partial a_1} > 0, \qquad \frac{\partial a}{\partial a_3} < 0.$$

As expected, a rise in the price of capital or the productivity of labor will increase the demand for labor; a relative increase in the productivity of capital will reduce the demand for labor.

Other parameters affect both the slope and the intercept of the labor demand function. For the remaining productivity parameters (nothing can be said about a_5), the effect is not at all clear since the slope and intercept are affected in different ways:

(15)
$$\frac{\partial a}{\partial a_2} < 0, \qquad \frac{\partial a}{\partial a_4} < 0,$$

$$\frac{\partial b}{\partial a_2} > 0, \qquad \frac{\partial b}{\partial a_4} > 0.$$

The final effect upon L_i of changes in a_2 and a_4 will depend upon the relative size of each of these partial derivatives and also upon the relative size of the two partial derivatives in equation (12).

The shift factor in the product demand equation acts in the expected way to increase the demand for labor when product demand increases:

(16)
$$\frac{\partial a}{\partial \gamma} > 0, \qquad \frac{\partial b}{\partial \gamma} > 0.$$

The following section will utilize this analytical framework as a foundation for empirical measurement. The model provides a guide to the form of the empirical function and the expected signs of its coefficients.

MODIFICATIONS OF THE MODEL FOR EMPIRICAL ESTIMATION

It is not possible to estimate directly the parameters of the model. Estimates would have to be obtained for the product demand functions, production functions, and the individual age-group supply functions. Because available data do not permit such estimates, the problem becomes one of formulating hypotheses that can be tested on the basis of what is available. If any meaningful predictions are to be made about changes in employment by occupation and age, one is forced to work with a modification of the underlying theory.

Instead of explaining the absolute level of employment for an age group and an occupation, say L_1, explanations of the change in employment over a decade prove to be more feasible. For this purpose the following expression is defined:

(17)
$$\text{Survival rate} = \frac{L_1 + \Delta L_{1,1 \text{ to } 2}}{L_{11}} = \frac{L_{22}}{L_{11}},$$

where the first subscript refers to age group 1 (the whole expression is for one particular occupation) and the second refers to the time period (1 for the beginning of the decade and 2 for the end of the decade). The survival rate is the proportion of those in an occupation and age group at the beginning of the decade who remain at the end of the decade. It is a net rate since it cannot measure movements into and out of the occupation during the decade but gives only the net result of both in- and out-migrations.[5]

Essentially, what is to be explained is the size of the term $\Delta L_{1,\ 1\ to\ 2}$. This is easier to explain than the absolute size of L_1, which requires estimates of all parameters of the model in order that the equilibrium point in the over-all market and individual age group markets can be determined. Nevertheless, the set of derivatives of L_1 with respect to changes in the various parameters provides a guide for estimating the difference term. If observable variables can be matched with changes in particular parameters, the set of derivatives provide an expected direction in which these variables should cause L_1 to change. Thus changes in L_I can be made a function of these observable variables, with some theoretical basis lurking in the background.

The size of the coefficients, as opposed to their signs, can only be determined from empirical evidence. The procedure constitutes, of course, indirect estimates of the parameters of the model, but there is no way to isolate the effects of the several parameters of each of the derivatives discussed in the previous section. In effect this amounts to measurement, not "without theory," but with only indirect theoretical support.

It is proposed that a simple single-equation regression model be used to explain levels and differences in net survival rates, within and between occupations and age groups and over time. The dependent variable in this equation will be the net survival rate. The actual rates used will utilize crude occupational death rates so that the influence of probable deaths may be removed. The independent variables will consist of data which a priori arguments would suggest can affect the parameters of the model presented in the previous section.

The purpose, then, of this function is to explain observed changes in net survival rates and to serve as a tool for predicting future net survival rates. There are several ways of arranging the available data to develop estimates of the function and/or predictions of future rates. This is illustrated in Figure 2. Survival rates can be computed for each decade from 1900 to 1960 for a group of 252 comparable occupations. For each occupation and decade, survival rates may be computed for each of five age groups.[6]

For each decade there is a matrix of survival rates for each occupation and age group. The goal is to predict as closely as possible the matrix for

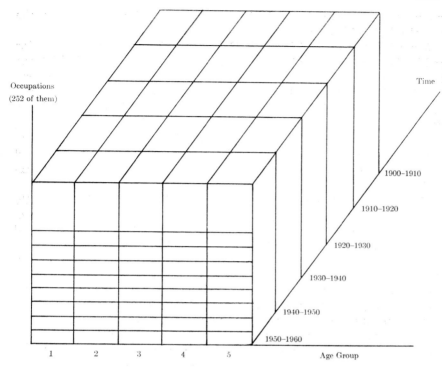

Occupations
(252 of them)

Time

1900–1910

1910–1920

1920–1930

1930–1940

1940–1950

1950–1960

1   2   3   4   5   Age Group

Figure 2
The Array of Available Survival Rate Data

the next decade. The simplest and most naive of all the methods is to assume that the matrix of survival rates next period will be the same as
the matrix for the current period. The prediction implies that none of the
parameters of the model in the last section change from one decade to the
next; or if they change, the changes neutralize each other to leave the
survival rates unchanged. As noted in the next section, some empirical
evidence begins to show that this is probably not a very good assumption.

The next step up in sophistication is to compute a trend of survival
rates over time for each age-occupation cell and extrapolate that trend to
the next decade. A trend is fitted to each cell in the front matrix of Figure
2 and the five cells directly behind it, which belong to the same occupation
and age group but to previous decades. Trend-fitting of this kind is entirely an empirical procedure having no basis in theory. There is no assumption made about stable parameters, nor is there any particular
pattern of change being assumed. The method can be justified only if it is

empirically accurate in its predictions. It can tell nothing about the causal relationships involved.

A much better method is to use these same observations (a particular cell in the front matrix of Figure 2 and five cells directly behind it) but to fit them to some explanatory function, namely the single-equation regression already described. Use of this particular group of observations comes closest to satisfying the assumptions under which the model was developed. The observations are homogeneous in the sense that they all represent just one age group and one occupation. As the independent exogenous variables affecting this particular age-occupation group changed over the decades, the empirical function could utilize these changes to explain changes in the survival rates over the decades.

Unfortunately, the approach seems to be impossible with presently available data. First, only six observations are attainable for each function, not nearly enough for estimating a function which contains several independent variables. Second, most of the independent variables cannot be observed in each decade. They are available only at isolated times during the time period covered, with many available only for the 1950 and 1960 census. Third, the survival rates computed for the early decades may not be very reliable.

Thus, it will not be possible to use the observed pattern of survival rates decade by decade for fitting explanatory regression functions. In terms of Figure 2, the information provided through the existence of several age-occupation survival rate matrices, one for each decade, cannot be fully utilized. The time variable, or time axis in Figure 2, must be ignored. The empirical work must proceed on the basis of just one matrix, similar, say, to the front face of the three-dimensional array shown in Figure 2. For the initial empirical work, the one matrix will consist of average survival rates, computed from the six observations for each age-occupation cell, one for each decade. (These are the same observations described above which might be used for fitting a trend or regression function.) The probable validity of the step, and the possibility of having to allow for the lost time dimension by using a trend factor in the empirical equation, will be discussed in the next section of the paper.

Since there is now only one matrix of survival rate values, some method must be used for obtaining observations to generate the desired regression function. The method adopted here is to use observations for the several occupations to derive a regression equation for each age group, i.e., a regression equation is fitted to each of the five columns of a matrix arranged like those in Figure 2. The regression equation for each column in Figure 2 now represents a cross-section analysis using a different occupation (but the same age group) for each observation. A difficulty in interpretation arises when one remembers that the model developed in the previous section was for one specific occupation, not for observations across several occupations. There does not seem to be any way to eliminate the difficulty entirely with the data available.

Some modification can be made, however, to bring the data a little closer to those for which the model was developed. Instead of fitting one function for each age group over all 252 occupations, it appears much more satisfactory to divide the occupations into the ten or so major occupation groups. For each age group one function is fitted across the occupations in each major occupation, restoring some homogeneity to the observations over which one function is fitted. Some empirical evidence, shown in the next section, indicates that there are substantial and persistent differences in values of survival rates and other variables between the major groups.

The guide furnished by the model can now be invoked to give a tentative form for the function. The general plan will be to take the available information which probably affects age and occupation differences in survival rates and to match the variables with the parameters of the model.

Ironically, it must be the demand side that is treated in the most perfunctory manner for this set of data, even though demand was most complete in the theoretical development. To get any measure of changes in the parameters on the demand side, or even some information on variables which will probably affect these parameters, some connection must be made between the workers in each occupation and their outputs. There is no way of observing anything about the output of workers in each occupation, except for the occupation-by-industry data provided by the 1950 and 1960 Census. No age breakdown is provided in the cross-classification, so that arbitrary assumptions will have to be made about how the different age groups are distributed for occupations which cut across a number of industries. Output data must come from the Census of Manufactures, with the three-digit level being the finest detail available for the occupation-by-industry cross-classification. It is possible that the aggregated industry data hide the effects of several different production and product demand functions which affect the occupations working within an industry grouping.

To avoid the difficulties in using output information, the growth rate of the entire occupation over time will be used as a proxy variable to represent any change in the product demand or production functions which will cause the labor demand curve to shift up or increase the algebraic value of its slope. In other words, increases in the total number hired of all age groups in an occupation is taken to mean that the labor demand curve also shifted in such a way as to increase the quantity hired, no matter what happened on the supply side within the individual age groups. In an empirical function with the net survival rate as the dependent variable, the growth rate should have a positive sign.

The first factor considered on the supply side will be the trait requirements for each occupation, the T variable in equation (6). This variable was collected into the constant term c in each of the supply equations of the complete model, equations (7). Trait requirements are expected to have a negative effect upon the constant; that is, the higher the requirements for a particular occupation, the small c is. Further, it is expected that some of these requirements would exert a stronger negative effect for older age groups than for younger ones.

Four relevant pieces of information are available for each occupation: the general education level needed, the amount of specific vocational or on-the-job training needed, the harshness of the working conditions encountered, and the physical abilities needed for the job.[7] Previous discussions in the literature suggest that the variables could enter an empirical function as three separate terms—all, of course, with negative coefficients.

The general education variable might possibly work in two different ways. A high required level in any occupation would tend to discourage workers from ever trying to enter the occupation, both at the entry level and at an older age. Further, if those now in the occupation have this high level of education, they might find it easy to transfer to other occupations as these others become more attractive or their present occupation becomes less attractive. Both of these effects indicate that the general educational variable will have a negative coefficient in the empirical function.

The specific vocational training variable may work in a slightly different manner. Like the general educational requirement, a great deal of required special training may discourage workers from trying to enter an occupation. In contrast, though, to the situation for general education, a large amount of special training acquired by those now in an occupation may make it harder, not easier, for them to transfer. In other occupations they may not be able to benefit financially from their present training. Also, as discussed by Becker,[8] one logical way in which firms can afford to offer specific training is to make the workers pay for it in the form of low wages during the training period. Workers can recoup this loss only by staying with the firm, and thus with the occupation. These two effects may work in opposite directions. While a negative sign would probably be expected, a positive sign could also be explained. In any case, it appears that this difference in effects warrants putting each of the training variables separately into the empirical function.

The harshness of the working conditions and the physical abilities requirement can be combined into one index of physical difficulties presented by the job. The obvious effect of this variable is the major reason why, e.g., different survival rates are observed for middle and older age groups of athletes as opposed to some types of service workers.

A variable is now developed to represent the attractiveness of other occupations, the S variable in equation (6). Like the T variable, it will have a negative effect upon the c's and thus will enter the empirical function with an expected negative coefficient. The variable is built up by first assuming that the main attractiveness of another occupation is a higher wage rate. A measure of each occupation's relative wage can be developed from the latest Census, though it is uncertain to which base the wage should be compared. The most meaningful procedure might assume that higher wages really exert some pull only if there is a possibility that the worker can, in fact, make the shift. In most cases it seems likely that it will be easier to make the shift within major occupation groups than between major groups.[9] Therefore, the pressure for occupational migration is the wage rate relative to the wage in all other occupations in the same major occupational group.

The mere appearance of a more favorable wage in another occupation does not necessarily mean that many workers will move or be able to move. The relative wage variable must be modified by some other factors before it is inserted into the empirical function. Four variables serve as modifiers. First, if the worker now has a high degree of education relative to the requirements of other occupations in the group, he could make the move more easily than if he presently had low education relative to the requirements of the rest of the group. Second, many workers can migrate among occupations only if there are a relatively large number of jobs available in other occupations. A high wage in a very small occupation cannot cause much migration. Therefore, a variable expressing the size of the occupation in which the worker is now working relative to the other occupations in the same major occupation group will be used to modify the pull expressed by the relative wage rate.

The last two variables express inhibitions to migration which are caused by the presence of specific vocational training requirements. They consist of the absolute amount of specific training needed in the job in which the worker is now employed and the amount of specific training required in other occupations within the same major occupational group.

The absolute amount of training reflects the loss of income incurred by the worker if he transfers to another occupation. Training for other occupations reflects the difficulty of inducing a firm to train the worker or his unwillingness to give up income during the training period. The precise way in which the four variables combine with the relative wage rate to serve as the S variable is discussed below.

The remaining variables consist of characteristics of the job or the market which will affect directly either the slope or the intercept of the supply curve, probably with different effects for different age groups, but do not fit neatly into either the S or T variables. Each one will be listed and briefly discussed:

(1) Degree of unionization. Several conflicting tendencies might arise in occupations which are highly unionized. The S_i's are likely to be lower and the sensitivity of the c_i's to changing market conditions less than in occupations where the market is more freely competitive. This would imply lower survival rates for growing occupations or favorable business cycle conditions, and higher rates for the reverse conditions. Union seniority rules will cause survival rates to be higher for older age groups when an occupation is declining and workers are being laid off. A negative effect for older age groups is the presence of forced retirements when pension plans exist. Unionization may be a good proxy variable for the presence of some pension plan or retirement policy. Since most of the data refer to relatively prosperous years and most unionized occupations are not among the declining ones, a negative sign would be expected for the coefficient of this variable.

(2) Fraction of the workers who are nonwhite. Under prosperous and growing conditions, nonwhites are less mobile, less able to shift occupations. Under declining conditions, they are more likely to be displaced first. In either case, they tend to have smaller slope and intercept changes over time in their supply curves, and thus impart this characteristic to occupations where they form a large portion of the workers. This variable should have a negative sign in the empirical function.

(3) Amount of migration. Occupations which contain workers who migrate between states a great deal would tend to have smaller survival rates, especially for the older age groups. The coefficient for this term should be negative.

(4) Proportion of workers who are self-employed. Workers who are self-employed should be more sensitive to market forces and adapt more easily to changing conditions (though farming may be a major exception). The effect of this factor is the reverse of the effect of unionization. Following the arguments given above, a positive sign would be expected

for this coefficient. A modification might have to be made since it is not certain that most of the self-employed are in nondeclining occupations, which would have to be true to insure that possible negative aspects of this effect do not override the positive effects.

(5) Availability of part-time work. The supply curves of occupations where a great deal of part-time work is available should have higher c_i's and perhaps higher α_i's. Like self-employed people, workers can more easily move into and out of occupations in which part-time employment is possible (for moving in) and less total income is involved (for moving out). A positive sign is expected.

While not exhausting the possibilities, this list seems to contain most of the important variables for which available data are comparable to that used for computation of survival rates (though even unionization might be questioned here). It should be clear that the emphasis of the explanation will be on the supply side rather than the demand side. As mentioned before, this is due primarily to differences in data availability. The empirical function which will be estimated now stands as:

$$NSR = \phi_1(G) + \phi_2(GED) + \phi_3(SVP) + \phi_4(Phys.)$$

(18)
$$+ \phi_5(RW)[(Rel.\ GED) + AO - SVP - (Rel.\ SVP)]$$

$$+ \phi_6(\%U) + \phi_7(\%NW) + \phi_8(\%M) + \phi_9(\%SE) + \phi_{10}(\%PT)$$

where

G = growth rate of this occupation,
GED = level of general educational development required for this occupation,
SVP = level of specific vocational training required for this occupation,
$Phys.$ = index of physical requirements for this occupation,
RW = relative wage rate of this occupation,
$Rel.$ = relative, either GED or SVP,
U = number of union members in this occupation,
NW = number of nonwhite workers in this occupation,
M = number of workers in this occupation who moved during the year previous to the Census,
SE = number of self-employed workers in this occupation,
PT = number of part-time workers in this occupation,
AO = relative number of opportunities available in other occupations in the same major occupational group.

There are ten terms in the equation. It is improbable that many of the estimated functions would contain ten significant coefficients. Indeed, the number of degrees of freedom available in some occupation groups would preclude ever trying as many as ten variables in a single equation. The final form of the function will vary for each occupation and age group, and will be determined only through actual confrontation with the data.

The exact form of the fifth term on the right-hand side of the equation, the term representing S, may be the subject of experimentation. The relative weighting of each of the four terms within the brackets must be determined. Further adjustment must be made to insure that the bracket never becomes negative, or the interpretation of ϕ_5 will be made unclear.

Finally, it must be emphasized again that this function makes no claim to an estimate for any of the structural equations of the theoretical model. Both supply and demand influences are included, and no identification is either attempted or achieved. The function is useful only if it yields good predictions. The empirical evidence presented in the next section suggests that it is likely to do so.

SOME EMPIRICAL RESULTS

Some preliminary computations indicate whether the method helps to explain the observed data. No attempt has been made as yet to estimate equation (18). The results, therefore, represent only an intermediate step and not the final working out of the ideas presented in the previous two sections.

Specifically, the questions considered are: (1) Does the age group make a difference in the survival rate pattern both within and between occupations and major occupational groups? (2) Can growth rates reasonably be used to represent demand influences leaving the rest to be explained by supply influences? (3) What is the effect of the passage of time upon the pattern of survival rates?

The basic source used for the computations was the complete set of net survival rates as set up in Figure 2, covering only male workers. From this set of rates it was possible to derive other descriptive measures, in particular: (1) The average net survival rate (AVSR) for a particular occupation and age group, averaged over the six decades considered. It is computed by taking each observation in the front matrix of Figure 2, and the five observations directly behind it, and finding the average.[10] (2) The average survival rate for a particular occupation and particular decade (DECSR) averaged across all age groups, the average of the rates appearing in each row of each separate matrix. (3) The trend of survival rates over time for each occupation and age group (TR). The same observations used for the AVSR are used to compute an ordinary least squares trend line. (4) The over-all average survival rate for each occupation, averaged both over time and across age groups (OVSR). Every survival rate referring to a particular occupation, including all age groups and every decade, is used to find the over-all average. (5) The over-all trend over time of each occupation, with all age groups combined (OVTR), is found by fitting a least squares trend line to the DECSR's for each decade. (6) The AVSR's are divided by the average decade growth rate of the whole occupation for the period of decades considered (GR). This measure is called (V).

The entire 252 occupations were ranked by each of these measures, including GR. A rank correlation coefficient was computed between each possible pair of measures. Since five age groups and five decades are available, there are twenty-three measures for each occupation leading to 253 correlations. The measure of rank correlation used was Kendall's tau.[11] Rank correlations were used here since the data showed a great deal of clumping around some small range of values, with just a few observations occurring away (sometimes a great deal away) from this clump. Eventually, of course, product-moment regressions must be fitted similar to equation (18). Rank correlations were computed within each major occupational group and between the average ranks for each of the major groups.[12] Limiting the observations for a correlation to those occurring within one major occupational group is consistent with the previously stated intention of maintaining as homogeneous groups of workers as possible despite the necessity of using a cross section of occupations as observations.

The purpose of Table 1 is to show the significant differences between the survival rate patterns for different age groups, both within each major occupational group and between the major group averages. The pattern of correlation coefficients, for each occupation group and between major occupation groups, is very similar. Each age group is usually significantly, though not very highly, correlated with the groups closest to it in age. As the age differences increase, i.e., as one gets farther off the diagonals in each section of Table 1, there emerges a weaker relation between the patterns of AVSR. Age seems to make a difference in the values of AVSR observed. This is corroborated when AVSR's are correlated with the over-all average rates. There is no significant correlation between the two. OVSR is a very poor approximation for the AVSR observed in any of the age groups. It seems imperative that each age group be analyzed separately.

Table 2 uses GR in conjunction with AVSR to give some indication of the relative usefulness of the growth rate as a proxy variable for demand

TABLE 1
Rank Correlation Coefficients between AVSR's for Different Age Groups

Between major groups

	2	3	4	5
1	.6111*	.2778	.3333	.0556
2		.5556*	.6111*	.3333
3			.8333*	.5556*
4				.6111*

Sales

	2	3	4	5
1	.3889	.0000	−.0556	.0000
2		.5000	.3333	.5000
3			.8333*	.7778*
4				.6111*

Professionals

	2	3	4	5
1	.3903*	.2365	.2764*	.1396
2		.5840*	.5442*	.3162*
3			.6524*	.3219*
4				.4986*

Craftsmen

	2	3	4	5
1	.6202*	.4101*	.1697	−.0909
2		.5475*	.3596*	.1071
3			.4929*	.3172*
4				.4970*

Farmers

	2	3	4	5
1	.4000	.4000	.4000	.4000
2		1.0000*	1.0000*	.6000
3			1.0000*	.6000
4				.6000

Operatives

	2	3	4	5
1	.5571*	.3464*	.0816	.0163
2		.6196*	.3977*	.2615*
3			.5170*	.4014*
4				.5170*

Managers

	2	3	4	5
1	.5238*	.2286	.0476	−.1429
2		.4762*	.2762	.0476
3			.5333*	.3619*
4				.5238*

Service

	2	3	4	5
1	.6725*	.1696	.1462	.0877
2		.2398	.3801*	.2982
3			.5322*	.4503*
4				.7544*

Clerical

	2	3	4	5
1	.6000*	.4182	.1273	.0182
2		.7455*	.4545	.3455
3			.7091*	.5273*
4				.6727*

Laborers

	2	3	4	5
1	.4966*	.1395	.0238	−.1395
2		.4320*	.3844*	.2313*
3			.6259*	.5510*
4				.7211*

The numbers bordering each table refer to the age groups described in Figure 2.

* Designates that the coefficient is significantly different from zero at about the 5 per cent level of significance. This symbol for significance will be used in Table 2. The critica ltau values were computed according to Kendall *op. cit.*, pp. 49–53

TABLE 2

Rank Correlation Coefficients between AVSR and GR

	Age Group				
	1	2	3	4	5
Between major groups	.2778	.1111	.3333	.1667	.2222
Professionals	− .0427	.3390*	.2877*	.3618*	.3162*
Farmers	.6000	.8000*	.8000*	.8000*	.4000
Managers	.1619	.4476*	.5524*	.4286*	.4095*
Clerical	.1636	.4909*	.6727*	.8182*	.6364*
Sales	.2222	− .0556	.1111	.0556	.0000
Craftsmen	.3414*	.3535*	.4545*	.4323*	.1556
Operatives	.1944*	.4918*	.5571*	.6634*	.4508*
Service	.1813	.2515	.3801*	.4269*	.3450
Laborers	.2330*	.5799*	.6276*	.5527*	.4065*

influences. Except for the entering age group, most age groups in most occupations show a significant, but not extremely high, correlation. The implication is that GR is a significant factor in explaining AVSR within each major group, but does not provide all the explanation. The rest of the explanation must be provided by supply forces. The singular behavior of the sales occupations will have to be investigated further. The results here also tend to corroborate what was said before about the relative homogeneity of the major occupational groups. Far more nongrowth factors (assumed here to be supply factors) will have to be found to explain the difference between major occupational groups than is necessary for the differences within each of the groups (except sales).

Further evidence comes from correlating AVSR and V. A correlation coefficient close to plus one means that dividing the survival rates by the growth rates did not change the order in which the occupations were ranked. This implies that the differences in survival rates between occupations were consistently more than the differences in growth rates between occupations. A negative correlation implies the reverse. A correlation near zero implies a mixed pattern of relative variation. The coefficients in this case were almost all positive, many significantly so. Within each group and between groups, the variation in survival rates between occupations was generally greater than the variation in growth rates. There is a persistent residual of variation in survival rates which must be explained by something other than growth rates.

A more meaningful measurement and explanation of the behavior patterns of the different age groups must await empirical estimation of a series of functions like equation (18), or some modification of it. The present computations only suggest that the patterns do differ and that there are some reasonable explanations for this difference.

Some indication of the danger run by collapsing the time axis in Figure 2 can be obtained by considering the DECSR's. A table constructed for the DECSR's analogous to Table 1 shows little consistent behavior between decades. The immediate reaction is to conclude that decades do differ and that time must be included in the empirical explanations in some way. This may be misleading, however, since all the previous discussion implies that there are significant differences in the behavior of the several age groups and that averaging across age groups (using the row averages in Figure 2) hides too many things.

More direct evidence can be found by considering the trends, TR. First, a frequency distribution of the TR's shows that the trends are not large (except for twelve observations in age group 1) and are centered around zero. The actual magnitude of the effect of trends must await prediction trials with an empirical function. Second, whatever trend effects have to be taken into account, there must be a differentiation by age groups. Correlation of TR with OVTR shows that OVTR cannot serve as an approximation to the TR's for individual age groups. Third, correlation of GR with TR shows that the TR's cannot be explained by saying that they are due to the over-all growth rate of the occupation. Each age group acts differently, and does not follow the occupation GR.

One last piece of evidence might be considered. Correlations between AVSR and the corresponding TR indicate whether increasing geographic and occupational mobility tend to make conditions in the different occupations more equal over time. The answer is generally no. A negative correlation between AVSR and TR would imply that the survival rates for the different occupations for a given age group are becoming more equal over time.

Some negative coefficients are observed, but few are significant and none are high. The equality tendency cannot be supported very well.

While trends do exist over time, the precise effects of these must await more detailed computations. The present computations do not reveal any meaningful patterns.

Comparison of the correlation coefficients does suggest that the proposed framework of the previous section should prove fruitful in explaining the observations. If this can be done, further insight into the realism and operation of the model outlined in the first section of this paper should be obtained.

Notes

1. Clearly, a complete explanation would require both occupation and industry groupings, but this also requires more data than are available for the period studied here. The problem is not too serious since, in large part, the occupational classification scheme follows industrial lines. There are about 450 detailed occupations in the more recent Census classifications. For comparable classifications going back to 1900 some aggregation was necessary. The computations in this study divide the work force into 252 occupations, still a good degree of disaggregation.

2. There is no particular tradition or evidence for choosing these production and demand functions. Their merits lie in the ability to derive from them a linear demand curve for labor, the simplest to match with a market supply curve which is aggregated from several individual age-group curves. If the more usual Cobb-Douglas production function and constant elasticity product demand function had been used, the demand function for labor would have been linear in the logarithms of the variables. Aggregation in logarithms on the supply side presents an intractable problem, even with the simple supply functions assumed here. Thanks are due to Professor Martin Beckmann for assistance in developing these two functions.

3. The empirical age groups used are: under 25, 25–34, 35–44, 45–54, 55–64, and 65 and over. By proceeding on the basis of only three age groups in the theoretical discussion, all important features of the model can be brought out by algebraic expressions which do not become overly long.

4. The general requirement is that the market price be high enough so that at least some workers of each age group are hired. With subscript i referring to the age group with the highest value for c_i/S_i, the conditions which insure that this requirement is met are:

$$\frac{a - c_j - c_k}{\alpha_j + \alpha_k - b} > -\frac{c_i}{\alpha_i},$$

where j, k refer to age groups which do not have the highest c_i/α_i value.

5. One of the major data deficiencies for detailed occupations is the lack of any information about shifts between occupations which occur over time. Such information is especially important if completely accurate measures of the forces affecting survival rates are to be made. This deficiency has still not been remedied in the 1960 Census. An attempt to separate the numbers of workers in any age cohort who died during the decade from those who migrated in or out of the occupation was made by A. J. Jaffe and R. O. Carleton, *Occupational Mobility in the United States, 1930–1960* (New York: King's Crown Press, 1954). Unfortunately, their procedures consist of a number of standardization operations and rather arbitrary assumptions about how the results should be interpreted. They had no direct observations upon which to base their estimates.

6. Three steps were necessary before these rates could be derived. First, a comparable detailed occupation series for the period 1900 to 1960 was needed. This was provided by the information in D. Kaplan and M. C. Casey, *Occupational Trends in the United States 1900 to 1950,* Bureau of the Census Working Paper No. 5 (Washington: Government Printing Office, 1958). Second, some means were needed to transfer this comparable series back to the occupational titles used in the original census so that age distributions of each occupation might be found. This was provided by copies of the worksheets behind the Working Paper No. 5, which were kindly provided by Mr. William Milligan of the Population Division of the Census Bureau. Third, the dissimilar age groupings for 1910 and 1920 had to be adjusted to match the groupings found in all the other census. A procedure suggested by A. Edwards, *Population: Comparative Occupation Statistics for the U.S., 1870–1940. 16th Census of the United States* (Washington: Government Printing Office, 1943), p. 154, was used. Though it is a simple and somewhat arbitrary method, nothing better is available.

7. The date came from the U.S. Employment Service, *Estimates of Worker Trait Requirements for 4,000 Jobs* (Washington: Government Printing Office, 1961).

8. G. Becker, "Investment in Human Capital: A Theoretical Analysis," *Journal of Political Economy*, LXX, No. 5, Part 2 (Supplement: October, 1962), 9–49.

9. See Note 6.

10. 1960 is not included in these computations, so there are only five cells over which an average is computed. The 1960 detailed occupational statistics were not published until late 1963.

11. M. G. Kendall, *Rank Correlation Methods* (New York: Hafner, 1955), especially pp. 3–8.

12. The usual list of eleven major occupational groups was condensed slightly by combining two groups into other groups. The Farmers and Farm Managers group was combined with the Farm Laborers and Foreman group to yield one group called Farmers. Private Household Workers were combined with the Service Workers, and the title Service retained.

PART III

MONEY MARKETS

A Commentary on Some Current Issues in the Theory of Monetary Policy[1]

Phillip Cagan

BACKGROUND OF CURRENT ISSUES

MONETARY theory is often ridiculed for lagging a decade behind the problems actually faced by the economy. While theory grapples with the problems of one decade and gradually influences public policy in one direction, conditions change and the policy forged for one problem muddles up another. Yet despite the swings in policy views, work in monetary theory has always pursued the same objective: to discover how and to what extent monetary factors affect prices and output. Nor has the nature of problems of policy changed basically, if one looks back more than a decade or two. It is just the answers that change. Whether they have also evolved and improved over time is less clear. In any event, interest in problems of monetary policy is currently high, reversing a long period of widespread indifference. In the latter 1930's and early 1940's many felt that money was unimportant, and then in the latter 1940's and early 1950's it was decided that money did matter after all, though how far monetary measures can stabilize the economy remains in dispute. Criticism has shifted ground from time to time but continues at full force, with the efficacy and proper role of monetary policy still the subject of most current work in the field.

The criticism intensified and took a new direction with Keynes' *General Theory*. Monetary theory is still trying to assimilate or cast off—as you prefer—his influence. Keynes initiated the modern emphasis in monetary theory on how money enters or leaves the economy. New money received by the public in exchange for other forms of wealth affects spending differently from new money received as additional income. The first has no immediate effect on spending, while the second has an effect over and above the initiating expenditure. Examples of the distinction appear in

135

earlier writings, but it had little influence on theory. Increases in the money stock, regardless of how produced, were typically viewed before Keynes as simply providing excess cash balances, which increased spending of all kinds.

In line with Keynes' shift in emphasis, theory now distinguishes between monetary and fiscal measures for increasing the money stock. In open-market operations by the central bank, money is exchanged for bonds on wealth account, while financing Treasury expenditures with new money augments national income. An increase in income will in large part be spent, and fairly soon, while exchanging money for bonds increases liquidity but affects spending only when those who initially become more liquid—generally banks and financial institutions, not the public at large—find borrowers for the extra funds. An expansion of borrowing takes time; hence by this route the effects on spending are slow and uncertain. That, it seems to me, is the essential and valid point for monetary policy of the "Keynesian revolution."

From this point of view, an open-market operation raises two questions: (1) How will a change in the liquidity of their portfolios affect the terms on which banks and the public offer loans to borrowers? (2) Under what terms and conditions will potential borrowers accept and spend the funds? The operation of financial markets is complicated. To simplify, current theory answers the first question by a liquidity-preference or demand-to-hold-money function, and the second by an investment function. The main variable in these functions is the rate of interest, though admittedly it stands as proxy for a host of factors at play. As a first approximation in theoretical models, these functions represent the main channel through which monetary measures affect spending. In bare outline the theory is that an open-market purchase of bonds by the central bank raises their price and lowers the yield. Because national income is not directly changed by the purchase,[2] no increase in aggregate spending will result except indirectly from the lower yield on bonds and on other securities to which the change spreads. Since the 1930's, monetary economists have wrestled with the question of how, and whether, spending responds to such changes in interest rates. An extreme view was that an increase in the money stock through open-market operations might not increase spending at all because investment expenditures would not respond to lower costs of borrowing. Even though banks acquired excess reserves and could expand deposits by buying bonds, the new money might sit idly in the bond sellers' cash balances.

My commentary on the development of these issues will be critical of the early criticisms of monetary policy, on the ground that the evidence affords them only limited support. The next section covers the response of investment expenditures to changes in interest rates. The third and fourth turn to the related question of whether the demand to hold money is affected by changes in interest rates. The fifth explores some of the implications for policy. The Keynesian approach emphasizes government deficits as a pivotal determinant of aggregate spending, with little attention to whether they are financed by bonds or new money. This ignores the temporary effects of deficits financed by bonds and leads to misinterpretation of their impact, a point taken up in the last section.

Monetary Effects on Investment Expenditures

In the *General Theory* Keynes contended that investment opportunities—in depression at least—might appear unattractive even at very low rates of interest. Of the many statistical studies carried out subsequently, most agreed with Keynes and claimed to find no effect of interest rates on investment, even for normal times. The initial studies seemed to support a widespread opinion at the time that lowering interest rates by monetary measures could not stimulate investment in a business recession. Later, the lack of response was also applied to restraining investment in a boom. Here the argument rested on much weaker ground: A sufficiently tight monetary policy could always force cuts in aggregate investment through inability to obtain financing; in a theoretical sense, borrowing costs would then rise to whatever level was necessary to bring the amount of funds demanded down to the limited supply. Nevertheless, it was maintained that only extreme tightening would have much effect, at which point there was allegedly danger of going too far and precipitating recession.

The view that interest rates do not influence investment swayed majority opinion for a time, but is now greeted with increasing scepticism. It proves too much. How could money then affect prices and output at all? Yet over the long run such effects can be shown to exist.[3] Studies of investment have demonstrated only that its response to interest rates is elusive and difficult to measure.[4] Negative results may reflect an insignificant response or simply failure to identify it. Since investment and interest rates rise and fall over the business cycle together with sales and profits, time series analysis has difficulty disentangling their separate effects, particularly if profit expectations—as is likely—play a dominant role.

Earlier discussion of monetary effects was deficient because of lack of evidence to back up the theory. One of the first to write in detail about the effects was Hawtrey,[5] who thought that changes in bank loan rates mainly affect short-term borrowing for carrying inventory stocks. His view was criticized for overlooking that interest charges are a small part of the total cost of carrying stocks, and hence that borrowing for that purpose may depend very little on interest rates.[6] Interest charges appear to be relatively large only on long-term capital investments. Yet here, too, it has been argued that the large risks involved and the uncertainties surrounding the prospective return may render interest costs of minor importance.[7]

These theoretical arguments were far from conclusive, and the inflationary conditions during and after World War II added doubts, for the accompanying easy-money policies appeared to stimulate the high and rising level of spending. It is now widely accepted, with more empirical justification, that interest rates affect spending on a wide range of products, including housing and many other consumer durables. By implication, the meaning of "investment" expenditures in monetary theory needs re-examination. It has typically meant purchases of capital goods, while in some models it represents autonomous expenditures (that is, expenditures not related to changes in income), and in many empirical studies it measures business expenditures on plant and equipment and changes in inventories. The various meanings are not identical. For monetary theory, the meaning of investment has broadened to comprise spending on the full range of durable goods as well as some services like business research, all of which can be influenced by the cost of borrowing. Such a definition may throw national income statisticians into despair, but that is another matter.

Interest-rate effects are also likely to be distributed over a long period of time, since investment expenditures by their nature require at least some and often extensive advance planning. Such lags are a further reason, perhaps, why empirical studies have trouble spotting the effects, in addition to the identification problem already mentioned. Another reason is that quoted interest rates are not entirely representative. They do not cover many kinds of negotiated loans on real estate and other physical capital. They also fail to reflect fully the availability of loanable funds,[8] which can influence indirect costs of borrowing, such as compensatory balances and other terms of loan contracts. Changes in these terms or in the ease of borrowing affect the "true" cost but are not reflected in quoted average rates paid and are probably not perfectly correlated with them. Nonprice rationing of funds is often important. In a tight money period like 1955–1956, banks shave down many applications for loans. It is sometimes overlooked that the purpose of monetary measures is to affect spending, not quoted interest rates, and that these rates may not fully register the effects being achieved, notwithstanding the simplified assumptions of theoretical models.

For various reasons, therefore, monetary effects are hard to trace. Evidence of an indirect nature points to long lags. Mayer[9] analyzed different kinds of investment expenditure for the time normally taken to plan and make payment after the initial decision to go ahead. He estimated that a change in direction of monetary policy takes a year or more to become effective. On a quite different approach, Friedman and Schwartz[10] have compared fluctuations in business activity and in the rate of growth of the money stock over a long period. They find a close correspondence between the two, with turns in monetary cycles leading turns in activity on the average by twelve months at troughs and sixteen months at peaks, though the lead varies considerably from cycle to cycle.

These findings help to reconcile two traditionally opposing views in monetary theory: One holds that changes in the money stock are an important source of instability in the economy, while the other claims that control over such changes is ineffective for promoting economic stability. According to the first view, if monetary effects occurred with little or no lag central banks ought—at least in principle—to be able to stabilize activity. If there are long lags, however, the two views are no longer inconsistent.

It is therefore somewhat surprising, though perhaps in keeping with tradition, that monetary controversy now rages hotter than ever. The interpretation of the evidence by Friedman and Schwartz is disputed. Two points are at issue. The first is their interpretation of the association between fluctuations in monetary growth and economic activity, which implies an effect running from money to activity. Though once quite popular, this proposition meets resistance today. To avoid that implication, one must argue that the response of the money stock to business cycles is fully responsible for the observed association. Over many mild business cycles—and particularly recent cycles—monetary growth has a synchronous, inverted cyclical pattern; that is, the growth tapers off and declines during business expansions, then revives and increases during business contractions.[11] The inverted pattern can indeed be attributed to the effects of business activity and of countercyclical monetary policies. Conceivably such effects can account for the impression that monetary growth has a long lead when compared with business cycles on a positive basis, that is, expansions in money with subsequent business expansions and similarly for contractions. Friedman and Schwartz, while not denying that business activity affects the money stock, claim that the association between the two is much closer for a positive than for an inverted comparison. If they are right, the positive association cannot be merely a reflection of the inverted one. There must be a mutual interaction, with money affecting activity after a long lag. The evidence for this interpretation is admittedly of a tentative nature; it is neither so crushing nor so weak as to stop all further research on the question.

The second point at issue concerns the appropriateness of relating changes in the rate of monetary growth to cycles in the *level* of economic activity, as Friedman and Schwartz do, rather than to cycles in the *rate of growth* of activity. The criticism is that the former comparison gives a spurious lead to money, on the ground that the rate of growth of economic time series generally has a cyclical turn before the level of the series does.[12] The lead is spurious, however, only if the mode of comparison is inappropriate. The evidence, to be sure, indicates that, over the long run, changes in the average rate of monetary growth tend to produce changes of equal amount in the average rate of change of prices. Suppose, however, that price adjustments lack the flexibility to match short-run cyclical changes in the monetary growth rate, though these cyclical changes still have an effect on aggregate spending. If prices do not adjust, real output bears the brunt of the spending effects. The pattern of the disturbance thus produced in real output is not obvious. Changes in the *level* of output may measure the disturbance more accurately than changes in its *rate of change*. Or the effects may be more complex than such simple relationships can handle. If monetary effects are distributed over time rather than discretely lumped at a point in time, and if there is feedback, the beginning of a movement is arbitrary and has no special significance. Yet the Friedman-Schwartz method need not for that reason be inappropriate. More elaborate analysis may, however, be necessary to bring out the timing relations in full clarity. How best to measure the relationship is yet to be settled.

Much of this controversy veers away from the main issue. Supposing that monetary effects had on the average only a moderate lag, substantial (and unpredictable) variability in the length of the lag would still cast serious doubt on our ability to use monetary controls effectively. Even though the method of dating turning points followed by Friedman and Schwartz may not appropriately measure the average length of the lag if it is distributed over time, their estimate of the lag could provide a reliable measure of the variability in its length, provided, of course, that the association does reflect the influence of money on activity. Their finding of large variability levels a severe criticism at traditional monetary policy, different in nature from the earlier charges of impotence but the same in the implication of ineffectiveness.

The Effect of Interest Rates
on the Demand to Hold Money

Since open-market operations exchange money for bonds in someone's portfolio but do not immediately increase anyone's income or spending, there must be some inducement to acquire and to hold the new money, at least temporarily. The inducement in theory is a rise in price of bonds outstanding, which reduces their yield and hence the opportunity cost of holding money. In technical terms, there is a movement down along the demand-to-hold-money schedule. At first the additional money is excessive relative to other forms of wealth held; the attempt by money holders to exchange their excess balances for other assets raises asset prices and lowers rates of return across the board. The decline in rates thus spreads to all financial and physical assets, so that an increase in the money stock may eventually stimulate new investment spending in many directions. The dependence of money holdings on interest rates and the slope of this relation have received considerable empirical study.

Many of the first studies correlating money holdings and interest rates left much to be desired. Since the nominal amount of money balances demanded is partly determined by individuals' wealth and volume of transactions, the demand can only be meaningfully measured relative to money national income or wealth. Many studies, following Keynes, assumed that one part of an individual's money holdings is actively used for transactions and is proportional to his income. The temporarily idle remainder was treated as unrelated to income and dependent only on interest rates. It is doubtful, however, that the dichotomy between "active" and "idle" balances holds up empirically. It is useful only for pedagogical purposes. The demand for idle balances will also be affected by the level of wealth and income, and the demand for transactions balances also by interest rates. A further difficulty with most of these studies was their coverage of just the four decades since the 1920's. Over that period, monetary velocity (that is, the ratio of national income to the money stock) and interest rates have both had two large movements, first down during the 1930's and early 1940's, then up until the mid-1950's. The two movements are by far the largest over the entire period and so dominate the regressions fitted to the data. The fit is deceptively impressive; one is sceptical of a correlation based essentially on only two movements, particularly since the other smaller movements are less closely related.[13] On this evidence alone, the association between velocity and interest rates may reflect, not a casual relation, but their similar response to depression and war.

Studies by Latané[14] and by Meltzer[15] avoid those difficulties by measuring the demand function for money in more sophisticated forms and by examining two earlier decades. Their results show a high correlation between interest rates and velocity. Moreover, Meltzer obtained consistent results for each decade of the whole period. It is not clear whether these results indicate a long-run or a short-run relation, or both. They are based on annual data and so probably measure a long-run relation, though the similar short-run cyclical fluctuations in velocity and interest rates no doubt add in some degree to the correlations found.[16]

Even if we grant that the demand to hold money depends on interest rates, the difficulties created by this dependence are constantly deplored but never adequately explained. To be sure, if the change in amount demanded for any given change in rates is infinite, as Keynes suggested was possible in deep depression at very low interest rates, rates could not fall lower through increases in the money stock because the public would sell all the bonds the Federal Reserve wanted to buy, at no increase in price. Monetary stimulation of the economy by open-market purchases is then virtually impossible.[17] It is doubtful that the economy has ever entered this strange world, even during the latter 1930's,[18] though no evidence is required to establish the self-evident proposition that such a "liquidity trap" does exist at rates of return of zero or slightly higher on all assets. Money is clearly preferable to any other asset fixed in nominal value and offering a negligible return. For interest rates normally prevailing, however, suppose that the response of demand to a change in rates is not infinite. What then? The precise degree of response determines the amount that interest rates will change for a given change in the quantity of money. A greater response requires a commensurately larger open-market operation to produce a given change in interest rates and hence to stimulate investment and aggregate spending. Yet why should this matter? If a certain change in interest rates is thought desirable, an open-market operation can, in principle, be large enough to produce it, whatever the size. Moreover, even if errors in forecasting the demand for money were large because its sensitivity to interest rates was high, the authorities should still be able, by a series of trial-and-error adjustments, to push a selected list of interest rates to any desired level.

The real problem is that the authorities can only guess what level of interest rates is appropriate at any time. This is not their fault. The problem is basically that the effects of open-market operations on spending take time and so cannot be quickly corrected by trial-and-error adjustments. A high interest-sensitivity in the demand to hold money does not itself add any further difficulties.

Having become aware of lags in investment spending, however, we may suspect that they occur in the demand to hold money also. If the response of demand to a change in interest rates is distributed over time, a large open-market operation taken to produce a given change in interest rates may gradually have a larger or smaller effect than is intended. Frequent attempts to offset unintended changes could subject interest rates to large fluctuations, disrupting the very stability that monetary policy is supposed to promote.

How real are such dangers? An assessment should take account of likely differences in behavior of various sectors of the economy. Households hold money as part of their wealth, equalizing the marginal rate of return that each asset offers in income or capital gain, liquidity, and risk. Nonfinancial businesses use money like any other factor of production, demanding more or less with changes in the cost of alternatives. In these two sectors, the interest-sensitivity of the demand to hold money is likely to be zero in the first instance but to increase gradually as a change in rates persists and time is allowed for adjustments.

Financial intermediaries and brokers are in the business of lending and borrowing money and so are expected to respond fairly quickly to a change in interest rates. As the middlemen of the money and capital market, they help to absorb short-run changes in supply. If the Federal Reserve buys bonds and lowers yields, bond dealers immediately provide the securities and then later buy securities on the open market to restock their inventory. If in the meantime yields do not stay down but rise, the dealers make a profit. When the Federal Reserve sells, the opposite behavior also produces a profit. Dealers exhibit what Keynes called the "speculative" motive for holding (or temporarily not holding) money. This is the explanation, perhaps, for the market's ability to absorb changes in the money stock from open-market operations in the very short run with only slight changes in interest rates.

But this short-run response need not last long, and over the intermediate run the response may be quite different. The dealers, together with other speculators, may not always expect interest rates to return to the original level; sometimes they may expect the direction of recent changes to continue and act to reinforce them. Such behavior can be observed from time to time, for example in the first part of 1958, when the Federal Reserve initiated an easy-money policy and professional and amateur speculators started a boom in government securities. That behavior implies, contrary to the usual formulation, that interest rates and the amount of money demanded move in the same direction. This has not been measured by time series studies, presumably because it happens too quickly or too infrequently.

As I interpret the limited evidence, in the short run the interest-sensitivity of the demand to hold money is fairly high, in the intermediate run it is low or sometimes perverse, and in the long run it is high or low depending on the long-run response of households and businesses. The varieties of behavior possible suggest that applying long-run relationships to short- or intermediate-run conditions is apt to mislead. In particular, the well-known cyclical fluctuations in the income velocity of money may not be an intermediate-run response to interest-rate changes at all. The fluctuations may reflect other cyclical factors, such as a temporary willingness to decrease or increase money holdings relative to the volume of expenditures as business prospects brighten or darken (though, to be sure, "business prospects" could be said to represent a rate of return on physical assets). Or, as one study suggests,[19] income velocity might improperly measure changes in the demand to hold money. Relative to wealth or "permanent" income, money balances do not fluctuate much over business cycles, and those quantities may be more appropriate than current income to indicate changes in the demand to hold money. There is therefore some basis for the view that, while the short-run sensitivity of the demand to interest rates is high, the intermediate-run sensitivity, which is of chief concern for countercyclical measures, is likely to be low, though it may also be less predictable.

FINANCIAL INTERMEDIARIES AND SUBSTITUTES FOR MONEY

The main determinant of the interest-sensitivity of the demand to hold money by households and businesses is the availability of substitutes. The growth of money-like claims has lately received considerable attention, attracted by the rapid growth of savings deposits held by households with financial intermediaries and of Treasury bills, commercial paper, and other liquid assets held by businesses. Various questions have been debated. One is the perennial favorite, "Is the traditional definition of money as currency and demand deposits too limited?" The discussion of this question has not progressed far, in part because of an understandable aversion to recognize as money anything for which the data are meager. The basic issue for policy, however, is whether the growth of money substitutes reinforces the sources of instability in the economy, and whether Federal Reserve control over the reserves of commercial banks is adequate. Such questions can be discussed in terms of cyclical swings in velocity, the subject of the preceding section. Financial intermediaries have received so much attention in the literature, however, that a survey of this kind would be remiss not to discuss them explicitly.

Financial intermediaries might increase short-run instability in two different ways. One is by changing their reserve ratios. Lending previously idle reserves puts money into circulation and thus raises spending. Any holder of cash balances can increase spending in the same way. As a matter of fact, the ratio of reserves to liabilities of financial intermediaries other than commercial banks is fairly stable over time.[20] There is no reason to single out such institutions on these grounds.

A second and more important source of short-run instability results from supplying substitutes for commercial-bank deposits. Tight money, for example, may induce depositors to shift funds from commercial banks to other financial intermediaries as the latter take advantage of rising market rates to increase the rate of interest paid on deposits. This raises the velocity of commercial-bank deposits. Conversely, easy money may bring the opposite shifts. Such shifts diminish the effect on cyclical swings in aggregate spending that tight or easy money is supposed to provide. It is true that the Federal Reserve can still control the supply of loanable funds by changing commercial-bank reserves and hence deposits in any amount desired,[21] so that the rapid growth of substitutes does not incapacitate traditional monetary controls. Yet the substitutes probably make the demand for commercial-bank deposits more sensitive to interest rates than it would otherwise be. As previously said, it is the difficulty of forecasting the distribution of the shifts over time rather than their magnitude that complicates monetary policy.

Concern over substitutes for money is, of course, not new. The Banking School of the mid-1800's in England thought that fluctuations in trade credit vitiated controls over the stock of currency set up by Peel's Act. Later, in this country, Henry Simons warned of the instability created by sudden shifts between demand deposits and short-term claims of all kinds.[22] Simons was mainly concerned about panics, which we now feel will be prevented even with short-term claims galore hanging precariously over the market. The problem now is mild cyclical shifts between those claims and commercial-bank deposits.

Shifts between money and other assets have been deplored so much that we tend to forget how little we know about them. We know that savings deposits and other liquid assets have grown rapidly relative to commercial-bank deposits. But beyond this we have to conjecture. Much of the long-run increase probably reflects a growing preference by the public for the services of intermediaries over direct holdings of stocks and bonds. Theoretically, the growth of liquid assets need not increase the interest-sensitivity of demand for commercial-bank deposits,[23] and no one has demonstrated that it does. Yet demand is always affected in this way by the availability of close substitutes, and it seems likely that most liquid assets, including commercial-bank deposits, are close substitutes for one another.

Although the interest-sensitivity of demand for these assets may be high, cyclical shifts to and from savings deposits do not appear to present a serious problem. The differential rate paid by savings and loan associations and mutual savings banks over the rate paid by commercial banks displays little cyclical fluctuation.[24] While the rates which commercial banks can pay are subject to a ceiling, the rates of other financial intermediaries, which have no ceiling, adjust to market conditions slowly. Moreover, individuals on the whole seem to respond slowly to changes in rate differentials. Except for a limited amount of "hot money," large and sudden shifts in and out of these assets appear unlikely.

In recent years, it is true, changes in certain rate differentials have been large and the induced shifts in holdings apparently also large. Those were special developments, however, not likely to be often repeated, certainly not as a regular feature of each business cycle. In 1950 Congress made the insurance offered savings and loan depositors virtually identical to the insurance offered commercial and mutual savings bank depositors. Also, during the 1950's, yields on mortgages and other securities rose; while ceilings prevented commercial banks from raising their rates very far, other financial intermediaries offered higher and higher rates. Many savers shifted their funds to the institutions paying more. Then, recently, the ceiling on commercial bank time and savings deposits was lifted, and they experienced rapid growth. These episodes prove that many people are rate-conscious, at least among assets that government insurance makes identical by assuming the risk of loss. There is no evidence, however, that such shifts quickly follow the changes in market rates typical of mild business cycles if government regulations are not altered.[25]

Proposals to moderate the effects of such shifts nevertheless abound. Simons, no man for half measures, would have abolished nearly all short-term claims. Present proposals have less dash. Since no one has devised an easy way to regulate the issue of commercial paper, trade credit, and other short-term claims with elastic supplies, attention has centered on the deposit institutions. Some benefit would come from removing rate ceilings on commercial-bank deposits, both time and demand; this price-fixing can be disruptive when changed, as it must be from time to time because competition has a way of seeping into the most tightly regulated markets. Removing the ceiling would also help to keep commercial-bank rates in line with the rates paid by other institutions over the cycle. Proposals have also been offered to require all savings banks to hold reserves with a government agency. If fixed as a percentage of deposits, such requirements would hold the total quantity of liquid assests constant whenever depositors shifted (for example) from commercial banks to savings and loan associations, assuming both institutions had to maintain the same reserve ratio. The shift would not then increase aggregate spending, as it can now.

The proposed reserve requirements could, however, introduce other sources of instability which are not now a problem. When the demand for savings deposits increased, savings banks would have to acquire additional reserves at the expense of commercial banks. Supplying savings deposits would therefore force a reduction in the quantity of commercial-bank deposits, unless the authorities increased total reserves. The resulting constancy of total liquid assets is appropriate if the shift to savings-bank deposits accompanies an equal decline in the demand for commercial-bank deposits, but not otherwise. If individuals sold bonds and put the proceeds into savings deposits, and the purchasers paid with funds acquired from maturing commercial paper or some other asset with a tractable supply, the demand for commercial-bank deposits would not change. Because commercial banks are nevertheless forced to contract, aggregate spending is curtailed.

Monetary policy could in principle offset these and other shifts. The point of such proposals is to reduce the sources of instability that require offsetting. The desirability of the reserve proposals for savings banks therefore depends on the importance of the shifts thereby rendered harmless relative to those that become a new source of instability. The difficulty of determining this makes the proposals unattractive, and lately they have received less attention.

THE DILEMMA OF MONETARY POLICY

Substitutes for money create more problems for monetary theory than for policy. Theory is called upon to analyze the demand and supply characteristics of money and its substitutes. Policy can largely overlook the gaps in that analysis and concentrate on supplying or withdrawing funds from the market to stimulate or restrain spending. Policy need not know how monetary measures work, only how to guide them and how to avoid difficulties. To judge from the behavior of rate differentials over cycles, financial intermediaries do not appear to be an important source of cyclical instability. The only real concern is whether they have or will become suppliers of nearly perfect substitutes for money. Contrary to the Radcliffe Report,[26] that danger seems remote, at least for the United States.

The problem faced by policy is rather that the effects of open-market operations on the prices of assets, and of changes in those prices on spending, take a long time. Policy therefore acts in the dark. At best, it lacks perfection, and the authorities are reduced to hoping that cautiously "leaning against the wind" does some good. At worst, policy adds a random source of disturbance to the market; or, if the lags are long enough, it may reinforce the very fluctuations it is piously striving to offset. This criticism goes considerably further than earlier contentions that monetary policy is ineffective. Before, critics admonished policy merely to refrain from extreme actions that might rock the boat; now, they advise it to pack up and go ashore.

An extreme proposal explicitly offered by Friedman[27] and by Shaw[28] advocates a constant rate of growth in the money stock at all times. A rate of 3½ or 4 per cent per year would allow for growth in the demand for money and keep prices roughly constant. Practically the same proposal is made by Angell,[29] who would have bank reserves grow at the estimated rate of growth of economic activity. The purpose of a constant rate is to avoid introducing variations in monetary growth that, though intended to mitigate current fluctuations in activity, may, because of long lags, generate fluctuations later. The Federal Reserve banks undoubtedly could produce a constant growth rate in the money stock except for minor deviations. To be sure, they often complain that they cannot prevent a decline in growth during recessions, when banks lack borrowers and excess reserves accumulate. In recent years, however, the reserve ratio of commercial banks (aside from changes in reserve requirements) exhibits very little fluctuation; banks have quickly purchased Treasury bills or other securities with new reserves when loan demand declined. Unforeseen variations in reserves from fluctuations in float and from currency or gold flows will make a constant growth rate in the money stock from week to week difficult, but from month to month it should be attainable.

The proponents of a constant growth rate do not claim that it would remove all instability from the economy. When for any reason loan demand declines, giving banks the same predetermined amount of reserves allows them to buy short-term securities and (if reserve ratios are not raised) to keep the money stock growing at the same rate. Sellers of the securities may just hold the money acquired, however, and not immediately spend it; in technical terms, the monetary expansion is offset in the first instance by a fall in velocity. Under these conditions it is tempting to favor a more aggressive expansion of bank reserves to try to make spending rise faster. Adhering to a constant rate of monetary growth appears defeatist to proponents of a discretionary countercyclical policy. Yet their position rests squarely on the assumption that a countercyclical policy does some good, which is the point at issue. The proponents of a constant rate argue that cyclical fluctuations in output, though not eliminated under the proposal, would have less amplitude than in the past, because variations in the monetary growth rate are an important source of instability in the economy.

One serious difficulty with a predetermined rate of monetary growth is that the selected rate may not keep prices constant over the long run, nor would it force them down when a persistent deficit in the balance of foreign payments required deflation. The rise in velocity during the 1950's, for example, made a lower growth rate of money desirable, although, had monetary policy not held interest rates so low during the 1940's, the postwar rise in interest rates and velocity would presumably have been much smaller. Such long-run swings in velocity may nevertheless occur, and from time to time an adverse balance of payments undoubtedly will. Adjustments required in the rate of monetary growth would have to be carried out in small steps, however, since every change is allegedly a source of instability to be avoided.

One might dislike this particular proposal but still agree that counter-cyclical monetary actions may be more disruptive than helpful because of lags. At the very least, policy should avoid large and sudden changes in the rate of monetary growth, though in such watered-down form the advice is hardly novel. Federal Reserve actions moved in that direction some time ago. Fluctuations in the monetary growth rate have been smaller since World War II than ever before for an extended period, though the results still fall short of a constant rate of growth.

The Alternative of Fiscal Policy

If monetary controls cannot stabilize the economy, it is natural to turn to fiscal measures. Government deficits pour additional dollars directly into the spending stream and so avoid the delays of open-market operations. To spread the dollars widely, tax cuts are superior to increases in federal expenditures on armaments or public works, which by nature mainly stimulate particular sectors of the economy, generally not those needing help the most. Yet obtaining congressional action to cut taxes promptly in a recession has been unsuccessful, and future prospects are bleak.

Even with full congressional co-operation, stabilizing the economy by varying the size of deficits or surpluses is not quite as simple as the "crude multiplier approach" implies. A permanent government deficit financed by selling bonds raises aggregate expenditures *over the long run* to the extent that monetary velocity rises. (For a given money stock, national income and velocity increase proportionately.) In theory, velocity will become moderately higher in the long run through an increase in interest rates produced by the government's sale of bonds to finance the deficit. Except for that effect, the rise in interest rates induces an offsetting reduction in private investment and—to the extent that saving is stimulated—also consumption. The reduction in private spending, resulting from the sale of U.S. bonds, takes time, however. The lag is very similar to the lag in the effect of monetary policy: Selling U.S. bonds raises their market yield, which gradually spreads to other assets and eventually curtails private investment. In the first instance, therefore, the budget deficit stimulates the economy by the full amount of the deficit plus the associated multiplier effects; the offsetting effect of the bond financing on private spending occurs slowly. Over the long run, the effect of a permanent deficit will be far smaller than the initial effects.

To the extent that the Treasury sells bonds to banks having excess reserves, of course, deficits are financed by new money, and while they continue, the effects remain at their initial strength. No offsetting effect on private spending occurs. Banks have not had large excess reserves in recent years, however, and the monetary authorities have generally not provided them specifically to absorb deficits. It may be that the stimulation of deficit spending induces some expansion of bank credit, although there is no evidence that such expansion accompanies deficits as a normal pattern except at special times, such as under the Federal Reserve bond-support program of the 1940's and early 1950's.

The effect of a deficit financed by selling bonds is therefore complicated and easy to misjudge. An accurate judgement must allow for the present and future effects of past levels of the deficit. The effect of a given rate of deficit is highest at first, then gradually fades, so that continued stimulus to the economy of the same initial amount requires a larger and larger deficit. Similarly, reducing a deficit of long standing is equivalent to running a surplus after having balanced the budget for a time. While financing a deficit with new money (by Federal Reserve purchases of the bonds issued by the Treasury) would maintain an undiminished effect, it would serve no purpose. For countercyclical purposes, fiscal measures need not last long, and over the long run their effects on aggregate demand can be achieved just as well by monetary measures.

With its rapid impact on aggregate demand, therefore, fiscal policy is primarily a countercyclical weapon. For that purpose budget policy should, ideally, increase the deficit gradually during business contractions, and at the onset of expansion reduce it gradually and then switch over to a gradually increasing surplus. Such a pattern occurs in part automatically through the interaction of income fluctuations with fixed tax rates and unemployment compensation. Although such automatic stabilizers cannot eliminate business cycles, they have done much in recent years to ameliorate them. We probably cannot, for practical reasons, go farther. Congressional changes in tax rates or in public expenditures are too slow and too often nonreversible.

Concluding Remarks on the Uses of Monetary and Fiscal Measures

With monetary theory raising grave warnings about the adequacy and dangers of traditional countercyclical policies and advising retrenchment, events, oddly enough, have thrust policy into a broader role. Monetary measures, together with what help our clumsy fiscal machinery can provide, are supposed to stabilize the economy, raise the growth rate of output, and stop the outflow of gold. It is enough to ruffle the most composed central banker. Theory helps to clarify the incompatibility of some of these goals. With easy money the authorities may perhaps stimulate investment and hence the growth of capital, but they cannot at the same time indefinitely avoid inflation unless the federal budget runs a substantial surplus. They cannot stimulate investment and at the same time expect to stop an adverse balance of payments unless the dollar exchange rate is allowed to fluctuate on the open market.[30] It is doubtful whether a discretionary monetary policy can do any more to stabilize the economy than has already been done without a more adept fiscal policy, and it might well try doing less. Lately, however, complaints of lagging economic growth outweigh those of instability, so that the goals of monetary policy may be changing, in part perhaps because the traditional goals of stabilization have been partially attained and further achievements appear out of reach.

Confronted with such diverse and conflicting goals, policy makers are susceptible to the appeal of nostrums. Juggling tax rates to spur investment for growth, along with export subsidies and import quotas to alleviate the adverse balance of payments, while deplorable on many grounds, at least help to attain the purposes intended. The policy of public expenditures directed at particular regions to attack pockets of persistent unemployment, though largely only a temporary palliative, at least recognizes that each region poses special problems and that a stimulant fed to the whole economy will not solve them. However, the recent disposition to use budget deficits for long-run problems of growth and unemployment, leaving monetary policy to look after short-run developments, cannot be defended. That disregards their comparative advantages. Budget deficits and surpluses have an immediate impact but (unless continually increased) accomplish little in the long run, while monetary measures affect the economy at large mainly in the long run, very little in the short run. Reliance instead on temporary deficits and surpluses to mitigate business cycles, and on monetary measures for longer-run objectives, will give more dependable results. Assigning separate domains to monetary and fiscal policy will also avoid setting them at cross purposes, an effect which too easily results from the confusing variety of national goals.

Notes

1. An earlier version of this paper was presented in September, 1963, at a monetary conference held by the Graduate School of Business of Columbia University. I am grateful to Albert Hart, Gottfried Haberler, and Richard Selden for comments.

2. Although the sellers of bonds have less earning assets and interest income, the Federal Reserve has more; hence, society's income has not changed. The redistribution of income between the public as taxpayers and as interest recipients is usually ignored.

Capital gains or losses from a change in bond prices affect wealth but not income. There are conflicting views on whether a change in wealth affects spending, but most agree the effect, if any in an ordinary operation, is small.

3. See my discussion of the evidence in Chapter 6 of P. Cagan, *Determinants and Effects of Changes in the Money Stock 1875–1960* (National Bureau of Economic Research, 1965).

4. In recent years an increasing number of studies point to an interest effect. See, for example, L. Klein, "Studies in Investment Behavior," in *Conference on Business Cycles* (National Bureau of Economic Research, 1951), pp. 233–304; S. J. Maisel, "A Theory of Fluctuations in Residential Construction Starts," *American Economic Review*, LIII (June, 1963), 359–383; J. Meyer and E. Kuh, *The Investment Decision* (Cambridge, Mass.: Harvard University Press, 1960); Y. Grunfeld, "A Study of Corporate Investment" in A. Harberger (ed.), *The Demand for Durable Goods* (Chicago: University of Chicago Press, 1960); W. Roberts, "Business Cycles, Residential Construction Cycles, and the Mortgage Market," *Journal of Political Economy*, LXX (June, 1962), 263–281; G. Stigler, *Capital and Rates of Return in Manufacturing Industries* (National Bureau of Economic Research, 1963). (The last reference deals with the rate of return on capital rather than the rate of interest.)

For a criticism of evidence from survey studies which claim to find no effect, see W. H. White, "Interest Inelasticity of Investment Demand—The Case from Business Attitude Surveys Re-examined," *American Economic Review*, XLVI (September, 1956), 565–587.

5. R. G. Hawtrey, *Currency and Credit* (4th ed.; London: Longmans, Green and Co., 1950), Ch. IV; J. R. Hicks, "Mr. Hawtrey on Bank Rate and the Long-term Rate of Interest," *The Manchester School*, X (1939).

6. R. S. Sayers, *Modern Banking* (1st ed.; Oxford: Clarendon Press, 1938), Ch. VI; J. M. Keynes, *A Treatise on Money* (London: Macmillan, 1930), Vol. I, pp. 185–200.

7. Such arguments, even if valid, do not necessarily imply, contrary to a widespread view, that the response of investment to changes in interest rates is low. Uncertainties may affect the mean and variance of expected returns, but not the density of potential projects arrayed along the schedule, which is all that is relevant for the elasticity of investment to changes in interest cost. See L. Tarshis,

"The Elasticity of the Marginal Efficiency of Capital Function," *American Economic Review*, LI (December, 1961), 958–985.

8. R. Roosa, "Interest Rates and the Central Bank," in *Money, Trade, and Economic Growth, Essays in Honor of J. H. Williams* (New York: Macmillan, 1951), pp. 270–295.

9. T. Mayer, "The Inflexibility of Monetary Policy," *Review of Economics and Statistics*, XL (November, 1958), 358–374, and "Dr. White on the Inflexibility of Monetary Policy," *Review of Economics and Statistics*, XLV (May, 1963), 209–211; W. H. White, "The Flexibility of Anticyclical Monetary Policy," *Review of Economics and Statistics*, XLIII (May, 1961), 142–147.

10. M. Friedman and A. Schwartz, "Money and Business Cycles," in *The State of Monetary Economics*, supplement to *Review of Economics and Statistics*, XLV (February, 1963), 32–64.

11. Cagan, *op. cit.*

12. One study—E. C. Brown, R. M. Solow, A. Ando, and J. Kareken, "Lags in Fiscal and Monetary Policy," in Commission on Money and Credit, *Stabilization Policies* (1963)—using quarterly data finds no difference in timing between turns in the rate of change of the money stock and of economic activity. The proper interpretation of this result is not clear, for the implied lag of less than three months is incredibly short.

13. L. H. Bean, " 'On Interest Rates and the Demand for Money': A Comment," *Review of Economics and Statistics*, XLII (August, 1960), 333–334; C. Warburton, "Monetary Velocity and the Rate of Interest," *Review of Economics and Statistics*, XXXII (August, 1950), 256–257.

14. H. A. Latané, "Cash Balances and the Interest Rate: A Pragmatic Approach," *Review of Economics and Statistics*, XXXVI (November, 1954), 456–460; "Income Velocity and Interest Rates: A Pragmatic Approach," *Review of Economics and Statistics*, XLII (November, 1960), 445–449.

15. A. H. Meltzer, "The Demand for Money: The Evidence from the Time Series," *Journal of Political Economy*, LXXI (June, 1963), 219–246.

16. Insofar as they do, there is danger that the effect is overestimated because of the failure to allow for the effect of income on interest rates via the investment-demand function. In statistical terms, this produces single-equation least-squares bias. Unfortunately, it cannot be easily handled until we are successful in specifying the investment-demand function.

There is another difficulty, pertaining to short-run movements, in that independent changes in the demand to hold money can produce changes in the supply of loanable funds and so affect interest rates. If the changes in money demand are produced by cyclical fluctuations in income, there is an appearance of a dependence of velocity on interest rates which actually reflects a relation running in the opposite direction.

17. Virtually but not entirely, because a sufficiently large increase in the money stock probably would create fears of inflation and greatly reduce the demand to hold money at any given level of interest rates.

18. A. H. Meltzer, "Yet Another Look at the Low Level Liquidity Trap," *Econometrica*, XXXI (July, 1963), 545–549.

19. M. Friedman, "The Demand for Money: Some Theoretical and Empirical Results," *Journal of Political Economy*, LXVII (August, 1959), 327–351.

20. W. C. Freund, "Financial Intermediaries and Federal Reserve Controls Over the Business Cycle," *Quarterly Review of Economics and Business*, II (February, 1962), 21–29.

21. J. Tobin and W. Brainard, "Financial Intermediaries and the Effectiveness of Monetary Controls," *American Economic Review Papers and Proceedings*, LIII (May, 1963), 383–400.

22. H. C. Simons, *Economic Policy for a Free Society* (Chicago: University of Chicago Press, 1948), pp. 166–171.

23. A. Marty, "Gurley and Shaw on Money in a Theory of Finance," *Journal of Political Economy*, LXIX (February, 1961), 56–62.

24. Cagan, *op. cit.*, Ch. 5.

25. Freund, *op. cit.*

26. *Report* of the *Committee on the Working of the Monetary System* (Cmnd. 827) (London: H. M. Stationery Office, August, 1959).

27. M. Friedman, *A Program for Monetary Stability* (New York: Fordham University Press, 1959).

28. E. S. Shaw, "Money Supply and Stable Economic Growth," in *U.S. Monetary Policy* (New York: American Assembly, 1958), pp. 49–71.

29. J. A. Angell, "Appropriate Monetary Policies and Operations in the United States Today," *Review of Economics and Statistics*, XLII (August, 1960), 247–252.

30. At present rates of outflow (1964), our gold stock in a few years will be close to minimum requirements. In future thereafter, we shall have to forgo the luxury, now so much appreciated in Washington, of procrastination in dealing with balance-of-payments difficulties.

The Bills Only Doctrine in Retrospect

Deane Carson

INTRODUCTION

AS an early and constant critic of the Federal Reserve System's bills only doctrine, the writer might be condemned for flaying a dead horse in proposing to survey the controversy once again—a controversy that has seemingly been laid to rest by the central bank's operations in longer-term securities since 1961. My defense is several-fold: First, it is far from certain that the Federal Reserve's view has fundamentally changed; second, the official policy of the 1950's, which was defended initially on basically institutional considerations, was later vested with theoretical trappings that deserve more complete critical consideration than they have received; and finally, a useful purpose can be served by pointing out the sources of conflict between the academic community and the Federal Reserve Board concerning the proper role of the latter in economic stabilization.

In reviewing and evaluating the rationale of the Federal's decision to confine its open-market operations to short-term securities,[1] one must first note that things were not what they seemed, at least to the outsiders, at the time the new ground rules were promulgated. Indeed, while the board emphasized its desire to improve the "depth, breadth and resiliency" of the government securities market by avoiding operations outside the short-term sector, the basic motivation certainly lay elsewhere. Briefly, the bills only doctrine appears in retrospect to have been an outgrowth of the long struggle for authority between the Federal Reserve Bank of New York, where open-market operations are executed, and the Federal Open Market Committee in Washington, where market policy is formulated. The board, along with some of the reserve bank presidents who sit on the Open Market Committee, wished to exercise greater control over the discretion exercised by the manager of the Open Market account in New York. Prior to bills only, the latter had considerable leeway with respect to the sector in which the general prescription of the Open Market Committee was executed.

In this connection, it is significant that the committee's objective of "maintaining orderly conditions in the government securities market" was changed to read "to prevent disorderly conditions in the market" at the time the bills only policy was adopted. This subtle distinction in mandate to the manager was of utmost significance, since it essentially abrogated Federal Reserve responsibility for the term structure of interest rates except at times of extreme market crisis.

In addition to the difference in views held by the New York Federal Reserve Bank and the board concerning the execution of open-market operations, the bills only doctrine was based upon the experience of postwar monetary management. This experience, which involved a continuation of wartime pegs on the government yield structure as a whole until 1947, and pegging of the long-term bond rate until the Treasury-Federal Reserve Accord in 1951, was interpreted by almost all observers, especially the board itself, as directly responsible for the postwar inflation. In its report to the full Open Market Committee, an *ad hoc* subcommittee continually referred to the period of market pegging and strongly suggested that long-term purchases or sales were equivalent to pegging the market.[2] This, of course, was nonsense; but one should not underestimate the trauma that gave rise to such statements and, given the subcommittee's own bias toward protecting the dealer market from exceptional hazards, its desire to avoid the very appearance of evil.

The principal recommendations of this subcommittee were adopted on March 5, 1953, following the submission of its report to the Open Market Committee in November. The proposals adopted were three in number: First, that open-market operations henceforth be confined to the short end of the market; second, that support of the market during periods of Treasury refinancing be discontinued; and third, that operations be conducted solely for the purpose of effectuating credit policy, and not for the purpose of supporting any pattern of prices and yields in the market.[3] The long-standing directive to the manager of the Open Market Account to "maintain orderly conditions in the Government securities market" was changed to one of "correcting disorderly conditions." While the latter phrase was not defined, it was interpreted to mean a qualification, in extreme circumstances, of the "bills only" doctrine contained in the first recommendation.

These changes were not only of technique, nor were they most significantly changes of method. Rather they reflect a view of the responsibility of the central bank in the realm of economic stabilization—a view which differs in some respects from that of many monetary theorists.

Underlying the thinking of the *ad hoc* subcommittee which resulted in the adoption of the new techniques was the belief that yields of government securities (and therefore the whole structure of interest rates) should be allowed to reflect the supply and demand forces of a free market. It was believed that the free play of such forces would improve the market for government securities. Replies by dealers in government securities to a questionnaire sent them by the subcommittee had strongly indicated the need for improvement, and the subcommittee appears to have been influenced by these opinions.[4] Its report contains little analysis, however, of the effectiveness of the new techniques from the standpoint of Federal Reserve's responsibility for economic stability. The proponents of the new techniques appeared to believe that they would not only serve to improve the government securities market, but that they would also be adequate to the task of monetary control.

On the assumption that the effective execution of operations to control bank reserves depends upon the existence of "depth, breadth and resiliency" in the market, the *ad hoc* subcommittee was concerned with the "thinness" which had characterized the long-term sector after the abandonment of the pegging technique in March, 1951. This condition was ascribed to the uncertainty of dealers as to the sector of the market in which operations would be conducted. To the subcommittee the remedy was apparent: Confine intervention in the market to that necessary to supply and withdraw bank reserves; operate exclusively in bills; and assure the market that these "ground rules" would henceforth prevail.

The subcommittee's concern with the structural characteristics of the government securities market is understandable. Since open-market operations are the medium through which a significant part of Federal Reserve credit policy is effected, success depends to some extent on the adequacy of the market. Given the large volume of the System's transactions, the desirability of a deep, broad, and resilient market is not subject to question. Such a market would be characterized by (1) orders to buy and sell both above and below the current market price, (2) a large volume of such orders, and (3) relatively small fluctuations in price due to quick response on the part of investors to small changes in market conditions. Furthermore, given the existing organization of the market, dealers must not only serve as brokers in government securities but act on their own account, taking positions in all sectors of the market, if depth, breadth, and resiliency are to be achieved.

It was the belief of the subcommittee that these characteristics could be developed only in a free market. The following excerpts from the subcommittee's report indicate the strength of this contention:

> . . . dealers must be confident that a really free market exists in fact, i.e., that the Federal Open Market Committee will permit prices to equal [sic] demand and supply without direct intervention other than such as would normally be made to absorb and release reserve funds.[5]
> . . . it is not enough for the development of an adequate market that the Committee's intervention be held to a strict minimum. It is important that the dealers be assured . . . that the Committee is prepared to permit a really free market . . . to develop.[6]
> . . . the guidance of economic decisions by free markets is a characteristic that has effectively served the American economy and for which there is no satisfactory substitute.[7]

These declarations were made with the full realization that "rates for Government securities are closely related to and affect interest rates on all classes of loans and investments."[8]

In commenting on the import of the new directives, Chairman Martin declared they "gave notice that the . . . Committee would not intervene to prevent fluctuations of prices and yields such as normally . . . occur as markets seek to establish equilibrium between supply and demand factors and to allocate savings. . . ."[9] It was his conviction, furthermore, "that we do the most service . . . consonant with the concept of private competitive enterprise by giving the play of the market the maximum influence that it can have without disruptive effects."[10]

The free market thesis was not unqualified; the System stood ready to correct disorderly conditions should they develop. This possibility was considered "remote."[11] Furthermore, "the System would be called upon rarely, if ever, to intervene in securities with longer than 1-year maturity and . . . the only justification for System intervention would be to correct disorderly conditions resulting from some emergency, such as an unexpected development in international relations."[12]

Further evidence of the commitment to a free market is inferred from the subcommittee's repeated assertion that the committee should restrict its intervention in the market. In general, this meant that operations should be conducted for the single purpose of regulating the reserve position of the banking system. In formulating its report, the subcommittee declared that "the present wording of the directive of the . . . Committee on 'maintenance of orderly conditions' carries with it an unduly, *and even dangerously strong,* implication of continuing intervention in all sectors of the market. This prospect . . . seriously impairs the ability of the market to stand on its own feet or to evaluate correctly the real forces of demand and supply in the economy."[13] Testifying in December, 1954, Chairman Martin stated that open market operations "have come to be limited to providing and withdrawing reserve funds. . . ."[14]

The emphasis of the *ad hoc* subcommittee report was placed upon the need for improving the technical performance of the government securities market. Rather less attention was given to the question of the impact of a bills only policy on the effectiveness of monetary control, although we are repeatedly assured that changes in short-term yields will be accompanied, after a (presumably short) lag, by same-directional changes throughout the yield curve via the mechanism of arbitrage. As Professor Samuelson has remarked, however, the relevant premise raised by the bills only policy is that "by confining operations to short terms, the monetary authorities can realize all the desired effects on credit and spending and can do this in the manner that is philosophically most compatible with the ethical goals of a free society."[15]

Before we turn to this issue, which much later concerned Federal Reserve economists,[16] a digression on the proper interpretation of the System's earlier views on its own role in economic stabilization is in order. While Professor Harris' statement that modern "developments in the theory of money and output seem largely to have escaped those responsible for monetary and debt policy"[17] is perhaps too strong, his analysis of the viewpoint of present Reserve officials is essentially correct:

They seem to consider the control of the rate of interest on Government securities merely as an attempt to raise artificially the price of these assets rather than (as they should) consider the control on this rate as a means of determining the rate of interest generally and hence influencing investment and output. . . .[18]

It is possible, and indeed rather probable, of course, that neither the *ad hoc* subcommittee nor members of the Open Market Committee actually wished their remarks on the subject of the free money market to be taken literally. In a sense, at least, they were addressed to themselves and to the layman, including market participants and legislators, rather than to the academic economist. The latter's view has nearly always been that the Federal Reserve should exercise a powerful influence on market rates of interest and their structure. On the other hand, central bank officials have nearly always attempted to minimize the public's image of their power, if not the power itself.

A prime example of the attempt to "play down" the impact of central bank action in recent years is contained in the phrase "leaning against the wind" used by Federal Reserve officials to describe their operations. Essentially, "leaning against the wind" implies that the central bank simply *modifies* the basic private forces making for expansion and contraction of credit and changes in the level of interest rates. Many economists, on the other hand, tend to assume that the central bank's role is either to *establish* the supply of funds available for bank credit or to *establish* rates of interest and their structure.

These different views of central bank power are not simply the products of difficulties in communication. The monetary economist is inclined to believe that there is a rate of interest, or a structure of rates, that is uniquely appropriate to the attainment of full employment without inflation. As a corollary, many contend that it is the task of the central bank to make this rate level and structure effective. The Federal Reserve's view has increasingly been that its task lies not in establishing interest rates but in modifying the availability of bank reserves on which credit expansion is based. In the quaint vernacular of a recently received undergraduate paper, the Federal Reserve seems to have "flushed the interest rate."

Two reasons may be given for the Federal Reserve position *vis a vis* its own market powers. On the theoretical level, the monetary authorities are inclined to doubt the utility of the academic economist's models as guides for policy. This in turn has led to one or the other of two attitudes: first, that the model (for example, the Hicks-Hansen-Lerner formulation) is so abstract that it does not adequately explain the forces that determine interest rates and the level of income, or, second, that to follow its prescription would involve the exercise of "arbitrary" power by the Federal Reserve. We will return to these attitudes when we discuss the Riefler-Young-Yager defense of the bills only doctrine which itself involves a model of monetary behavior.

The second reason for the present view of the Federal Reserve *vis a vis* its responsibilities is largely political in nature. The position of the American central bank in the governmental structure is, if not unique, at least unusual. Its basic responsibility is to Congress, modified by both legal and extra-legal and informal relationships to the Executive. Congress itself is made up of hundreds of individuals representing various economic and regional interests, and with varying degrees of responsibility and power. Federal Reserve officials tend to be highly sensitive to the views of this heterogeneous body in general and to those of certain more powerfully placed members in particular. Criticism of its policy is pervasive, unrelenting, and at least occasionally unjustified and uninformed. There is not a little sentiment in Congress that the System is part of a monstrous conspiracy of the banking community to destroy the small farmer and businessman; at the same time, it has been accused of being an engine of inflation. Tight money policies invariably generate an-guished complaints from constituents whose congressmen duly reflect them in the multitude of committee hearings at which Reserve officials are asked to testify.

Given this responsibility to Congress, and the need to serve the na-tional interest, the Federal Reserve is forced to explain its sometimes politically distasteful policies in ways that will minimize political hos-tility. This is done, if our interpretation is correct, by de-emphasizing the role that the Federal Reserve plays in determining the level and struc-ture of interest rates, and by adopting operating techniques which, while somewhat arbitrary, give the appearance of impersonality and, in fact, are less arbitrary than some available alternatives. This involves re-liance principally on the purchase and sale of short-term securities (in which market sector the *price* effect will be least) to modify the aggregate supply of excess reserves available to the member banks. The resulting increase (or diminution) in commercial-bank reserves is then allocated to loans and investments or to idle cash as the banking system desires; interest rates in the various markets for funds, furthermore, respond to the changes that have taken place in asset portfolios according to pri-vately determined choices. Finally, the structure of rates is allowed to reflect free market allocation of funds and private demand, with no at-tempt being made by the monetary authority to establish a particular pattern. This image of the board's powers is certainly more acceptable to the general public than that of a monolithic monetary authority; un-fortunately, the desire to project it may lead the central bank to adopt attitudes and techniques that interfere with its own—as well as the pub-lic's—ultimate goals. And, ironically, it does not appear that criticism is blunted by the projection of a "weak" central bank.[19]

THE RIEFLER DEFENSE OF BILLS ONLY

In response to criticism of the bills only doctrine which the System adopted in 1953, economists connected with the Federal Reserve Board in Washington developed a further rationale for the policy. This work was largely the responsibility of W. W. Riefler, a long-time economist of the board and assistant to Chairman Martin.[20] Thus it represents official board thinking at the time of its publication in late 1958.

Riefler's analysis, while avoiding the explicit reference to a free money market that had so confused monetary theorists who had read the *ad hoc* subcommittee report in early 1955, rests, to a great extent, on an implicit preference for minimizing the impact on interest rates of any given operation by the central bank. His major points are listed and discussed below.

(1) Bill operations are preferable to long-term security transactions because "operations by the System in long-term securities can give rise to expectations not only regarding the direction of general monetary policy but also regarding specific prices and yields of long-term securities—a double set of possible misinterpretations. Bill operations lead mainly to expectations about general monetary policy."[21]

(2) Market arbitrage by government securities dealers, and the high degree of substitutability of securities and credit instruments that exists for many lenders and borrowers, result in the transmission of sustained changes in yields in one market sector to other sectors, with or without a time lag.

(3) The effect of open-market operations on interest rates is predominantly the result of change in bank free reserves and only slightly due to the addition or withdrawal of securities in a certain sector of the government securities market.

(4) Since (2) and (3) above lead to the conclusion that it really doesn't matter whether the System's open-market operations are conducted in short- or long-term securities as far as the interest rate effect is concerned, (1) above is the basic justification for operating in the short-term sector.

(5) Interest rate changes are a means to an end, not an end in themselves. The effectiveness of monetary policy rests upon its ability to modify the supply of bank reserves and the flow of bank credit. Changes in interest rates are thus conceived of as the by-product of the reserve effect.

Riefler's central point, (1) above, requires elaboration. Centrally located in the money market are some twenty dealers in government securities whose function is not only to serve as brokers, matching buy and sell orders, but also to make markets in various maturity sectors. The latter requires them to take positions (accumulate inventories) in various issues on their own account, using relatively small amounts of their own capital and relatively large amounts of borrowed money. Their willingness to undertake the latter function depends upon profit expectations. These are determined by a set of conditions involving the availability and cost of borrowed money, anticipated changes in prices of potential inventory, and the yield of such securities during the inventory-carry period.

Dealers will be encouraged to assume positions in longer-term securities, and thereby to stabilize the market, whenever (1) financing is readily available, (2) the cost of financing is favorable relative to the yield on carried securities, and (3) there is an expectation of an increase in the price of the security over the inventory-carry period. In brief, the dealer must expect to realize a carry-profit after all explicit and opportunity costs have been deducted. Future expectations as to (1) and (2), as well as (3), are important in the decision process.

Since dealers operate on extremely thin margins, small changes in the price of a long-term security held in inventory cause large changes in the rate of profit on capital invested. At the same time, *ceteris paribus*, the more costly are borrowed funds relative to the yield of long-term bonds (as in periods of extremely tight money), the less the attraction of speculative carries in the long-term sector of the market.

To continue with Reifler's argument, dealers constantly seek to discover and correctly interpret Federal Reserve policy. Since they handle all System purchases and sales, they can easily discover the volume of System operations. But this is not enough, for they must also correctly assess the *meaning* of the transactions if their speculative activity is to yield a profit. A somewhat lengthy quotation from Riefler points out the consequences of a misinterpretation of Federal Reserve intentions by market professionals:

> There is always the possibility that they may assume that a given purchase or sale [in any market sector] by the System foreshadows larger changes in bank reserve positions than in fact develop. In such cases, they may take positions and establish, for a period, an unsustainable level of prices or yields that is inconsistent with the actual supply-demand situation.
>
> [The above possibility] is a major reason for the System's policy of non-intervention in the intermediate- and long-term sectors of the market. Its operations in longer-term securities would be much more subject to comment and possible misinterpretation by market professionals than are its operations in Treasury bills. . . . The very fact that the System took the initiative in buying or selling long-term securities, where the market is almost always thin as compared with the bill sector, would indicate a feeling on the part of Reserve authorities that existing prices and yields on long-term securities were out of line. Market professionals perforce would have to try to assess this implication in their subsequent trades.[22]

While the above analysis is essentially correct, it hardly constitutes a compelling reason for avoiding long-term operations. In essence, the argument is that long-term operations increase the uncertainties to which dealers and other professionals are subject when monetary control is exercised through the bill market. Furthermore, however, the fact is that dealers, misinterpreting the objective of a given volume of long-term operations, will tend to operate in the same direction as the Open Market

Committee, thus bringing about a change in yields that is inconsistent with basic conditions of demand and supply in the capital markets. That is to say, dealers will seldom go against a trend which they believe the Federal Reserve is trying to establish.

A yield inconsistent with basic supply-demand forces will, according to Riefler, cause later congestion in the capital market if the market has initially been brought to an abnormally low level by dealer expectations generated by System long-term purchases. Indeed, "the lower yields will tend to persist for a period until the volume of prospective [capital] issues, previously withheld but currently seeking a place on the calendar, grows to the point where nervous congestion develops and the true nature of the basic supply-demand position is disclosed."[23]

Although Riefler is not entirely clear on this point, the basic supply-demand position to which he refers is apparently determined in part by the supply of bank reserves. In this context, if the System wishes to augment reserves by, say, $100 million through long-term bond purchases, the following effects obtain. First, yields fall as prices are bid up by the System. Second, dealers and others, riding with the expected trend of monetary ease, also purchase long-term securities, thus further reducing long-term yields. But while the initial fall in yield was consistent with the new supply of bank reserves, the secondary decline is not. One can also infer that the desired increase in investment was consistent with the initial change in yield and additional bank reserves, while the secondary change in yield brings into the new capital issue market an increase in demand that is greater than the supply of loanable funds. This is the basic cause of "congestion" in the capital market.

Riefler does not carry this part of the analysis to its conclusion. In the first place, the excess of capital demand over the supply of loanable funds at the new lower yield induced by both System operations and dealer expectations will not be stable. The long-term yield will tend to rise until the market is cleared, quite possibly at the level originally reached as a result of the initial System purchases. The congestion cannot possibly last for very long. Some prospective investors will be disappointed, of course, but unless investment demand is very elastic with respect to interest rates, the magnitude of congestion will be of little consequence. On the other hand, dealers who have taken positions in long-term issues will be "burned" as prices of long-term bonds rise to reflect the basic supply-demand position. We will return to this particular effect after further considering the conclusions that follow from Riefler's analysis.

A second conclusion to be drawn is that induced dealer expectations which bring long-term yields to an abnormally low point (given the initial assumptions) imply that a relatively small System operation in this market can generate relatively large changes in long-term yields.[24] In recession, when the latter tend to be sticky and in some cases have tended to *rise*, this effect constitutes a powerful argument for System purchases in the longer maturities! In such cases, when lenders are shifting to more liquid assets, dealer expectations of the sort Riefler contemplates, so far from being a disruptive market force, actually serve monetary policy objectives rather well.

At this point we must distinguish between normal day-to-day defensive operations of the System, and operations undertaken to effect changes in basic monetary conditions.[25] The former involve both purchases and sales to counteract factors bringing about changes in bank excess reserves that are not desired from the standpoint of existing monetary policy. These include such things as gold flows, changes in Federal Reserve float, and currency shifts. In this type of open-market operation, there is no particular reason for preferring long-term purchases and sales to short-term. Indeed, the latter should be preferred on the basis that Riefler suggests: In this sector, while "false" expectations can be generated by System operations, the impact on the security prices is much smaller and, therefore, somewhat less disruptive to the performance of dealer functions. Riefler, however, makes no distinction of this sort.

Riefler further defends bills only on the grounds that the effect of operations in the short-term sector are transmitted to the long-term sector through dealer arbitrage and the high degree of lender asset substitution that exists between market sectors. The discussion of the latter is particularly perceptive. His general position is that the existence of these links between market sectors accounts for the smoothness of the yield curve and provides the transmission lines through which changes in short-term yields and bank reserve positions are carried to the longer-term sectors. He concludes that the existence of these links makes the choice of sector in which the System should conduct its operations a matter of indifference, if there were no other considerations.

The common observation that long- and short-term interest rates tend to move in the same direction has tended to obscure the really important policy considerations involved. Reserve officials contend that short-term operations which increase or decrease short-term yields will bring about similar directional effects, perhaps with a lag, in the intermediate- and long-term sectors. As a corollary, they believe that direct purchases and sales in the latter maturities are unnecessary. This position is untenable as a defense of bills only *dynamic* operations on two grounds.

First, the time lag between an easy money condition in the short-term market and its subsequent impact on long-term yields and investment expenditures has been extensive at certain times in the past. The classic example of this is the depression of 1929–1932, when short-term yields were brought to an extremely low level without noticeable impact on long-term yields. Only after the financial system had been flooded with liquidity in subsequent years did the long-term yield decline. Timing of this sort is certainly incompatible with accepted goals of countercyclical monetary policy.

But even if the time lag does not present a problem, changes in the direction of monetary policy initiated in the bill market may exert a weak impact on the long-term rate. The latter typically moves sluggishly upward or downward relative to similar changes in bill yields. On the other hand, the *price* of long-term bonds drops sharply with a relatively small increase in yield, and vice versa. As far as inhibiting or encouraging long-term investment expenditures is concerned, it is the yield effect which is of paramount importance in monetary control.

In recession, for example, short-term open-market purchases by the System usually bring down long-term rates very little in terms of what a countercyclical expansion of long-term spending on investment would require where demand is inelastic. On the other hand, during an investment boom (conceptually, the investment demand schedule shifting to the right), long-term yields may not move up sufficiently to have much dampening effect.

The bills only approach to monetary control is ill-suited to the problems presented by large changes in investment expenditures and income. Since sustained booms and depressions present many other control problems to the authorities, it seems unwise to limit the arsenal of defense so severely.[26]

Riefler's final point in defense of bills only may be passed over rather quickly. He contends in point (3) above that most of the interest rate effect of open-market operations derives from the resulting change in bank reserves, and only a small fraction of the effect can be attributed to the withdrawal or addition of securities in a particular market sector.

To test this hypothesis, he examines a period of Treasury refunding in early 1958 in which a substantial volume of maturing securities was exchanged for long-term bonds. Since the refunding did not in itself cause a change in bank reserves, he observed the security-supply effect on long-term yields more or less in isolation. Making the assumption that the swap of very short-term debt for long-term bonds was equivalent to a system open-market sale of an equivalent amount in the long-term sector, he was led to conclude that the resulting small increase in yield was significant.

Like many other similar experiments, this one is not immune to criticism of its design. In the first place, a Treasury refunding of the kind observed is *not* equivalent to System sales in the long-term market in one important respect. When the Open Market Committee sold $1.5 billion in this market (the amount actually involved in the refunding), dealers would very quickly appraise the operation as intended to raise long-term rates. The exceptional effect that Riefler discusses would lead dealers to ride the trend, mark down prices, and liquidate their own positions, thus raising interest rates by more than the amount generated by the open-market operation. Dealers had no reason to expect that the Treasury's move was anything more than its usual attempt to lengthen the debt during recession periods.[27]

In the second place, interest rates did not rise as much as might be expected under other circumstances. The testing period was one that immediately followed a shift in monetary policy from extreme stringency to active ease. Member bank free reserves averaged (—) **$476** millions in September, 1957. By January, 1958, the date of announcement of the Treasury's refunding terms, free reserves averaged (+) **$122** millions. The Federal Reserve Bank of New York discount rate was reduced both in November, 1957, and *during* the period between the announcement of terms and the completion of the refunding on February 5, 1958. These are hardly conditions in which one might expect a System sale of $1.5 billion in the long-term market. Riefler's test is at best inconclusive regarding the interest rate effect of long-term operations by the System, and more statistical testing of this matter is clearly needed.

Supplemental Views on "Bills Preferably"

As a backstop to Riefler's defense of bills only, two other members of the Federal Reserve Board staff subsequently published additional views on the problem.[28] Quite aside from the rechristening of the doctrine "bills preferably," which did not change the official position in the least although it provided a more accurate descriptive title,[29] Young and Yager offer largely the same defense as did Riefler, with some additional analysis. To this we now turn.

Major attention is devoted in this analysis to the suggestion that the System should endeavor to reshape, at certain times, the yield curve in the government securities market. Much of what we have argued in the preceding section would lead to this conclusion. Young and Yager deny that this is either desirable or feasible.

Pointing out that although long-term yields may indeed fail to decline during recessions after an initial fall, or fail to rise after an initial increase during booms, the authors argue that this is no evidence of monetary policy failure, let alone failure of the links between market sectors. Taking the recession of 1957–1958 as a case in point—a case in which the differential between long- and short-term rates reached a record high level—they contend that this disparity "suggests that, by the Spring of 1958, monetary policy had come to make its maximum contribution to economic recovery."[30] That long-term yields did not fall further, after the initial decline, "reflected strong private and governmental demands for funds, current and prospective, at the reduced levels of long-term rates."[31]

Examination of flow of funds and saving data for this period indicates that credit and equity funds fell from an increase of $11.8 billions in the fourth quarter of 1957 to an increase of only $3.0 billion in the first quarter of 1958. The third quarter of 1957 increase had been about $900 million higher than the fourth quarter. Long-term government bond yields fell from 3.73 to 3.30 in the fourth quarter of 1957, when investment demand was still high, and only to 3.25 by the end of the first quarter of 1958, when demand had fallen to a very low quarterly level. In the second quarter (spring) of 1958, funds raised increased by $13.7 billion over the previous quarter and then fell again to an increase of 5.9 in the third quarter of 1958. Beginning in the spring quarter, long-term bond yields began to increase. Most of the increase came in the slack third quarter when the average yield went from 3.19 to 3.75. This was prior to the very large fourth-quarter 1958 increase of $22.7 billion in equity and credit funds raised.

These data tend to indicate a substantial lag between changes in long-term rates and changes in spending and are not inconsistent with the Young-Yager hypothesis stated above. However, for every fortuitous example of the benefits that flow from a hands-off policy in the long-term market, the economist can offer a different period to illustrate the need for intervention. From the beginning of the recession in the early summer of 1953 to the end of November, for example—a period of seven months —long-term bonds fell by just more than ⅛ of 1 per cent. One could hardly describe this stability as the result of heavy prospective and present demand for funds.

As a second major defense of bills only, Young and Yager assert that "little empirical evidence is available to illuminate the problem of the relative elasticities of financing demand and total demand to changes in long- and short-term interest rates. It can hardly be contended, accordingly, that a firm basis exists for specifying what shape of yield curve is most appropriate to the given stage of the economic cycle."[32] This contention leads to the conclusion that the central bank should confine itself to the control of bank reserves on which credit is based, leaving to private market forces the tasks of allocating available funds between market sectors and establishing interest rates.

This argument is really not against long-term operations, but rather against an attempt by the Federal Reserve to establish a particular yield curve during a particular phase of the economic cycle. That the two kinds of arguments differ can be seen from the fact that the System could conduct its dynamic open-market operations in the long end of the maturity range, leaving short-term rates to adjust to their own level. While it is true, furthermore, that the appropriate yield curve is not always known, much can be inferred from particular existing yield curves. Failure of monetary policy to stem inflationary investment booms in the period following the Accord suggests that, at least possible, the yield curves that developed were *not* appropriate. These were marked by rapidly rising short-term yields, slowly rising long-term yields, and, often, a pre-recession yield curve in which short-term securities were yielding nearly as much as, or more than, long terms. This suggests that booms are rather insensitive to short-term yield changes and that higher long-term rates would have been appropriate. This is also suggested by economic theory.[33]

Young and Yager would prefer the use of market techniques that yield the least possible market disruption and undesirable "feedback" effects consistent with the achievement of policy goals. This would be agreed to by all students of the problem. A difficulty exists, however, in that long-term operations, which we have contended will be desirable at certain times, are more disruptive to dealer functions than short-term purchases and sales. As we have seen, dealer functions include taking risk positions in all sectors of the market. Such positions in the long-term sector are more hazardous, and therefore less likely to be assumed, when the System is operating in the long maturities.

The writer believes that the disturbances in the long-term market occasioned by System purchases and sales have been considerably exaggerated by the proponents of bills only. In the first place, there is little evidence that System withdrawal from intervention in this sector materially improved its depth, breadth, and resiliency. One empirical study of the matter offers the conclusion that the market behaved less well in the period after the adoption of bills only than before. Price spreads became wider on a day-to-day basis (lack of depth); the ownership of debt has not widened when important investor groups are considered (lack of breadth); and nonself-correcting price movements have occurred in at least two periods (lack of resiliency).[34]

In the second place, the proper functioning of the long-term market depends at least as much on adequate dealer financing of inventory as on the possible impact of System intervention. Indeed, dealers complain of the forced withdrawal from long-term positions occasioned by tight-money policies. When dealer financing is short and expensive, a clear-cut tendency to avoid taking positions in long-term securities is often observed. In this view, a poorly functioning long-term market is the natural concomitant of tight money. If long-term operations are at times required, and dealers cannot live with them, it would seem that, so far from seeking to accommodate the present market institutions, the feasibility of other arrangements should be explored.

Bills Only and the Term Structure of Interest Rates

In one very important sense, the bills only controversy involves the question of whether the central bank can affect the term structure of interest rates, apart from its acknowledged power to influence the *level* of the yield curve of government securities. This question is of considerable practical importance at certain times; for example, when the economy is in severe recession and the spread between short- and long-term rates is unusually large, or when international payments considerations appear to dictate high short-term yields at a time when domestic economic conditions dictate lower rates and monetary expansion. At such times the ability of the central bank to generate a yield curve different from that which would obtain in the absence of its direct intervention in various maturities is of crucial importance and involves the validity of hypotheses concerning the term structure of interest rates.

. One such hypothesis which has dominated monetary thought is that long-term rates are averages of current and expected short-term rates. This expectational hypothesis has been challenged by the institutional hypothesis, according to which the term structure of interest rates is influenced by the existence of suppliers of funds to certain segments of the market for whom securities of other maturities are not perfect substitutes. According to the latter view, yields in any maturity sector may be permanently affected by the *supply* of securities in that sector, a result that cannot be explained by the expectational hypothesis.[35]

In his recent work on the term structure, Meiselman has reconciled the two theories by pointing out that the expectational hypothesis only requires that

market excess demand schedules of securities of given maturities tend to be infinitely elastic at rates consistent with current and expected short-term rates. Of course, it is not necessary that all transactors have infinitely elastic schedules . . . . It is only necessary that one class of adequately financed transactors have [such a schedule] . . . . Speculators with given expectations adjust quantities of securities taken from or supplied to the market *in order* to maintain the structure of rates consistent with expectations.[36]

It is apparent that the institutional hypothesis is consistent with the probable success of central bank attempts to impose a given yield structure in the market. As long as excess demand schedules are highly inelastic at current and expected short-term rates, so long can the monetary authority (or the Treasury, for that matter) permanently impose a given yield structure by controlling the relative supplies of securities in particular maturity sectors.

The interposition of "adequately financed transactors" with infinitely elastic excess demand schedules complicates the central bank's task. For example, if the bank wishes to bring down long-term yields *relative* to short-term yields, the impact of its operations in the long-term market (purchases) may be largely offset by sales by speculators, the purpose of which is to maintain the structure of rates consistent with their expectations. Since the proceeds of such sales are unlikely to be kept idle, the speculators will undoubtedly purchase short-term securities, a fact which, given our initial assumptions, should lead to concurrent sales by the central bank. In effect, this situation leads to a two-way swapping operation between speculators and the central bank.

The outcome of the game would seem to depend upon the resources of the players. Here Meiselman's qualification that transactors be "adequately financed" is not important; what is required is that speculators have enough long-term bonds in inventory (or power to issue them) to offset the purchases of bonds by the central bank. Since the bank is at worst constrained by its supply of short-term securities, it seems unreasonable to suppose, given the supplies of securities in the Federal Reserves portfolio, either that (1) speculators' supplies will be adequate or that (2) ultimately expectations will not be modified by the central bank's action.[37] In effect, speculators can ignore the central bank in their calculations only if the bank is in fact committed to a neutral policy with respect to "the rate of interest."

CONCLUSIONS

The bills only controversy has engaged the attention of academic economists and Federal Reserve officials for more than a decade. Until recently, the latter tended to a rather adamant position against the use of direct operations in long-term government securities. This position has been based upon both broadly philosophical grounds, stressing the values of a "free money market," and upon pragmatic considerations involving the possible impact of such intervention on the functioning of the securities markets and the effectiveness of monetary policy.

Most academic economists have argued that circumstances and the objectives of monetary control can best be served at times by direct purchase and sales of long-term bonds. They contend that private market allocation of funds does not always result in a structure of interest rates that is most appropriate to monetary control. We have concluded that this view is essentially correct.

The contention that long-term operations are justified at certain times is made in spite of full agreement with Federal Reserve officials that day-to-day defense operations can best be effected in the short-term maturities. This, however, should not obscure the fundamental differences between monetary theorists and practitioners that have come to light as a result of the bills only controversy. Needless to say, many of these remain to be resolved.

Notes

1. See Board of Governors of the Federal Reserve System, *Annual Report*, 1953, p. 88, for a complete statement of the new "ground rules" governing open-market operations.
2. The full text of this report is published in *U.S. Monetary Policy: Recent Thinking and Experience*, Hearings before the Subcommittee on Economic Stabilization of the Joint Committee on the Economic Report, 83rd Congress, 2nd Session. Hereafter referred to as *Hearings*.
3. Board of Governors of the Federal Reserve System, *Annual Report*, 1953, p. 88. These "ground rules" were rescinded by the Open Market Committee on June 11, 1953, on motion of Mr. Sproul, only to be reinstated at the next meeting held September 24, 1953. Members Sproul and Powell were alone in opposing the latter action.
4. For *ad hoc* subcommittee analysis of these replies see *Hearings*, pp. 292–299.
5. *Ibid.*, p. 266.
6. *Ibid.*, p. 267.
7. *Ibid.*, p. 300.
8. *Ibid.*, p. 301. For an interesting discussion of the relationship between the Treasury bill rate and the customer loan rate see D. A. Alhadeff, "Monetary Policy and the Treasury Bill Market," *American Economic Review*, LII (June, 1952), 326–346.
9. *Hearings*, p. 23.
10. *Ibid.*, p. 229.
11. *Ibid.*, p. 304.
12. *Ibid.*, p. 298. The fact that long-term federal bonds "broke 90" without System intervention shortly after the new directives were adopted indicates the strength of its conviction in this respect.
13. *Ibid.*, p. 268, italics mine.
14. *Ibid.*, p. 21.
15. *The Three Banks Review*, No. 29, March, 1956.
16. Perhaps as a result of much academic criticism of the bills only policy: cf. P. A. Samuelson, *loc. cit.;* Deane Carson, "Recent Open Market Policy and Tech-

nique," *Quarterly Journal of Economics,* LXIX (August, 1955); Alvin Hansen, "Monetary Policy," *Review of Economics and Statistics,* XXXVII (May, 1955); E. Wood, "Recent Monetary Policies," *Journal of Finance,* X (September, 1955); S. Weintraub, "Monetary Policy: Comment," *Review of Economics and Statistics,* XXXVII (August, 1955); Deane Carson, "Federal Reserve Support of Treasury Refunding Operations," *Journal of Finance,* VI (March, 1957); D. G. Luckett, "Bills Only: A Critical Appraisal," *Review of Economics and Statistics,* XLII (August, 1960). A more favorable academic view of the Federal Reserve's position is found in D. Fand and I. O. Scott, Jr., "The Federal Reserve Ssystem's 'Bills Only' Policy: A Suggested Interpretation," *The Journal of Business of the University of Chicago,* January, 1958.

17. *Hearings,* p. 55.

18. *Loc. cit.*

19. See, for example, Allan Meltzer's testimony before the House Banking and Currency Committee's subcommittee on Domestic Finance on February 11, 1964.

20. W. W. Riefler, "Open Market Operations in Long-Term Securities," *Federal Reserve Bulletin* (November, 1958), pp. 1260–1274.

21. *Ibid.,* p. 1264.

22. *Ibid.*

23. *Ibid.,* p. 1267.

24. Riefler, in fact, states this explicitly on page 1263.

25. An excellent discussion of defensive and dynamic System operations is found in R. V. Roosa, *Federal Reserve Operations in the Money and Government Securities Markets* (Federal Reserve Bank of New York, 1956).

26. Since early 1961 more flexibility has been adopted in response to peculiar domestic and international balance of payments conditions.

27. Unfortunately, the use of debt management as a countercyclical device has been inhibited by lack of demand in booms and emerging demand in recession. Dealers have come to expect the Treasury to lengthen debt whenever conditions are favorable.

28. R. A. Young and C. A. Yager, "The Economics of 'Bills Preferably'," *Quarterly Journal of Economics,* LXXIV (August, 1960).

29. The System, in fact, did not confine its operations to Treasury bills during the period. Other short-term debt was involved, ranging up to eighteen months in maturity.

30. Young and Yager, *op. cit.,* p. 366.

31. *Ibid.,* p. 367.

32. *Ibid.,* p. 365.

33. Young and Yager apparently feel that one "received theory" is as good as another, or perhaps equally bad, as a guide to monetary policy. Their reference to the theory that short-term rates are of primary causal importance to the business cycle was last seriously entertained by R. G. Hawtrey in the 1920's, and had reference to an economic organization that probably antedated World War I.

34. D. G. Luckett, " 'Bills Only': A Critical Appraisal," *Review of Economics and Statistics,* XLII (August, 1960), pp. 301–303.

35. See F. A. Lutz, "The Structure of Interest Rates," *Quarterly Journal of Economics,* LX (1940–1941), 54–55 n.

36. David Meiselman, *The Term Structure of Interest Rates* (Englewood Cliffs, N.J.: Prentice-Hall, Inc., 1962), p. 57. Italics mine.

37. If one accepts the expectations theory, or better, Meiselman's variant of expectations theory, the conclusion is inescapable that long-run changes in the yield curve consequent upon Treasury or central bank alterations in the supply of securities of various maturities must be accompanied by a change in expectations as to "the interest rate".

Some have cited the "failure" of "operation twist" or "nudge" in the period after 1961 as evidence that the monetary authorities cannot permanently change the shape of the structure of rates. See J. R. Schlesinger, "The Sequel to Bills Only," *Review of Economics and Statistics,* XLIV (1962), 184–189. On the contrary, this episode is not conclusive, since the Federal Reserve's operations in the long-term market were neither vigorous nor sustained.

The Integration of Simple Growth and Cycle Models

Hyman P. Minsky

INTRODUCTION

VARIOUS ceiling models of cycles or cyclical growth have appeared.[1] In all except one, Kurihara's model, the rate of growth of the ceiling is exogenous. However, the saving and investing that takes place as income is at or below the ceiling implies that the ceiling grows. This paper investigates the conditions under which the rate of growth of ceiling income, as generated by the demand-determined division of income between investment and consumption, is sufficiently large that self-sustained growth can take place.

Existing econometric income models can be divided into two broad classes: short-run forecasting and long-run growth. The short-run forecasting models are basically extensions of the simple Keynesian aggregate demand-determining models. The long-run growth models assume that sufficient aggregate demand always exists and investigate the implications of various patterns of input changes for the growth of capacity.

In many ways, the most interesting analytical and forecasting range is neither the very short run nor the very long run. An intermediate horizon, of ten to fifteen years, is of great practical interest for economic policy, for this is the time span that encompasses the possibility of major or deep depression cycles. Although it is legitimate in constructing short-run forecasting models to ignore the impact of investment upon productive capacity and of finance upon the stock of financial instruments outstanding, over a ten- or fifteen-year period these small changes will cumulate and be of decisive importance in determining system behavior. On the other hand, the standard strategy in constructing long-run models is to assume that the impact of financial variables

175

can wash out. Thus, both practical and theoretical possibilities open up when an intermediate horizon is adopted.

Recent work in the long waves in economic growth rates[2] and on mild and deep depression cycles[3] also indicate that a complete model of the income-determining process that can be iterated to generate a ten- to fifteen-year time series is of interest.

Both the short-run and the long-run models are one-sided, in that they are concerned with either aggregate demand or aggregate supply, and incomplete, in that they do not include, in any deep sense, monetary and financial phenomena. Friedman and Schwartz[4] have imputed the observed pattern of cycles to the behavior of quite narrowly defined money; Tobin,[5] implicitly, and Minsky,[6] explicitly, have examined the implications of financial factors for the longer waves. Aside from the previously mentioned paper by Kurihara, scant attention has been paid to how the productive capacity ceiling is generated, or to the interaction of the production ceiling with demand determination. In this short paper we shall undertake only a part of the total analytical work, and we shall essentially ignore the monetary-financial feedbacks in the growth process. What will be undertaken is to integrate aggregate demand and supply determination in an income model.

Special attention will be paid to those conditions which must be satisfied if self-sustained growth is to take place. Our results show that self-sustained growth is not likely, except as an intermittent phenomenon, unless inflation succeeds in curtailing consumption, or technological progress, whether embodied or disembodied, raises the rate of growth of ceiling income. With a sufficiently rapid rate of growth of ceiling income, the ceiling constraints will not necessarily trigger a downturn. Thus, once again, we have to turn to the characteristics of the aggregate demand-determining relation to generate a downturn. In the conclusion it is suggested that if the coefficient of induced investment decreases as a result of financial changes, a downturn can take place because the rate of growth of ceiling income needed to maintain growth increases. That is, as a self-sustained growth process matures, it becomes necessary to run faster in order to stay in the same place.

THE INGREDIENTS

A simple income model that allows for both the behavior of aggregate demand and supply can be built out of well-known ingredients. To be precise, the model that will be discussed here consists of:

(1) a demand generating relation which is the familiar Hansen-Samuelson[7] accelerator-multiplier model,

(2) a maximum supply (or productive capacity or ceiling income) generating relation derived from the Harrod-Domar[8] growth models,

(3) a minimum supply (or floor income) generating relation which is based on the assumption that there exists (a) a part of consumption (and perhaps investment) demand which is independent of current income, although not necessarily of past incomes or of the value of the capital stock, and (b) a maximum to the disinvestment that can take place per period, which is related to the size of the capital stock and hence to the maximum supply.

(4) a reconciliation relation which states that actual income equals aggregate demand unless aggregate demand exceeds the maximum aggregate supply or falls below the minimum aggregate supply, in which case actual income will equal the appropriate aggregate supply.

Due to our present interest in self-sustained growth, the implications of assumption (3) will be ignored. This will enable us to simplify our demand-determining functions and write these as homogeneous relations. In another paper,[9] I have examined how the nonhomogeneous portions of these equations affect both the interval of time for which self-sustained growth can take place, if the ceiling is not growing rapidly enough to sustain growth permanently, and the depth of the depression.

Self-sustained growth takes place when actual income and maximum supply income grow without the existence of any exogenous growth stimulating factor, i.e., an internally sustained state of steady growth. Within the framework of the Hansen-Samuelson plus Harrod-Domar integrated model under discussion, this means that the maximum aggregate supply is growing at a sufficiently high rate so that, with actual income equal to this maximum supply income, the demand induced by the achieved level and rate of change of income is sufficient to utilize fully the increasing productive capacity.

Standing by itself, the Hansen-Samuelson model states that income is determined by aggregate demand. In periods when demand is not constrained by aggregate supply, this Keynsian assumption is valid, especially if the nonhomogeneous part of the consumption function depends upon wealth which, of course, is a reflection of the economy's capital stock. With this interpretation of the Hansen-Samuelson model, the consumption function of this part of the integrated model is said to determine *ex-ante* consumption, and the accelerator based investment function is interpreted as determining *ex-ante* investment.

The second-order difference equation of the Hansen-Samuelson model is simple framework that yields the variety of time series necessary for cyclical analysis and also the possibility of a *one-shot* turning point based upon initial conditions, which is vital for our analysis.

We assume that at any date the maximum available supply depends upon the existing capital stock. This capital stock changes by the amount of net investment. The rate of change of aggregate supply depends upon the net investment that occurs, and its productive efficiency. This obviously means that the saving coefficient of the Harrod-Domar part of the integrated model is an *ex-post* saving coefficient.

The productive efficiency of investment put into place relates the change in aggregate supply to the change in capital stock. As such it is an incremental output/capital coefficient. The way in which the Harrod-Domar growth model is typically written focuses attention on the reciprocal of the output/capital coefficient, the capital-output ratio. This way of writing the productive efficiency of investment makes it easy to assume that the productive efficiency of investment in the aggregate supply-determining relation is the reciprocal of the coefficient of induced investment in the demand-determining relation.

The coefficients of induced investment and of the productive efficiency of investment are two quite different things. The coefficient of induced investment—the accelerator coefficient in the relation that determines *ex-ante* investment—is in part based upon the productive efficiency of investment, but it is also related to the willingness of investors to take risks and the terms upon which investors can finance their endeavors. In spite of this recognition of the difference between the coefficients of induced investment and the productive efficiency of investment, we will initially assume that they are equal. This enables us to focus on the extent to which adjustments in consumption make it possible for self-sustained growth to occur.

The reconciliation relation, as used here, is a purely formal assertion that supply is, if necessary, an effective constraint. The really deep economics in any ceiling model focus on how supply is rationed. Whether consumption or investment demand, or both in varying degrees, are cut back is a result of market processes.

The model as set out here is not sufficiently complete to cover these phenomena. The function of financial markets is to ration investment funds. The available nominal supply of investment funds depends upon the functioning of the financial system. The ability of the financial system to constrain consumption depends upon the existing and desired portfolios of households. An integration of financial phenomena with the real demand- and supply-generating relations would be necessary to enable us to deal more precisely with the reconciliation relations.

We can look at the rationing process a bit more closely even without constructing a formal model of the financial system. In the diagram below,

Log Y_c is the ceiling income and at each date t, aggregate demand is greater than the ceiling, i.e., the ceiling is an effective determinant of income. Given that the demand for consumption goods is determined by

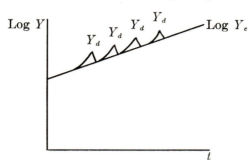

income of the t-1st period, consumers have the "cash in hand" to finance, at existing prices, the purchase of the consumption component of Y_d. However, investors, independent of the separation between saving and investing units, have to finance investment in excess of planned saving.

This presumably requires changes that increase velocity or the money supply. To the extent that investment can be cut back to the difference between productive capacity and planned consumption without any rise in interest rates, the income-generating process need not be affected. However, if the rationing phenomenon results in a rise in interest rates (or its equivalent, a rise in the price of investment goods as against consumption goods), then the income-generating process will be affected. If we make the Keynsian assumption that consumption demand is independent of interest rates, but assume that investment demand, and hence the β coefficient, depends upon interest rates, then a rising set of interest rates will lower the β coefficient. A fall in β raises the minimum rate of growth of capacity that leads to demand's rising faster than capacity, when income is at the ceiling. Thus the reconciliation process can affect the effect of the ceiling by raising the rate of growth required to sustain growth.

The assumption that changes in the size of the capital stock are the sole determinants of the rate of growth of productive capacity is, of course, heroic. The alternative is to adopt a production function which allows for factor substitution and relate ceiling output growth to the growth of the labor force as well as capital equipment. However, once we assume that technological change occurs, the growth of capacity will not be dependent solely upon the growth of the capital stock. As is usual, the technological change coefficient becomes a catchall that allows not only for technical progress, but also for differential growth rates of the labor force and capital and the improvement of the labor force due to education, public health, etc.

As a result, within a Harrod-Domar framework for the growth of capacity, we allow for both embodied and disembodied technical change. Embodied technical change works by way of the capital put into place and, in our formulation, will result in a rise in the productive efficiency of investment. Disembodied technical change results in a rise in productive capacity that is independent of the amount of investment put into place. Such "progress" is as inevitable and well-nigh as universal as the passage of time; and, like time, it covers a multitude of sins.

THE FORMAL MODEL

The formal model can be written as:

$$(1) \qquad Y_n^s = Y_{n-1}^s + \frac{I_{n-1}^a}{\bar\beta}$$

$$(2) \qquad C_n^d = \alpha Y_{n-1}^a$$

$$(3) \qquad C_n^s = \bar\alpha Y_n^s$$

$$(4) \qquad C_n^a = \lambda_1 C_n^d + \lambda_2 C_n^s$$

$$(5) \qquad I_n^d = \beta(Y_{n-1}^a - Y_{n-2}^a)$$

$$(6) \qquad I_n^s = (1 - \bar\alpha) Y_n^s$$

$$(7) \qquad I_n^a = \lambda_1 I_n^d + \lambda_2 I_n^s$$

$$(8) \qquad Y_n^a = C_n^a + I_n^a$$

$$(9) \qquad \lambda_1 = 1 \quad \text{if} \quad Y_n^d = C_n^d + I_n^d \le Y_n^s$$
$$= 0 \quad \text{otherwise}$$

$$(10) \qquad \lambda_1 + \lambda_2 = 1.$$

C, I, and Y have their usual meanings, the superscript a means actual, d means demand and s = supply, α = ex-ante marginal (= average in these models) propensity to consume, β = ex-ante coefficient of induced investment, $\bar\alpha$ is the ex-post marginal (= average in these models) propensity to consume, and $1/\bar\beta$ = ex-post productive efficiency of investment (i.e., the marginal output per unit of investment coefficient). The switching coefficients λ_1 and λ_2 have no interpretation aside from their definition in equations (9) and (10). The subscripts $_{n'n-1}$ on Y, C, and I refer to the dates.

Behavior of Aggregate Supply

Equation (1) states that the change in aggregate supply depends upon the investment put into place. Equation (1) plus equation (6) yields us the familiar Harrod-Domar growth model where the rate of growth depends upon the saving and the investment coefficients. For we have

$$Y_n^s = Y_{n-1}^s + \frac{(1 - \bar{\alpha})}{\bar{\beta}} Y_{n-1}^s$$

(11) $$\bar{v} = Y_n^s / Y_{n-1}^s = 1 + \frac{1 - \bar{\alpha}}{\bar{\beta}}$$

and

$$Y_n^s / Y_{n-2}^s = Y_n^s / Y_{n-1}^s \cdot Y_{n-1}^s / Y_{n-2}^s = \left(1 + \frac{1 - \bar{\alpha}}{\bar{\beta}}\right)\left(1 + \frac{1 - \bar{\alpha}}{\bar{\beta}}\right) = \bar{v}^2,$$

so that

(12) $$Y_n^s = Y_0 \bar{v}^n$$

where $\bar{v}$ is the rate of growth of aggregate supply when income actually equals supply income. The above is the familiar result: that the rate of growth of income is a constant, given that the *ex-post* saving coefficient and the *ex-post* marginal output-capital ratio are constants. This result, of course, holds within our model when $\lambda_2 = 1$. If $\lambda_1 = 1$, then

$$Y_n^s = Y_{n-1}^s + \frac{\beta(Y_{n-2}^a - Y_{n-3}^a)}{\bar{\beta}},$$

$$v_{n-1}^s = Y_n^s / Y_{n-1}^s = 1 + \frac{\beta}{\bar{\beta}} \frac{Y_{n-1}^a}{Y_{n-1}^s} \left(\frac{Y_{n-2}^a - Y_{n-3}^a}{Y_{n-1}^a}\right),$$

(13) $$v_{n-1}^s = 1 + \frac{\beta}{\bar{\beta}} \frac{Y_{n-1}^a}{Y_{n-1}^s} \left(\frac{v_{n-3}^a - 1}{v_{n-3}^a v_{n-2}^a}\right).$$

The rate of growth of the maximum available supply depends upon:
(1) the ratio of the coefficient of induced investment to the capital-output ratio,
(2) the ratio of actual income to the maximum aggregate supply, and
(3) the rate of change of actual income in the previous two periods.
As (2) and (3) are variables, the rate of growth of maximum supply income is also a variable. Of course v_{n-3}^a can be less than 1, which means that the maximum supply income can decrease.
Note that as long as

$$\beta(Y_{n-2}^a - Y_{n-3}^a) < (1 - \bar{\alpha})Y_{n-1}^s, \qquad v_{n-1}^s < \bar{v},$$

there is no way that lost growth in productive capacity can be made up unless $v_{n-1}^{\bullet} < \bar{v}$ implies that subsequent $1/\bar{\beta}$'s will be larger than they otherwise would have been.

BEHAVIOR OF AGGREGATE DEMAND

Equation (2) plus equation (5), together with a definition of income as $C^d + I^d$, yields the Hansen-Samuelson accelerator-multiplier model. As is well known, the characteristics of the time series which this model will generate depend upon the values of α and β. We assume that normally a certain minimum buoyancy of entrepreneurs and investors exists so that the coefficient of induced investment is sufficiently greater than 1 that in the solution equation

$$(14) \qquad\qquad Y_n = A_1\mu_1^n + A_2\mu_2^n,$$

we have that $\mu_1 > \mu_2 > 1$. The values of μ_1 and μ_2 are

$$(15) \qquad
\begin{aligned}
\mu_1 &= \frac{\alpha + \beta + \sqrt{(\alpha + \beta)^2 - 4\beta}}{2}, \\[2mm]
\mu_2 &= \frac{\alpha + \beta - \sqrt{(\alpha + \beta)^2 - 4\beta}}{2}.
\end{aligned}$$

The values of A_1 and A_2 are determined by the initial conditions.

Assuming that the two initial conditions are Y_0, $Y_1 > 0$ and that $Y_1 = \tau Y_0$, $\tau > 1$. We then have

$$Y_0 = A_1 + A_2$$

$$\tau Y_0 = A_1\mu_1 + A_2\mu_2$$

so that

$$(16) \qquad
\begin{cases}
A_1 = \dfrac{\tau - \mu_2}{\mu_1 - \mu_2}\, Y_0 \\[4mm]
A_2 = \dfrac{\mu_1 - \tau}{\mu_1 - \mu_2}\, Y_0
\end{cases}$$

if $\mu_1 > \tau \geq \mu_2$, $A_1 \geq 0$, $A_2 > 0$; however, if $\mu_1 > \mu_2 > \tau$, then $A_1 < 0$. As A_1 is the coefficient of the larger root, $A_1 < 0$ implies that in time $A_1\mu_1^n + A_2\mu_2^n < 0$, so that the "explosion" of income will be in the direction opposite from the initial displacement. Even if the roots of the solution equation are real and greater than 1, the time series generated by the solution equation can generate one turning point. The cause of this turning point lies in the initial conditions. If the initial conditions do not supply a sufficient push to income, a turning point will result. The minimum push that will yield a monotonic explosive series is given by μ_2, the smaller root of the solution equation.

BEHAVIOR OF THE INTEGRATED MODEL

We can now sketch how the integrated model operates. The essential question is what happens when demand income exceeds supply income. As the pattern of behavior of the model is independent of where we begin, we can in all generality assume that the two initial incomes, Y_0 and Y_1, are both less than the maximum supply income and that

$$Y_1/Y_0 = \tau > \mu_2$$

so that a particular solution of the income-generating function $Y_n^d = A_1\mu_1^n + A_2\mu_2^n$ with $A_1, A_2 > 0$ and $\mu_1 > \mu_2 > 1$ will be set in motion to generate future demands. As long as $Y_n^d < Y_n^s$, actual income will be determined by this particular income-generating relation. However, as $A_1 > 0$, the rate of change of actual income will in time approach μ_1, the larger of the two roots. But values of α, β which lead to a μ_2 in the neighborhood of achieved rates of growth, generate a μ_1 that is far larger than observed rates of growth. Hence in time

$$Y_n^d = A_1\mu_1^n + A_2\mu_2^n > Y_n^s$$

will result. This means that actual income will be Y_n^s and all of demand will not be realized.

Before examining how the reconciliation process is carried out when $Y_n^d > Y_n^s$, and noting the implications of some reconciliations for the generation of self-sustained growth, it is best if we interpret the switch that occurs when $Y_n^d > Y_n^s$. Y_n^d is the result of a self-sustaining demand-generating process based upon the structural characteristics of the economy and some initial conditions. Such an income-generating process once set in motion will not generate actual incomes for all times in the future. The path of actual income will be affected by exogenous events and constraints as well as the structural elements and history embodied in the ruling demand-generating relation. These exogeneous events and constraints are interpreted as determining new initial conditions for a particular demand-determining relation that will determine aggregate demand as long as no external event or constraint prevents this demand income from being realized. Hence whenever $Y_n^a \neq Y_n^d$, Y_n^a and Y_{n-1}^a are new initial conditions for a demand-determining relation. Within our framework this new demand-determining relation will determine actual incomes until the incomes so determined are inconsistent with the supply constraints, for we are ignoring external shocks in this paper.

When Y^d is inconsistent with Y^s, then actual values of C and/or I will differ from their demand or *ex ante* values. The problem now becomes to what extent the cutback Y^d to Y^s takes the form of a reduction of consumption or of a reduction of investment. Equations (3) and (6), which tell us how income, when it is equal to aggregate supply, is divided between consumption and investment, do not describe how the reconciliation process affects consumption and investment.

When $Y_n^d > Y_n^s$, then $Y_n^a = Y_n^s$. This means that new initial conditions, Y_n^s and Y_{n-1}^a, determine A_1 and A_2 in a specific demand-generating relation. If $Y_n^s/Y_{n-1}^a < \mu_2$, then $A_1 < 0$ and a single turning point will be generated, whereas if $Y_n^s/Y_{n-1}^a \geq \mu_2$, then $A_1 \geq 0$ and $Y_{n+1}^d/Y_n^s > Y_{n+1}^s/Y_n^s$ will be generated so that Y_{n+1}^s becomes the $n + 1^{st}$ period's actual income. In this case we know that $Y_{n+1}^s/Y_n^s = \bar{\nu}$ and steady growth will take place if $\bar{\nu} \geq \mu_2$ and a single turning point will be generated if $\mu_2 > \bar{\nu}$. Steady growth is the result of setting off new demand-generating processes each period which in the next period generate demand that is equal or greater than supply, whereas the turning point with the accompanying fall of income below supply occurs if the demand-generating process leads to a smaller increase in demand than in supply.

Hence, whether steady growth or a cyclical downturn occurs when the available supply becomes a determinant of actual income depends upon the rate of growth of aggregate supply; this model is a ceiling model of cycles and growth. However, as aggregate supply is growing, it is the rate of growth of aggregate supply rather than the existence of some fixed ceiling to productive capacity that is the critical factor. As there is no doubt that the rate of growth of supply that can be sustained when the economy is at or close to full employment is lower than the rate of growth of income that does take place when the economy is recovering from a depression, a decrease in the rate of growth of actual income occurs when income approaches aggregate supply income. This decrease in the rate of growth of actual income is the critical constraint in this model.[10]

THE POSSIBILITY OF SELF-SUSTAINED GROWTH

The rate of growth of aggregate supply is given by

$$\bar{\nu} = 1 + \frac{1 - \bar{\alpha}}{\bar{\beta}}$$

and the lower root of the solution equation is given by

$$\mu_2 = \frac{\alpha + \beta - \sqrt{(\alpha + \beta)^{2-4}}}{2}.$$

From these equations we get:

(17)
$$\beta = \frac{\mu_2(\mu_2 - \alpha)}{\mu_2 - 1},$$

(18)
$$\bar{\beta} = \frac{1 - \bar{\alpha}}{\bar{\nu} - 1},$$

which are straight lines in α, β and $\bar{\alpha}$, $\bar{\beta}$. (Given that $\mu_2 > 1$, the domain of α and β is restricted.) If we assume $\alpha = \bar{\alpha}$, $\beta = \bar{\beta}$, $0 < \alpha < 1$, and $\beta > 0$, then for any α, β pair $\mu_2 > \bar{\nu}$; that is, the rate of growth of productive capacity will be below the minimum rate of growth of income that must take place if self-sustained growth is to occur.

This is illustrated in Figure 1. For example, at point A, $\alpha \approx .92$ and $\beta \approx 2.825$ yield $\mu_2 = 1.05$ and $\bar{\nu} = 1.03$. Hence, if $Y_n^d = Y_n^s$, $Y_{n-1}^d = Y_{n-1}^s$ the demand-generating relation set into motion with Y_n^s, Y_{n-1}^s as initial conditions will have $A_1 < 0$ which implies that growth will not be self-sustained.

For self-sustained growth to occur, it is necessary for α and β to be "greater" than $\bar{\alpha}$ and $\bar{\beta}$. For example, if α and β are such that they lie along the line $\mu_2 = 1.04$, then $\bar{\alpha}$ and $\bar{\beta}$ must be such that they lie on or below the line $\bar{\nu} = 1.04$ if self-sustained growth is to occur. In Figure 1, self-sustained growth would be attainable if the set of lines $\bar{\nu} = 1.03$, etc. could be shifted upward so that for every $\bar{\nu} = \mu_2$ the line for $\bar{\nu}$ would lie above the line for μ_2. For this to occur, some combination of factors that tend to yield $\bar{\alpha} < \alpha$ and $\bar{\beta} < \beta$ must be operative.

Ex-Ante and Ex-Post Consumptions

The assumption that $\alpha = \bar{\alpha}$, given that $C_n^s = \bar{\alpha} Y_n^s$ and $C_n^\alpha = \alpha Y_{n-1}^s$ and that $Y_n^s = \bar{\nu} Y_{n-1}^s$, implies that $C_n^s = C_n^\alpha > C_n^d$. The rise in income between the nth and the $n - 1^{st}$ period results in ex-post consumption being larger than ex-ante consumption. As supply income effectively determines income because $Y_n^d > Y_n^s$ and $C_n^a > C_n^d$, the entire burden of adjustment is upon investment.

Rather than assume that ex-post consumption exceeds ex-ante consumption, we can assume that ex-post consumption equals ex-ante consumption. If this occurs,

$$Y_n^s = Y_{n-1}^s + \frac{Y_{n-1}^s - \alpha Y_{n-2}^s}{\bar{\beta}},$$

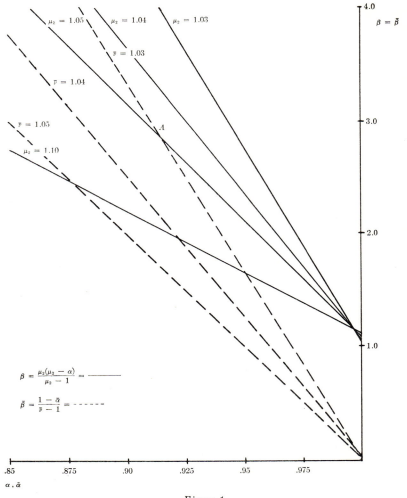

Figure 1

$$\nu_n = 1 + \frac{1 - \alpha/\bar{\nu}}{\bar{\beta}}.$$

From this we get

(19) $$\bar{\beta} = \frac{\bar{\nu} - \alpha}{\bar{\nu}(\bar{\nu} - 1)}.$$

As is illustrated in Figure 2, the lines for equation (19) also lie below the lines for equation (17), so that for any given α, $\beta = \bar{\beta}$ pair $\mu_2 > \bar{\nu}$. Even if *ex-post* consumption is restricted to *ex-ante* consumption, the adjustment process still results in *ex-post* investment being lower than *ex-ante* investment. The rate of growth of supply that results is too low to maintain self-sustained growth.

THE IMPACT OF INFLATION

In order to have $\bar{\nu} \geq \mu_2$ it is necessary that when $Y^d > Y^s$ (recall that we are assuming that $\beta = \bar{\beta}$), *ex-post* consumption be less than *ex-ante*

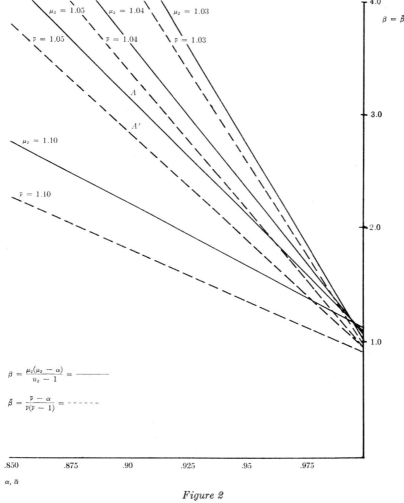

Figure 2
Ex-post C = Ex-ante C

consumption. One way in which consumers can be *forced* to lower their consumption below the *ex-ante* level is for consumer prices to rise; this is, of course, particularly true if a large portion of consumers use all their income for consumption and have no means by which they can spend more than their income. Writing p^* for $p_n/p_n - 1$, we have

$$\bar{\nu} = 1 + \frac{Y^s_{n-1} - \dfrac{\alpha Y^s_{n-2}}{p^*}}{Y^s_{n-1}\bar{\beta}}$$

$$= 1 + \frac{1 - \alpha/\bar{\nu}p^*}{\bar{\beta}}$$

so that

(20) $$\bar{\beta} = \frac{\bar{\nu}p^* - \alpha}{\bar{\nu}p^*(\bar{\nu} - 1)}.$$

Assuming $p^* > 1$, there exist values of α and β which generate rates of growth of aggregate supply that are larger than the lower root of the demand-generating relation. This means that if inflation that decreases consumption below *ex-ante* consumption occurs, self-sustained growth can take place. (Even though consumption is lowered below *ex-ante* consumption by inflation, with a constant rate of increase in consumers' prices, real consumption will still be growing:

$$\left(\frac{\alpha Y^s_{n-2}}{p^*} \Big/ \frac{\alpha Y^s_{n-3}}{p^*} = \bar{\nu} > 1 \right).$$

In Figure 3, point A shows that if $\alpha \approx .875$, $\beta \approx 3.675$ then $\mu_2 = 1.05$ and $\bar{\nu} = 1.05$ with $p^* = 1.02$. That is, if *ex-post* consumption is approximately 98 per cent of *ex-ante* consumption so that $Y^s_{n-1} - .98\alpha Y^s_{n-2}$ can be invested, real supply will grow at 5 per cent. Points B and C have similar interpretations.

It is doubtful that in the United States, as now organized, inflation is an efficient or an effective way of depressing consumption in order that investment be sufficient to generate a growth rate of income large enough to satisfy the conditions for self-sustained growth.

The Effect of Technological Change

We can distinguish two types of technical change. Disembodied technical change, where productive capacity increases independently of investment, and embodied technical change, where investment is the carrier of technical change.

Disembodied Technical Change

To take technical change into account, we write

(1¹) $$Y_n^s = \tau \, Y_{n-1}^s + \frac{I_{n-1}^a}{\beta}, \qquad \tau > 1.$$

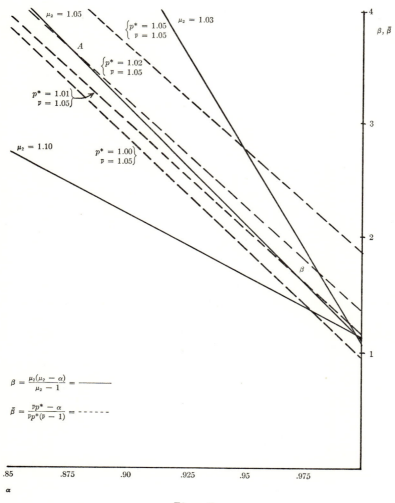

$$\beta = \frac{\mu_2(\mu_2 - \alpha)}{\mu_2 - 1} = \text{_____}$$

$$\bar{\beta} = \frac{\bar{\nu}p^* - \alpha}{\bar{\nu}p^*(\bar{\nu} - 1)} = \text{- - - - - -}$$

Figure 3
Effects of Inflation

This results, when income is at the ceiling, in

$$\frac{Y_n^s}{Y_{n-1}^s} = \tau + \frac{1 - \bar{\alpha}}{\bar{\beta}}$$

and, with less than capacity income, in

$$\frac{Y_n^s}{Y_{n-1}^s} = \tau + \frac{\beta}{\bar{\beta}} \frac{Y_{n-2}^a - Y_{n-3}^a}{Y_{n-1}^s}.$$

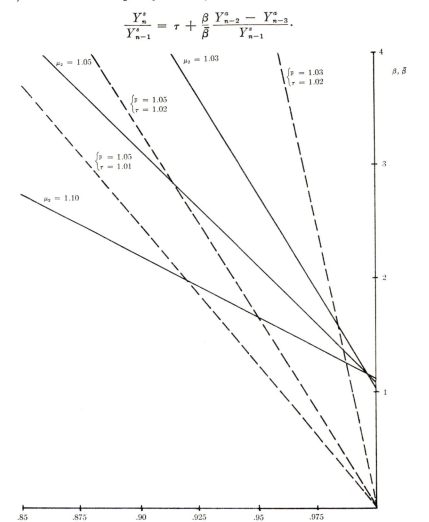

Figure 4
Disembodied Technological Change

The rate of growth of ceiling income, when income is at the ceiling, is

$$\bar{\nu}_1 = \tau + \frac{1 - \bar{\alpha}}{\bar{\beta}}$$

which yields

$$\bar{\beta} = \frac{1 - \bar{\alpha}}{\bar{\nu} - \tau}.$$

As is shown in Figure 4, with a 2 per cent per year growth in productive capacity due to disembodied technical change, it is possible with $\alpha = \bar{\alpha}$, $\beta = \bar{\beta}$ for the rate of growth of ceiling income $\bar{\nu}$ to be greater than the critical value μ_2 derived from the demand-generating relation.

Embodied Technical Change

We will assume that embodied technical change results in $\bar{\beta} < \beta$; i.e., the productive efficiency of investment is higher than "expected" because of technological progress.

In Figure 2, note that if $\alpha = .9$ and *ex-post* consumption equals *ex-ante* consumption, $\beta = 3.15$ and $\bar{\beta} = 2.85$ will yield $\mu_2 = \bar{\nu} = 1.05$, i.e., it takes but a small decline in $\bar{\beta}$ below β to satisfy the conditions for self-sustained growth.

CONCLUSIONS

Given that technological change, whether embodied or disembodied, takes place, and that the effect of technological change is to increase the rate of growth of ceiling income beyond that which would result just from accumulations, it has been shown that the ceiling income can grow fast enough so that self-sustained growth is possible. Therefore, in a technically dynamic world, we have to look beyond productive capacity constraints to explain the observed pattern of cyclical growth.

The coefficient of induced investment β is not a technical production function characteristic as is $\bar{\beta}$, but rather reflects investors' and entrepreneurs' attitudes toward risk. Thus, β would be a variable that depends, at least in part, on the menu of financial instruments available to asset owners and the liability structure of investing units.

In the demand-generating relation, the smaller root of the solution equation was the critical value for sustaining growth. However, the derivative of this coefficient, μ_2, with respect to β, the coefficient of induced investment, is negative.[11] Anything that tends to lower β will raise μ_2 and thus increase the minimum rate of growth of ceiling income that will sustain growth.

Cumulative unbalanced changes in the menu of available financial instruments take place during a period of self-sustained growth. The unbalanced nature of financial developments should affect the relative interest rates at which the public and financial institutions are willing to hold their available stock of primary liabilities; this, together with the fact of increasing risk as the independence of the expected performance of financial assets decreases,[12] will feed back upon the willingness to invest. Thus the rate of growth of ceiling income (including the effect of technical change) that is sufficient to sustain growth with one set of portfolios can become inadequate with another. A cyclical growth pattern can emerge due to cumulative changes that affect demand rather than from any necessary insufficiency of the rate of growth capacity.

It seems evident that the integration of ceiling models of growth with the financial flows that accompany growth is a fruitful research path in any attempt to develop econometric models that have the interesting intermediate time horizon.

Notes

1. R. M. Goodwin, "The Non-Linear Accelerator and the Persistence of Business Cycles," *Econometrica*, January, 1951; J. R. Hicks, *A Contribution to the Theory of the Trade Cycle* (New York: Oxford University Press, 1949); K. Kurihara, "An Endogenous Model of Cyclical Growth," *Oxford Economic Papers*, October, 1960; R. C. L. Mathews, "A Note on Crawling Along the Ceiling," *Review of Economic Studies*, XXVII (1) No. 72 (October, 1959); H. P. Minsky, "A Linear Model of Cyclical growth," *Review of Economics and Statistics*, XLI (May, 1959), reprinted in R. A. Gordon and L. R. Klein, *Readings in Business Cycles* (Homewood, Ill.: Richard D. Irwin, 1965).

2. M. Abromowitz, United States Congress, 86th Congress, Joint Economic Committee, *Employment, Growth and Price Levels, Hearings Part 2, Historical and Comperative Rate of Production, Productivity and Prices.*

3. M. Friedman and S. J. Schwartz, "Money and Business Cycles," *Review of Economics and Statistics*, Supplement (February, 1963), p. 55.

4. *Ibid.*

5. J. Tobin, "An Essay on Principles of Debt Management," in *Fiscal and Debt Management Policies*, Commission on Money and Credit (Englewood Cliffs, N. J.: Prentice-Hall, Inc., 1964).

6. H. P. Minsky, "Financial Crisis, Financial Systems and the Performance of the Economy," *Private Capital Markets*, Commission on Money and Credit (Englewood Cliffs, N. J.: Prentice-Hall, Inc., 1964).

7. P. A. Samuelson, "Interactions Between the Multiplier Analysis and the Principle of Acceleration," *Review of Economics and Statistics*, XXI (May, 1939). Reprinted in *Readings in Business Cycles* (Philadelphia: Blakiston and Co., 1944).

8. R. F. Harrod, *Toward a Dynamic Economics* (London: Macmillan, 1948); E. D. Domar, *Essays in the Theory of Economic Growth* (New York: Oxford University Press, 1957).

9. Minsky, "A Linear Model of Cyclical Growth."

10. The formal apparatus is set out in Minsky, *ibid.*

11. Minsky, *ibid.*, p. 137, footnote 12.

12. Tobin, *op. cit.*

PART IV

INTERNATIONAL MARKETS

The Effects of Devaluation in a
Growing Economy[1]

George H. Borts

INTRODUCTION

IN this paper I shall examine the effects of exchange-rate devaluation on the balance of payments of a growing economy. Since I shall adopt an approach somewhat different from that employed by earlier writers, it will be necessary to explain how they handled the problem. They analyzed devaluation as a possible cure for an excess demand for foreign exchange. A very clear statement of this approach was made by Professor Machlup: "The problem is how to analyze the probable effectiveness of a devaluation undertaken to remove or reduce an existing excess demand for foreign exchange without the use of direct controls, when money incomes have been stable, and when no autonomous capital movements take place either before or after the devaluation."[2]

In the view cited, an excess demand for foreign exchange, presumably arising from a current account deficit, is met by an outflow of gold or an inflow of short-term capital. The deficit could not be met by a private long-term capital inflow, because it would then be consistent with equilibrium of the foreign exchange market. The purpose of the cited analysis is to discover whether devaluation can reduce the excess demand by raising exports relative to imports. If exports rise relative to imports, there is a corresponding rise in saving relative to investment, implied by national income accounting. The rise in saving over investment is taken over by the central bank and transformed into foreign assets, as a means of reversing the drain of foreign exchange or repaying short-term foreign borrowing.

Different assumptions and a different analysis are employed in this paper. I shall assume that an initial position of equilibrium holds in both the foreign exchange market and the domestic market for goods and

195

services. I shall investigate two questions: First, starting from equilibrium, what is the effect of devaluation on the balance of payments, when both the current account and the capital account are open to change? Second, assuming a specific disturbance to balance-of-payments equilibrium, under what circumstances will devaluation provide a cure? The approach implied by these questions may be expressed in terms of the following definitions: The deficit or surplus in the balance of payments may be written as the sum of the balances on current account and on long-term capital account. Short-term capital movements are considered to be part of the deficit or surplus, while other entries in the balance of payments are excluded. Let B_g denote deficit or surplus, B_c the current account balance, and B_k the capital account balance.

By definition we have:

$$B_g \equiv B_c + B_k.$$

In the older approach, B_k is regarded as constant, so that changes in the current account B_c are solely responsible for changes in the surplus or deficit B_g. In this paper, the capital account balance B_k is not constant. It is regarded as a function of the difference between interest rates in this country and abroad, where the foreign interest rate is taken as given. If the domestic interest rate exceeds the foreign rate, B_k will be positive. On balance, there will be a net increase in foreign holdings of our long-term assets and a net decrease in our holdings of foreign long-term assets.

$$B_k = f(r - r_F)$$

$$r_F = \bar{r}_F$$

The function f is assumed to be perfectly elastic in the long run at $r - r_F = 0$. It is less than perfectly elastic in the short run. Consequently, I assume that in the long run $r = r_F$, that $B_k \equiv -B_c$, and that $B_g \equiv 0$.[3]

One might be curious about the role devaluation plays under the ideal assumption that the over-all balance of payments is always in equilibrium ($B_g \equiv 0$). Why analyze devaluation under the assumption that a perfectly elastic supply of long-term capital ($r = r_F$) assures the financing of current account deficits? In answer, devaluation will have four effects: It will, in conjunction with institutionally determined money wage levels, influence the level of employment. Second, it may influence the rate of exports and imports, and consequently influence the long-term debtor or creditor position of the country. The latter is a concern of government policy and debates in Canada, Australia, France, and Germany. Third, devaluation will have short-run effects on the over-all balance of payments as the economy adjusts its capital stock to a higher employment level. Recall that the supply of foreign long-term capital is perfectly elastic in the long run but not in the short run. Finally, devaluation may be a useful way of eliminating disequilibrium produced by other disturbances.

In the following discussion I shall focus on changes in savings and investment as a means of describing how the current account responds to devaluation. I shall assume that initially the current account is in balance, and savings equal investment. I shall examine the system for changes of this type: percentage change in savings minus percentage change in investment. Where this term is positive, it is clear that the current account has improved, and where it is negative, the current account has deteriorated. In this respect, the analysis goes beyond the development by earlier writers who dealt mainly with variations in savings. It is only recently that induced changes in investment have attracted any attention.[4]

Two types of economies will be examined. In the first, there is a single type of output which is consumed, exported, or invested to increase the stock of capital. In the second type of economy, two goods are produced: a capital-intensive export good, and a labor-intensive domestic good. The domestic good is partly consumed and partly invested.

I shall examine these economies when they are at full employment, and when they suffer unemployment due to institutional determination of the money wage. I shall assume that these economies trade with the rest of the world under conditions in which it is possible to ignore the repercussions of variations in the current account balance on the world supply and demand of exports and imports. That is, I assume that world supply and demand functions do not shift in response to variations in this country's current account balance.

In terms of the questions posed above, the analysis yields the following results:

(1) Starting from the equilibrium, what is the effect of devaluation on the balance of payments, when both current and capital accounts are open to change?

At full employment, the effects of devaluation accord with the purchasing power parity doctrine. The equilibrium money wage rises in proportion to the devaluation of the exchange rate, and all physical magnitudes are unchanged.

At less then full employment, the situation is quite different. Provided that certain traditional restrictions are met on the price elasticities of demand, devaluation will raise the level of employment and induce the economy to shift upward from a lower to a higher growth path. Second, devaluation is likely to worsen the current account balance and lead to an induced import of capital. This will almost certainly occur in the short-run transition to a higher growth path, and may also occur in the long run, when the economy is completely adjusted to the new growth path. The reason for the deficit in the short run is that devaluation's stimulating effect on investment and output raises imports by more than the price changes improve the current account. In the process, devaluation raises the marginal efficiency of investment; specifically, it raises the level of investment more than it raises the level of savings. Consequently there will be a net import of capital into the country.

If devaluation leads to a return to full employment, it will imply a temporarily higher interest rate. Depending upon the willingness of foreigners to purchase this country's securities, this could lead to a temporary but nevertheless sharp balance-of-payments surplus. Note that the possibility of a surplus appearing depends on the supply of foreign long-term lending. For in this transition to full employment, the current account deteriorates. These very important results indicate that policies other than devaluation might be investigated if a country wishes to improve its long-run debtor postiion.

(2) Assuming a specific disturbance to balance-of-payments equilibrium, under what circumstances will devaluation provide a cure? We may distinguish two types of disturbances to the balance of payments: those arising from exogenous changes in the money supply, and those arising from changes in consumer preferences for imports and exports.

At full employment, we again obtain very traditional results. A current account deficit produced by an exogenous rise in the money supply will be offset by an equiproportionate rise in the money wage and devaluation of the exchange rate. A current account deficit produced by a rise in demand for imports or a fall in demand for exports will be offset by either a fall in the money wage or a devaluation of the exchange rate. The latter events depend upon the traditional stability conditions for the sum of price elasticities of demand for imports and exports.

With less than full employment, the results are again quite different. An exogenous rise in the money supply will lead simultaneously to a rise in the level of output and to a current account deficit. Devaluation cannot cure this current account deficit, because it has additional stimulating effects on the level of output.

A rise in demand for imports or a fall in demand for exports will lead to a fall in the level of output. In the long run, there will be no current account deficit or surplus, consequently no disequilibrium. This last result follows from the nature of the economy's adjustment from one growth path to another, and it will be explained below.

A ONE-PRODUCT ECONOMY

Description of the Model

I shall first specify and analyze the variables and functional relations for a one-product economy at full employment. Next I shall introduce unemployment.

The economy produces a single product X with factor inputs L and K. The production function is homogeneous of the first degree, and technological change is assumed absent.

$$(1) \qquad X = X(L, K)$$

The money wage is equal to the value of the marginal product of labor. Perfect competition is assumed in both factor and product markets.

$$(2) \qquad w_x = P_x \cdot f_L$$

The rate of return on capital, a pure interest rate, is equal to the marginal physical productivity of capital. This follows from the assumption that X may be reinvested to produce more X.

$$(3) \qquad r \equiv f_K$$

The output X may be consumed, exported, or invested. The capital stock is thus the accumulation of past investments.

$$(4) \qquad X = X_c + X_e + X_I$$

The world demand for X is a function of the price of X and the world population, the latter an exogenous variable.

$$(5) \qquad P'_x = [X_e/L_w]^{-\beta}$$

where -1β is the price elasticity of world demand.

$$(6) \qquad L_w = L_{\bar{w}}$$

The exchange rate ρ is fixed by government policy.

$$(7) \qquad \rho = \bar{\rho}$$

$$(8) \qquad P_x = P'_x \rho$$

where P_x is the price in domestic currency. The value of income produced is the money value of X.

(9)
$$Z_p = XP_x$$

Income is disbursed by households in the form of savings, the consumption of X, and the consumption of an import N.

(10)
$$Z_d \equiv X_c P_x + NP_n + S$$

Savings are a constant fraction of income.

(11)
$$S = sZ_p$$

In equilibrium, income produced equals income disbursed.

(12)
$$Z_p = Z_d$$

The share of income spent on the domestic commodity is a function of the relative prices of the two consumer goods. It is assumed that the income elasticity of demand for the two goods is unity.

(13)
$$X_c P_x / Z_d = [P_x / P_n]^{-\gamma}$$

Note that γ may be positive or negative. The supply elasticity of imports is assumed infinite.

(14)
$$P'_n = P_{\bar{n}}$$

(15)
$$P_n = P'_n \cdot \rho$$

There is full employment of labor in the sense that the demand for labor L equals the momentarily fixed supply L_s.

(16)
$$L = L_s$$

There is also full employment of capital.

(17)
$$K = K_s$$

where K_s is the momentarily fixed supply.

In addition to the above static relationships, we have the following conditions holding over time: The rate of growth of the labor force in this country and in the world are demographically determined constants. In addition it is assumed that they are equal. Note the use of starred superscripts to denote percentage changes.

(18)
$$L_s^* = \lambda$$

(19)
$$L_w^* = \lambda$$

The rate of growth of the capital stock is defined equal to the ratio of investment to the capital stock.

$$(20) \qquad K^* \equiv X_I/K$$

The rate of return on capital is, in equilibrium, equal to the going rate of return in the world market. There is in the long run an infinitely elastic supply of investment funds and investment opportunities.

$$(21) \qquad r = \bar{r}_F$$

It might appear on first glance that the last equation is redundant in view of the fact that I have specified initial given values of L and K which determine a marginal physical product of capital. This is not so. The last equation implies that in equilibrium the values of L and K satisfy a specified ratio initially and through time.

GROWTH UNDER FULL EMPLOYMENT

In the absence of disturbances, this economy grows at the constant proportional rate λ, the rate of growth of the labor force. We may see this conclusion through the following argument: The full employment conditions determine the level of output. The fixed equilibrium level of interest requires that the quantity of capital and output grow at the same rate as the labor force. This determines the level of investment; $X_I = K_s K^*$, and $K^*, = \lambda$; therefore $X_I = K_s\lambda$. Solving for X_e and X_c, we have

$$(i) \qquad X - X_I = X_e + X_c = L_w \left[\frac{P_x}{\rho} \right]^{-1/\beta} + X \left[\frac{P_x}{\rho} \right]^{-\gamma} P_{\bar{n}}^{\gamma}.$$

The price level is determined by the demands for exports and for consumption of the domestic good in conjunction with the output remaining after investment requirements are satisfied. $X - X_I$ is determined. Equation (i) may be solved for P_x.

By assumption, the world demand for exports grows at the same rate as the growth of the economy's capacity. Consequently, there is no secular change in the terms of trade. The economy grows with an unchanged price level, with stable shares of output devoted to consumption, exports, and investment.

If the exchange rate were to be devalued, the only effect would be an equal rise in the money wage and in the price level. This may be seen from the fact that equation (i) may be solved for (P_x/ρ). Devaluation leaves unchanged both X, the level of output, and X_I, the amount of output devoted to investment. Consequently, X_e, the quantity of exports, plus X_c, the consumption of X, remains unchanged. This means that the price of X must in equilibrium rise in equal proportion to the devaluation. In addition, the money wage will rise in equal proportion to the price level, since the equilibrium capital-labor ratio is left unchanged. The above results are hardly surprising and are true of most full-employment economies in the absence of money illusion.

The current account deficit produced by a rise in the demand for imports or a fall in the demand for exports could be eliminated by a fall in the money wage or a devaluation of the exchange rate relative to the money wage. The condition necessary for this to occur is the familiar stability constraint on the elasticities of demand for imports and exports:

$$\eta_n + \eta_x < -1.$$

Also note that at full employment the quantity of money does not play an independent role in determining the equilibrium of the economy. The price level, level of output, and interest rate are already determined. If we were to introduce money as an explicit variable, it would be a monetary requirements equation, e.g.,

$$(22) \qquad M_D = kZ,$$

and the quantity of money would not play an independent role. There is nevertheless a monetary equilibrium implied by the model, for aggregate demand equals aggregate supply, and there are no money flows between this country and the rest of the world. The absence of money flows is assured by the assumption of a perfect world capital market, which in the long run provides unlimited borrowing or investment facilities at a fixed rate of return. If exports exceed imports, then in equilibrium those who are accumulating foreign balances are willing to invest them abroad at the world rate of interest, and conversely if imports exceed exports. Thus the supply of money must identically equal the demand for money, and no money flows are possible between this country and the rest of the world. No independent monetary policy is possible in such an economy. Any attempt to set a supply of money which diverged from the demand for money would permanently push the system away from equilibrium and force the abandonment of the level of the exchange rate. Consequently, a balance of payments deficit produced by a monetary disturbance, would lead to a rise in money wages, prices, and a devaluation of the exchange rate. This would eliminate the deficit.

GROWTH WITH UNEMPLOYMENT

Let us now alter the scene by introducing unemployment. I shall introduce an institutionally determined money wage and replace equation (16) with the new statement.

$$(16') \qquad\qquad w = w_0.$$

It is assumed that w_0 is above the wage necessary for full employment. I assume that the equilibrium restriction on the capital-labor ratio is unchanged. Consequently, a higher money wage implies a higher price of output. This in turn implies a lower level of exports, and a smaller share of output devoted to consumption. The net effect is a lower level of total output. We may see the over-all effect of a fixed money wage by writing the following expression for output as the sum of consumption, exports, and investment. It is assumed that the level of output is below the full employment level.

$$(ii) \qquad X = X\left[\frac{P_x}{\rho}\right]^{-\gamma} P_n^{\gamma} + L_w^0 \exp\{\lambda t\}\left[\frac{P_x}{\rho}\right]^{-1/\beta} + \frac{K}{X} XX^*$$

It is assumed that P_x is determined by the fixed money wage. The second and third term bear explanation, as they are written in different form than earlier. The level of exports depends upon a relative price term $[P_x/\rho]^{-1/\beta}$, and upon the level of world population L_w, which grows over time at the constant rate of λ. The level of investment, defined equal to KK^*, is also equal to $(K/X)XX^*$, since $K^* = X^*$.

The above differential equation may be solved to yield the following:

$$(iii) \qquad\qquad X = X_0 e^{\lambda t},$$

where

$$(iv) \qquad\qquad X_0 = \frac{X_e^0}{1 - \dfrac{X_c^0}{X_0} - \dfrac{X_I^0}{X_0}},$$

and

$$(v) \qquad\qquad X_e^0 = L_w^0\left[\frac{P_x}{\rho}\right]^{-1/\beta},$$

and

$$(vi) \qquad\qquad \frac{X_c^0}{X_0} = \left[\frac{P_x}{\rho}\right]^{-\gamma} \cdot P_n^{\gamma},$$

and

(vii) $$\frac{X_I^0}{X_0} = \frac{K_0}{X_0} \cdot \lambda.$$

Thus, whether at full employment or not, the economy grows at the rate λ, the growth of world demand for exports. If at less than full employment, however, the economy moves along a parallel growth path which is at a lower level than the full employment path. Note that along any given growth path, there is a stable ratio of investment to output. There is also assumed to be a stable ratio of savings to output. Consequently, if the current account is in balance at one point on a given growth path, it is in balance at all points on that path. Also note the growth path at less than full employment is determined solely by the money wage and the exchange rate, without reference to the money supply. The quantity of money is still an endogenous variable in the sense that even with unemployment the system has a solution without reference to an exogenous money supply.

The effect on output of an institutionally determined wage may be seen by differentiating equation (iv). Use starred superscripts to denote percentage changes, and note that by assumption the price P_x and the wage w_x move equiproportionately. We have

(viii) $$\frac{X^*}{P_x^*} = \frac{-\gamma \dfrac{X_c}{X} - \dfrac{1}{\beta}\dfrac{X_e}{X}}{X_e/X}.$$

In this context X^* denotes the shift from one growth path to another.

The value of expression (viii) is not necessarily negative, since γ may be negative. It is proved in the appendix that the expression is negative when the traditional stability conditions are met with regard to demand elasticities. The price elasticities of demand for imports and exports must sum to a value less than minus unity.

$$(\eta_n + \eta_x < -1)$$

To conclude, if a money wage is set above that money wage implied by full employment, then the economy will be forced to a lower-level growth path. It remains to be seen how the economy carries out the transition from one growth path to another.

The Effect of Devaluation on the Growth Path and on the Current Account

We may now introduce devaluation as a policy designed to raise the economy back to the full-employment growth path. Here we have a number of alternatives to consider. In moving from a higher to a lower growth path a certain amount of capital was made redundant. The reason is that investment along a growth path equals $K_s\lambda$, where K_s is the amount of capital needed to sustain the output at a moment of time along that path. A drop from one path to another, with an unchanged capital-output ratio, will require less capital and thus implies a sharp rate of disinvestment. It might also imply a departure from the equilibrium capital-output ratio while the transition to a new equilibrium was carried out. These considerations apply in reverse when we analyze the shift from a lower to a higher growth path, and they will be analyzed in some detail. I shall assume that the economy has been on the lower growth path for some time, and that the stock of capital has adjusted to the equilibrium capital-output ratio. There is full employment of capital, and less than full employment of labor.

The movement from a lower to a higher growth path, as a consequence of devaluation, implies the following changes in the components of aggregate demand: Consumption of X rises as a consequence of the rise in output and the rise in the price of imported consumer goods. The latter is true if $\gamma > 0$. Exports rise as a consequence of the drop in the foreign price of X. Investment rises as a consequence of the rise in output. Investment must be sufficient to provide the extra capital for the jump to the higher path $[(K/X) \triangle X]$ plus the normal growth of capital along the higher path $(K/X) X_F\lambda$, where X_F refers to full employment output along the higher path. Consequently we may write the following expression for the level investment would attain after the devaluation, with an unchanged capital-output ratio:

(ix) $$X_I = \left(\frac{K}{X}\right)[X_F\lambda + \Delta X].$$

On the other hand, prior to the devaluation, investment was equal to

(x) $$X_I^0 = \left(\frac{K}{X}\right)X_u\lambda,$$

where X_u refers to the output along the lower growth path. Assuming that the capital-output ratio remained unchanged, we would have the following percentage rise in investment due to devaluation:

(xi) $$X_I^* = X^*\left(1 + \frac{1}{\lambda}\right),$$

where X^* is the percentage shift in the growth path due to devaluation.

A numerical example will clarify the situation and reveal the unstable expansion. We may use equation (viii) to calculate the per cent rise in output implied by a devaluation. This follows from the symmetric relation between prices and exchange rates. Assume, for example, that $\gamma = 0$, and $\beta = 1$. A 10 per cent devaluation will imply a 10 per cent shift in the growth path, that is a 10 per cent rise in output. Consumption and exports will rise by 10 per cent each, while investment will rise by 10 per cent multiplied by $(1 + 1/\lambda)$. If $\lambda = 2$ per cent, then investment rises by 500 per cent. The implied expansion means that output would rise beyond the level of the new growth path, if resources were available. Assuming that the new growth path is the full employment level, or ceiling, the implied expansion would run up against the ceiling.

I propose to examine what adjustments have to occur to permit the economy to attain and maintain this ceiling level of output. I have indicated above that some reconciliation must occur among the inconsistent demands for increased output among consumers, exporters, and investors. I shall assume that the economy achieves this reconciliation by departing temporarily from the fixed capital-output ratio and the fixed rate of return on investment which it implies. Let us assume that as output and employment rise in response to devaluation, the capital-output ratio falls. This has two implications. First, the rate of return on investment rises. Second, the price level rises, as a consequence of a fixed money wage and a decline in the marginal productivity of labor. The fall in the capital-output ratio will prevent investment from rising as much as it might have. The rise in the price level will prevent consumption and exports from rising as much as they might have. The net result is that the rise in output is rationed among the three sectors, with investment nevertheless expanding more rapidly than output. Because investment expands more rapidly than output, the capital-output ratio will rise in the long run back to its equilibrium level. The price level, the rate of return on capital, and the ratio of investment to output then fall to their pre-devaluation levels. Thus, the transition to the higher growth path is completed. The above adjustments are depicted below graphically. The mathematical relations are derived in the appendix, where it is proved that investment must expand more rapidly than output during this adjustment of the capital stock to the new growth path. It is also shown that the price level and rate of return on investment must rise during the transition.

What about the balance of payments? What effect will devaluation have on the current account? Let us assume that initially the current account was in balance with savings equal to investment. Then it can be shown that during this transition period between t_0 and t_2 the cur-

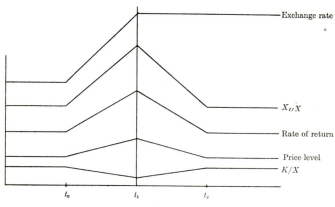

Figure 1

t_0 = pre-devaluation
t_1 = post-devaluation transition
t_2 = post-devaluation permanent state

rent account will be in deficit with imports in excess of exports, and investment in excess of savings. This point may be demonstrated by comparing the savings-income ratio with the investment-income ratio. The former is assumed constant, while the latter rises and remains above its secular value during the transition. Thus if investment equalled saving before devaluation, it would be in excess of saving until t_2. Once the economy has adjusted its capital stock to the higher growth path, this deficit will disappear and balance will return to the current account. However, the consequence of regaining the full employment growth path is a temporary deterioration of the current account and a certain amount of borrowing from abroad.

THE ROLE OF DEVALUATION IN CORRECTING DISTURBANCES TO THE CURRENT ACCOUNT

Monetary Disturbances

At less than full employment, monetary disturbances may alter both the level of the growth path and the current account balance. For example, the government could raise the level and growth rate of output by purchasing goods for money. The growth rate could be raised above λ until the economy reached full employment. Call this new growth rate λ_G. This policy will lead to a current account deficit because of a rise in imports. The effect of devaluation on the current account then depends upon the precise nature of monetary policy. For devaluation also leads to a rise in the demand for output. If the monetary authority is willing to supply the money necessary for the devaluation-induced rise in output, then devaluation will not improve but will worsen the current account as described earlier. If the monetary authority refuses to allow a faster growth of demand than λ_G, then devaluation could improve the current account by squeezing government expenditure to provide more exports. Similarly, once monetary policy restores full employment, devaluation can eliminate the current account deficit, for there is a "correct" exchange rate needed to keep the economy on the full employment growth path. The "correct" exchange rate would then replace government demand in keeping the economy at full employment.

Real Disturbances

At less than full employment, a rise in demand for imports or a fall in demand for exports will have short-run effects on the current account. In the short run, these disturbances lead to a decline in the level of output, a deceleration of investment, a drop in the price level, and a drop in the rate of return on investment. This is the opposite of the expansion process implied by the shift to a higher growth path. While the process of decline is going on, the balance on current account would become *favorable*, because investment falls short of savings. Once the capital stock becomes adjusted to the new lower growth path, prices and the rate of return on capital rise back to their old levels, savings once again equal investment, and the current account surplus disappears. The above disturbances have no long-run effects on the current account.

For the same reasons a rise in demand for exports, or a fall in demand for imports, would in the short run lead to a current account deficit. Devaluation may not eliminate this deficit, but enlarge it. This again depends on the precise nature of monetary policy. Devaluation raises the demand for output. If monetary policy acquiesces in this faster growth of output due to devaluation, then the current account will not be improved.

Thus we see that at less than full employment, devaluation has uncertain effects on current account deficits. Before devaluation can correct a current account deficit, the growth path of output must be stabilized either by the full-employment constraint or, without full employment, by some positive monetary policy. Otherwise, the destabilizing effects of devaluation on aggregate demand, real output, and investment, outweigh the corrective effects operating through relative prices. These remarks are in sympathy with earlier discussions by Machlup and by Tsiang. (See notes 2 and 4.)

THE SUPPLY OF FOREIGN LONG-TERM CAPITAL

I showed earlier that starting with equilibrium at less than full employment, the current account would turn passive as a consequence of devaluation. It would remain passive until the capital-output ratio returned to equilibrium, at which point, the current account would again be balanced. What about the long-term capital account? I shall examine in detail assumptions made concerning the supply of foreign long-term capital. This variable is considered to be a function of the interest differential between this country and the rest of the world:

$$B_k = f(r - r_F).$$

It is assumed that in the long run f is infinitely elastic at $r - r_F = 0$, while it is less than infinitely elastic in the short run. The functions are depicted in the following charts:

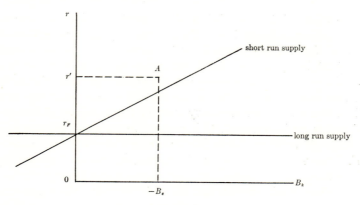

Figure 2

The interest rate may in the short run be higher or lower in this country than abroad.

We have seen that the short-run effect of devaluation is to raise the rate of return on capital and to cause a deterioration of the current account. These effects are depicted in the above diagram as the point A, with coordinates $(r', - B'_c)$. There is no reason why this point should fall on the short-run supply function B_k. If it does, then the over-all balance of payments will be unchanged with a capital account surplus offsetting a current account deficit. As shown on the diagram, however, the capital account surplus more than offsets the current account deficit, with an over-all balance-of-payments surplus resulting. While this result is a short-run phenomenon, it does have certain implications for monetary policy which will be examined below. It should be noted, however, that when the adjustment of the capital stock is completed, the rate of return will fall back to r_F, and the current account deficit and the capital account surplus will disappear.

The short-run effects of devaluation have certain implications for monetary policy. If point A lies above the short-run supply function B_k, the over-all balance of payments turns favorable. The monetary authority will gain gold and lose domestic assets. On the other hand, if point A lies below the short-run supply function B_k, the over-all balance of payments shows a deficit. The monetary authority will gain domestic assets and lose gold. The conclusions concerning the balance sheet of the monetary authority may be seen by writing the following identities:

$$\text{Imports} - \text{Exports} = \text{Investment} - \text{Savings}$$

$$\text{Imports} - \text{Exports} = B_k - B_g$$

Assume that point A lies below the supply function B_k. Assume that the current account deficit is 100, the capital account surplus B_k is 80, and the over-all deficit B_g is $-$ 20. Then the monetary authority finances the deficit of 20 by giving up gold. At the same time it buys the excess supply of securities which were not taken up by domestic or foreign savers. The excess supply also equals 20. The purchase of securities implies the willingness of the montary authority to go along with the present rate of return on investment. If it refused to purchase the excess supply of securities, it would be imposing an interest rate on the market higher than r'. This would slow down the movement to the full employment growth path.

On the other hand, assume that point A lies above the supply function B_k. Devaluation will cause the capital account to improve by more than the deterioration in the current account. A balance-of-payments surplus will occur. The monetary authority will purchase gold and sell securities (out of its portfolio) to foreign savers. The reason for selling securities is again to pursue a policy consistent with the interest rate r'.

Thus the effect of devaluation on the balance of payments is seen to depend on the long-run capital account and its response to interest differentials. In the short run, the current account will turn passive and the interest rate will rise. The capital account will show a surplus, but this may be too large or too small for over-all balance. In the long run, devaluation has no effect on the over-all balance of payments.

If the monetary authority is willing to go along with the rate of return on investment r', then its role is limited to exchanging securities for gold. If it attempts to set some other interest rate, then it will interfere with the adjustment process. If it tries to set a higher interest rate than r', it will slow down the movement to the higher growth path, since it will enforce a lower capital-output ratio, and a higher price level. If it tries to set a lower interest rate than r', it will set off a familiar inflationary process. The monetary authority would then be faced with offers of securities by individuals who wish to borrow at a rate lower than r' and buy physical capital which yields r'. This process implies an increase in the quantity of money which will be impossible to sustain in the long run at the going exchange rate, for the monetary authority will be financing a portion of the current account deficit.

I should like to summarize the role of monetary policy in the preceding discussion.

At full employment, with the B_k function infinitely elastic in the long run, money is an endogenous variable. The level of output, the price level, and the interest rate are determined without the need for an exogenous money supply, or a specific monetary policy.

At less than full employment, with B_k infinitely elastic in the long run, the money supply may be endogenous, for the same reasons as before. However, there is a possible role for monetary policy. The government could raise the level of output and the growth path by purchasing output in exchange for money. This would lead to an accelerated rise in investment. The result would be a deterioration of the current account because of rising imports. The effect on the over-all balance of payments would then depend on whether the interest rate was raised, and on the induced flow of long term capital B_k. Depending upon the short-run elasticity of B_k, some current deficit can be financed by foreign long-term borrowing. This result has already been analyzed by Fleming and Mundell and will not be explored further.[5]

In the rise to the full-employment growth path produced by devaluation, there will occur a current account deficit and a capital account surplus. Over-all, the devaluation will lead to a balance of payments surplus or deficit depending on the elasticity of B_k. If the monetary authority tries to prevent a surplus by preventing a rise in interest rates, then we have an inflationary expansion of the money supply as described above. If the monetary authority tries to prevent a deficit by raising the interest rate above r', this slows the rise of investment and output.

TWO-PRODUCT ECONOMIES

The conclusions described above are not substantially altered when we consider two-product economies. However, the analysis becomes much simpler because of my assumption that capital is used only for the production of exports. In consequence, investment and changes in investment are functions solely of the level of export demand. In the following discussion I shall skirt the pitfalls uncovered earlier. In particular, I shall not assume that devaluation achieves a return to the full-employment growth path. Thus it will be possible to keep the assumption of an unchanged rate of return on capital. It will also be possible to keep the assumption of an infinitely elastic supply of long-run capital, B_k. Further, it will not be necessary to introduce the role of monetary policy. The adjustments to be described do not require any explicit monetary policy, and it will be sufficient to assume again that the quantity of money is an endogenous variable. I shall also ignore disturbances to the balance of payments and concentrate on the effects of devaluation when the economy is in equilibrium.

There is one important difference between the two models. In the two-sector model to be presented, devaluation may have a permanent effect on the current account, so that capital is imported indefinitely. In the preceding model, devaluation had only a transitional effect until the rate of return came back to equilibrium.

Description of the Model

As before, I shall state the variables and functions of a full-employment economy and then proceed to analyze devaluation under unemployment conditions.

(1) $X = X(K, L_z)$. Production function for exports, assumed homogeneous of the first degree.

(2) $Y = L_y \cdot \pi$. Production function for Y, the domestic good. It is assumed that Y uses only labor in production.

(3) $w_x = P_x \cdot f_L$. The money wage equals the value of the marginal product of labor.

(4) $w_y = P_y \cdot \pi$

(5) $w_x = w_y$

(6) $rP_y = P_z f_K$. The rent per unit of capital equals the value of the marginal product of capital.

(7) $r = \bar{r}_F$

(8) $Y = Y_c + Y_I$. The domestic good may be consumed or invested.

(9) $P_x = P'_x \cdot \rho$

(10) $\rho = \bar{\rho}$

(11) $P'_x = (X/L_{\bar{w}})^{-\beta}$. Demand function for exports.

(12) $Z_p = XP_x + YP_y$. Definition of produced income.

(13) $Z_d = Y_c P_y + N \cdot P_n + S$. Disposition of income into consumption of domestic good $Y_c P_{y'}$ of imports $NP_{n'}$ and into savings S.

(14) $Z_p = Z_d$

(15) $Y_c P_y/Z = (P_y/P_n)^{-\gamma}$. Demand function for consumption of the domestic good.

(16) $P_n = P_{n'} \cdot \rho$

(17) $P'_n = P_{\bar{n}}$

(18) $S = sZ_p$. Savings are a given fraction of income.

(19) $L_x + L_y = L_s$. There is full employment of labor.

(20) $K_x = K_s$. Full employment of capital.

(21) $L_s^* = \lambda$. The labor force grows at the rate λ.

(22) $L_w^* = \lambda$. The world population grows at λ.

(23) $K^* \equiv Y_I/K_x$.

(24) $M_d = kZ_p$. Demand for money stock.

The above model economy grows at λ, the rate of growth of the domestic labor force and world population. Both investment and export output grow at the rate λ, maintaining a constant capital-output ratio. This ratio is determined again by the rate of interest as seen by substituting equations (3) and (4) into (6) to obtain

(i)
$$r = \frac{\pi f_K}{f_L}.$$

Under the assumption that the production function is homogeneous of degree one, the capital-output ratio in the export industry is determined by equation (i). Also note that the equilibrium is again determined without reference to the supply of money, and that at full employment, devaluation would alter the price level and the money wage in the same proportion and leave all physical magnitudes unchanged.

Let us introduce unemployment into this economy by replacing the full-employment condition with (19'), $w = w_0$. It is assumed that this institutionally determined wage level exceeds the old equilibrium level and leads to a lower level of exports and employment. As a result, the economy shifts to a lower growth path, in the same fashion as before. In the appendix it is shown that the wage rise leads to a lower level of real output, if the following restriction on elasticities is satisfied.

(ii)
$$\eta_x + k(\eta_n + 1) < 0;$$

where η_x and η_n are price elasticities of demand for exports and imports, and k is the ratio of imports to the sum of exports and investment.

Growth along the lower path proceeds at the same rate as along the upper path. The shift to the lower path makes a certain amount of capital redundant in the same way as before. However, the problem of capital stock adjustment will not be re-examined, as the same conclusions hold. I shall assume that the capital stock has become fully adjusted to the equilibrium capital-output ratio, and that capital is fully employed, while labor is not fully employed.

Let us see how this economy reacts to devaluation of the exchange rate. I shall examine the difference between the growth of savings $[S^*]$ and of investment $[I^*]$, both in money terms, measured in domestic prices. This analysis will be carried out in two parts. The reason is that there is a short-run accelerator-type reaction to the devaluation followed by a long-run reaction. Prior to devaluation, the demand for exports and for capital grows in proportion to the growth of world population. Devaluation raises the demand for exports and the demand for capital in equal proportion. The reason is that devaluation does not change the capital-labor ratio in exports. In the short run the demand for investment rises by a large multiple of the rise in the demand for capital. Once the capital stock reaches the desired level, however, it again grows at a secular rate determined by the secular growth of world demand for exports. Investment falls almost as sharply as it has risen.

The reaction of savings and income to the devaluation is not as sharp. In the short run, the level of income rises for three reasons: a rise in export receipts measured in domestic currency, a rise in consumption of the domestic good due to its lower relative price, and a rise in the use of the domestic good for investment purposes. Income does not rise as sharply as investment because of the dampening effect of the first two components. I assume that the devaluation does not return the economy to the full employment growth path, so that expansion is possible with an unchanged capital-output ratio.

The long-run reaction to the devaluation differs from the short-run. In the long run all physical magnitudes again grow at the secular rate of growth of world population. Savings and investment also grow at the same rate. They may nevertheless be unequal in the long run if, in the short run, capital and income had grown at unequal rates. These possibilities are illustrated in the following numerical example. I shall then derive the analytic expressions for the short-run and the long-run effects on the current account.

Period	Demand for Exports	Demand for Capital	Demand for Investment	Income	Savings	Consumption of Y
0	100	100	10	1000	10	890
1	110	110	11	1100	11	979
2	135	135	27.5	1300	13	1137.5
3	148.5	148.5	14.85	1414.6	14.15	1251.25

All entries in the above table are measured in unchanged money wage units. Exports rise by 10 per cent per year due to the assumed rise of world population at that rate. Initially, investment is equal to savings, and savings are 1 per cent of income. The events from Period 0 to Period 1 depict the secular growth process, with all magnitudes growing at 10 per cent. In Period 1 the currency is devalued, and exports rise by the secular percentage (10 per cent), plus a rate reflecting the devaluation. The demand for capital rises by an equal amount, and investment must rise by an abnormally large amount. It must bring the quantity of capital up to the level necessary to produce 135 units of exports. The previous period's investment of 11 had brought the quantity of capital up to 121. Thus we require an investment of 14 units of capital. In addition, investment must take care of the normal 10 per cent growth of the capital stock necessary to bring exports up by another 10 per cent in the subsequent period. This requires investment of 13.5 units of capital; 27.5 units in all.

The rise in exports and the sharp rise in investment produces a sharp but less violent rise in income. Also shown is a rise in consumption of the domestic good due to devaluation and due to the rise in income. Savings rise from period 1 to 2, but by a smaller proportion than investment, and the current account balance of payments turns unfavorable. In period 3, exports, the stock of capital, and consumption are again growing at 10 per cent. Investment, however, has declined from its previous level. The accelerator effect is over. Income therefore grows by less than 10 per cent between periods 2 and 3, as investment declines. The permanent effect of the devaluation on income consists of three elements: the permanent rise in the level of exports; the permanent rise in investment necessary to keep a larger capital stock growing at 10 per cent; and the permanent rise in consumption of the domestic good. As shown in the example, investment permanently exceeds savings, for capital grew at a higher rate than income during devaluation. The cause is the failure of consumption to grow more rapidly. If consumption of the domestic good grew at the same rate as exports, then income in period 3 would be 1485, and savings would equal investment. Consequently, the long-run effects of devaluation depend upon the rise in consumption of the domestic good. This relation will be seen below.

Let us now turn from the numerical example to an analysis of the effects of devaluation. In terms of the model it is shown in the appendix that the percentage rise in savings attributable to the devaluation may be written:

(iii)
$$S^* = \left[\frac{1}{\beta} + \frac{J[a\gamma + b/\lambda\beta]}{1 - aJ}\right] \cdot \rho^*,$$

where ρ^* is the per cent rise in the price of foreign exchange. The rise in investment attributable to the devaluation may be written:

(iv)
$$I^* = \rho^*\left[\frac{1}{\beta} + \frac{1}{\lambda\beta}\right].$$

The terms β, $\dot{\gamma}$, and λ have been defined previously. J refers to YP_y/Z, the proportion of income generated in the domestic sector; a refers to Y_c/Y, the proportion of the domestic good which is consumed, and $b = 1 - a$. The expression $I^* - S^*$ reduces to

(v)
$$I^* - S^* = \left[\frac{\dfrac{1 - J}{\lambda\beta} - Ja\gamma}{1 - aJ}\right],$$

a term which is likely to be positive for reasonable values of λ, β, and γ. It will be recalled that λ is the rate of world population growth, $(-1/\beta)$ the price elasticity of demand for exports, and $-\gamma$ the price elasticity of consumer demand for domestic goods. The expression will be positive *if*

(vi)
$$\frac{1 - J}{aJ} > \beta\gamma\lambda.$$

It is shown in the appendix that this inequality is satisfied when

(vii)
$$\frac{\eta_n + 1}{\eta_x} < \frac{1}{\lambda}$$

where η_n and η_x are respectively the price elasticities of demand of imports and exports, and λ is the rate of growth of world population. Using a figure $\lambda = 10$ per cent from the previous example, it may be seen that the above condition is very likely satisfied. This conclusion becomes stronger with lower, more reasonable rates of population growth. The rate of world population growth plays an important role in the above condition, for it partially determines the magnitude of the accelerator. The lower the value of λ, the lower the level of secular investment and the greater the percentage rise in investment due to devaluation of a given magnitude.

The above expressions depict the short-run reaction to devaluation, resulting from the accelerated rise in the demand for investment. In the long run a different set of conditions is present. In the long run the demand for investment and the demand for exports rise by the same proportion. If the demand for domestic goods also rises by this proportion, then income and savings will rise by this proportion as well. If this were the case, in the long run devaluation would have no effect on the current account. On the other hand, if the demand for domestic goods rises by a smaller proportion, then income and savings will not rise at the same rate as investment; the current account will remain passive.

It is shown in the appendix that in the long run the per cent rise in savings due to devaluation is

(viii) $$S^* = \left[\frac{1}{\beta} + \frac{aJ\gamma}{1 - aJ}\right] \cdot \rho^*$$

while the rise in investment due to the devaluation is

(ix) $$I^* = \rho^*/\beta.$$

The expression $I^* - S^*$ is then positive if $\gamma < 0$. In terms of the relevant price elasticities, this will occur when $\eta_n > -1$, that is, when demand for imports is price-inelastic. Thus, even in the long run it is possible that the current account remains passive. Note that this condition depends only on the price elasticity of demand for imports. The reason is that exports and investment change in equal proportions in the long run. Even though investment and savings grow at the rate λ in the long run, investment may permanently exceed savings.

CONCLUSION

I have shown that in growing economies the effects of devaluation depend upon factors over and above those considered by other writers. The traditional stability conditions for price elasticities of demand are seen to play an expanded role. They determine whether devaluation can raise the level of effective demand in an economy characterized by unemployment and an institutionally determined money wage.

I have shown that in the short run, devaluation is likely to produce unfavorable movements of the current account because of the stimulation to investment. Even in the longer run, when the acceleration of investment has died out, there is a strong possibility, in the two-sector economy, that investment will continue to exceed savings. This possibility is shown to depend solely on the elasticity of demand for imports. This last conclusion depends on the premise that capital is used only in the export sector, and that the domestic sector is a handicraft. If capital has domestic uses, then the analysis of the two-sector economy would be similar to that used earlier for the one-product economy.

I have shown that devaluation has additional repercussions if it leads to a return to full employment; for then the investment accelerator with an unchanged capital-output ratio must give way to an analysis involving a transitional decline in the capital-output ratio, a rise in the price level, and a rise in the return on investment. These transitional changes yield a deficit in the current account and a surplus in the capital account. They may also lead to a surplus in the over-all balance of payments. In the period of transition there is a role for monetary policy which has been pointed out. However, once the rate of return goes back to equilibrium, money is again an *endogenous* variable. I have also shown that there is a role for monetary policy, if in the long run the rate of return on investment is not determined by an infinitely elastic supply of foreign capital.

Do these models have policy implications? There is always a strong temptation to jump from a model to a policy in the belief that the world conforms in behavior to a hypothetical set of equilibrium relationships. Indeed, if one did not harbor such a belief, the construction of these models would produce very little satisfaction.

The models do appear to have policy implications for those countries where they provide a reasonable although abstract description of the economy's operations. I would surmise, for example, that the models might fit Canada or Australia, or any other country whose income fluctuations have little effect on world income levels.

The following policy implications have been brought out:

(1) Starting from equilibrium, full employment or otherwise, devaluation is not likely to improve a country's position with respect to its current account. Consequently, devaluation will not improve a country's long-run debtor position.

(2) Starting from equilibrium, devaluation may produce a temporary over-all balance-of-payments surplus, but in the long run, it will not influence the over-all balance of payments. This short-run surplus depends on the supply elasticity of foreign long-term lending.

(3) In only two clear cases does devaluation appear to be a corrective policy with regard to the over-all balance of payments. This is (a) where the monetary authority attempts to set a money supply

greater than that consistent with full employment and a given exchange rate, and (b) where, at full employment, there is a rise in demand for imports or fall in demand for exports. These are well-known results.

(4) Finally, devaluation is a corrective policy for underemployment caused by an institutionally determined money wage above the equilibrium level.

MATHEMATICAL APPENDIX

MODEL I—ONE-PRODUCT ECONOMY

A. To show that

(1) $$X = X_0 e^{\lambda t}$$

is the solution to the equation

(2) $$X = X\left[\frac{P_x}{\rho}\right]^{-\gamma} P_n^{\gamma} + L_w^0 e^{\lambda t}\left[\frac{P_x}{\rho}\right]^{-1/\beta} + \left[\frac{K}{X}\right]XX^*$$

where

(3) $$X_0 = \frac{L_w^0\left[\frac{P_x}{\rho}\right]^{-1/\beta}}{1 - \left[\frac{P_x}{\rho}\right]^{-\gamma}P_{\frac{\gamma}{n}} - \frac{K_0\lambda}{X_0}} :$$

Denote the following terms as constants:

$$a = \left[\frac{P_x}{\rho}\right]^{-\gamma}P_n^{\gamma}; \quad b = L_w^0\left[\frac{P_x}{\rho}\right]^{-1/\beta}; \quad c = \left[\frac{K}{X}\right].$$

Then equation (2) may be written as:

$$X = aX + be^{\lambda t} + c\frac{dX}{dt}.$$

This equation has the solution:

(4) $$X = \left[\frac{b}{1 - a - \lambda c}\right]\exp\{\lambda t\} + \left[X_0 - \frac{b}{1 - a - \lambda c}\right]\exp\left\{\left[\frac{1-a}{c}\right]t\right\}.$$

Note that the bracketed constant in the second expression is zero.

B. To show that equation (5) is negative when

$$\eta_n + \eta_x < -1:$$

(5)
$$\frac{X^*}{P^*} = \frac{-\gamma\left[\dfrac{X_c}{X}\right] - \left[\dfrac{1}{\beta}\right]\dfrac{X_e}{X}}{X_e/X}.$$

First note that by definition

$$\eta_x = -\frac{1}{\beta}.$$

Next note the following definition of total consumption C, where $C = (1 - s)Z$:

(6)
$$X_e P_x + N P_n = (1 - s)Z.$$

Taking percentage changes, we have

(7) $N^* = X^* + \left(1 + \dfrac{\gamma A}{1 - A}\right)(P_x^* - P_n^*)$,   where $A = X_e P_x/C$.

Consequently, η_n, the elasticity of demand for imports with respect to the price ratio P_n/P_x equals $(-1 - \gamma A/(1 - A))$, and

(8)
$$\gamma = \frac{1 - A}{A}(-1 - \eta_n).$$

When the elasticity definitions are substituted in equation 5, we obtain:

$$\frac{-X^*}{P_x^*} = -1 - \eta_n - \eta_x.$$

C. To show that investment expands more rapidly than output as the consequence of devaluation, that the price level rises, and that the rate of return on investment rises. We may derive the per cent rise in investment as follows. Prior to devaluation the level of investment equals

$$X_I^0 = K_0\lambda.$$

As a result of devaluation and any associated price rise, investment consists of two components: The first is the extra capital associated with the rise in output to the new growth path and with any change in the capital-output ratio. The D term represents this disturbed percentage rise in the capital stock. The second term consists of the secular growth of capital along the higher path.

$$X_I' = K_0 D + K_1\lambda$$

Since $K_1 = K_0(1 + D)$, we have the following expression for X_I^*, the percentage rise in investment:

(9)
$$X_I^* = D(1 + 1/\lambda).$$

Let us now derive D, the disturbed percentage rise in the capital stock. We may in general write the production function as

$$X^* = K^* + \alpha Q^*, \quad \text{where} \quad Q^* \equiv L^* - K^*.$$

(10)
$$K^* = X^* - \alpha Q^*.$$

This is the disturbed term we seek. We may write Q^* in terms of a price rise by looking at the equilibrium condition for the use of labor.

$$\bar{w} = P_x f_L$$

Taking logarithmic derivatives, we have

$$0 = P_x^* + v Q^*,$$

where $v \equiv f_L^*/Q^*$ is the elasticity of the marginal productivity of labor. Consequently,

$$P_x^* = -v Q^*.$$

It may be shown that $v = (\alpha - 1)/\sigma$, where α is the share of output paid to labor and σ the elasticity of substitution.[6] Assume $\sigma = 1$, and write $Q^* = (1 - \alpha)P_x^*$. Substitute in equation (10). We have

(10′)
$$D = K^* = X^* - \left(\frac{\alpha}{1 - \alpha}\right) P_x^*.$$

Consequently, the percentage rise in investment may be written:

(9′)
$$X_I^* = \left[X^* - \frac{\alpha}{1 - \alpha} P_x^*\right] \cdot \left(1 + \frac{1}{\lambda}\right).$$

I shall derive the expression $X_I^* - X^*$ and show that it becomes positive as a result of devaluation. In order to do so it is necessary to solve for the rise of prices P_x^*, which in the short run rations the increment of output among users. The following procedure will be used: Equation (5) shows the per cent fall in the growth path from a given percentage rise in the money wage and the price P_x. Because of the symmetry between the price P_x and the exchange rate, equation (5) also shows the per cent rise in the growth path from a given devaluation. As explained in the text the output level at the full employment growth path is, in the short run insufficient to satisfy the total demand for output. Consequently, the price level rises and the capital-output ratio falls, as seen by $Q^* > 0$.

To continue the proof, we have shown in equation (5) above that $X^* = B\rho^*$, where ρ^* is the percentage devaluation of the exchange rate, and X^* the upward shift of the growth path. We shall prove below that

$$P_x^* = C X^* = C B \rho^*.$$

Consequently,

$$X_I^* > X^* \quad \text{if} \quad 1 > \frac{\alpha}{1 - \alpha} C.$$

We may solve for the rise in prices by writing the following expression for the per cent rise in the growth path:

(11) $X^* = jX_c^* + kX_e^* + mX_I^*;$ where $j = X_c/X \quad k = X_e/X$

$m = X_I/X$ and $j + k + m = 1$

(12) $X_c^* = X^* - \gamma P_x^* + \gamma \rho^*$

(13) $X_e^* = -\frac{1}{\beta} P_x^* + \frac{1}{\beta} \rho^*$

(9') $X_I^* = \left(X^* - \frac{\alpha}{1 - \alpha} P_x^*\right)\left(1 + \frac{1}{\lambda}\right).$

Also recall from equation (5) that

(14) $X^* = \rho^*\left[\dfrac{\gamma j + \dfrac{1}{\beta} k}{k}\right] = B\rho^*.$

When these definitions and solutions are substituted in equation (10), we obtain CB and C

(15) $P_x^* = \rho^*\left[\overbrace{\dfrac{Bm/\lambda}{kB + \dfrac{m\alpha}{1 - \alpha}\left(1 + \dfrac{1}{\lambda}\right)}}^{BC}\right] = X^*\left[\overbrace{\dfrac{m/\lambda}{kB + \dfrac{m\alpha}{1 - \alpha}\left(1 + \dfrac{1}{\lambda}\right)}}^{C}\right].$

We see that

$$1 > \frac{\alpha}{1 - \alpha} C \quad \text{if} \quad 0 < \gamma j + \frac{k}{\beta} + m \frac{\alpha}{1 - \alpha}.$$

We have already proved in Section B of this appendix that $\gamma j + k/\beta$ is positive. Thus, the whole expression will be positive. This means that investment expands by a greater percentage than savings, and that the price level rises. Finally, it remains to be shown that the rate of return on investment rises. This last is given from:

$$r = f_K, \quad \text{so that} \quad r^* = f_K^* = uQ^*,$$

where u is the elasticity of the marginal productivity of capital. It can be shown that $u = \alpha/\sigma$. Assuming that $\sigma = 1$, we may write $r^* = \alpha Q^*$ which is positive.

MODEL II—TWO-SECTOR ECONOMY

A. To show that an exogenous rise in the money wage lowers the level of real output and moves the economy to a lower long-run growth path. I shall also show that when there is unemployment, devaluation raises the level of real output and moves the economy to a higher long-run growth path.

From equation (12) in the text, we have the definition of income,

$$Z \equiv XP_z + YP_y.$$

Using starred superscripts to denote percentage changes, we have:

(1) $Z^* = (1 - J)[X^* + P_z^*] + J[Y^* + P_y^*]$ where $J \equiv YP_y/Z.$

From equations (3), (4), (6), and (7) we may derive:

$$w_z^* = P_z^* + f_L^*$$
$$w_z^* = P_z^* + f_K^*,$$

from which it follows that

$$f_L^* = f_K^* = 0; \qquad L_z^* = K_z^*;$$

and

(2) $w^* = P_z^* = P_y^*$

From equations (9) and (11) we may derive:

$$X^* = -\frac{P_z'^*}{\beta} + L_w^* = -\frac{(w - \rho^*)}{\beta} + L_w^*.$$

I shall ignore the secular term L_w^* in this analysis as we are dealing with a shift from one growth path to another with the same secular rate of growth L_w^*. Further denote $D = -(w^* - \rho^*)$, so that

(3) $X^* = D/\beta.$

From equation (8), we have

$$Y = Y_c + Y_I.$$

Taking percentage changes, we have

(4) $Y^* = aY_c^* + bY_I^*.$

From equation (15), we may derive

(5) $$Y_c^* = Z^* - w^* + \gamma D.$$

From equation (23), we have

$$Y_I = KK^* = \left(\frac{K}{X}\right)XK^*.$$

Since K/X and K^* are constant along the long-run growth paths, we have

(6) $$Y_I^* = X^* = D/\beta.$$

We may substitute equations (3), (4), (5), and (6) in equation (1), to obtain

(1′) $$Z^* - w^* = D\frac{\left[\dfrac{1 - J + bJ}{\beta} + \gamma aJ\right]}{1 - aJ}.$$

Note that $1/\beta = -\eta_x$, the elasticity of demand for exports, and

$$\gamma = \frac{1 - A}{A}(-1 - \eta_n),$$

where η_n is the elasticity of demand for imports. Substituting above, we have

(1″) $$Z^* - w^* = D\left[-\eta_x + \frac{NP_n(-1 - \eta_n)}{XP_x + Y_I P_y}\right].$$

We expect the bracketed term to be positive. This will occur when $-\eta_x + k(-1 - \eta_n) > 0$, where k is the ratio of the value of imports to the sum of the money value of exports and investment.

B. Let us now turn to the short-run effects of devaluation. In the short run, the following terms describe the rise in savings and investment:

(7) $$Z^* = \rho^*\left[\frac{1}{\beta} + \frac{J(a\gamma + b/\beta\lambda)}{1 - aJ}\right]$$

(8) $$I^* = \rho^*\left[\frac{1}{\beta} + \frac{1}{\beta\lambda}\right].$$

We may derive these terms using the same procedure as in Section A above. Write the per cent growth of output, noting that we are dealing with devaluation only, and $w^* = 0$.

(9) $$Z^* = (1 - J)X^* + J(Y^*).$$

Since $w^* = 0$, we have

(3′) $$X^* = \rho^*/\beta,$$

(5') $$Y_c^* = Z^* + \alpha\rho^*.$$

The term for the rise in investment will contain an accelerator. We have an unchanged capital-output ratio, so that $X^* = K^*$. Prior to devaluation we have the following expression for investment:

$$Y_I^0 = K_0\lambda.$$

Following devaluation, investment must make good any shortfall in the capital stock, and make allowances for the normal growth of the capital stock. We have the expression for investment following devaluation:

$$Y_I' = K_1\lambda + \left(\frac{K}{X}\right)\Delta X, \quad \text{where} \quad K_1 = K_0 + \left(\frac{K}{X}\right)\Delta X.$$

Therefore

(6') $$Y_I^* = X^*\left[1 + \frac{1}{\lambda}\right] = \rho^*/\beta(1 + 1/\lambda).$$

This gives us equation (8). When equation (3'), (5'), and (6') are substituted in (9), we obtain equation (7). When $I^* > S^*$, the following condition holds:

(10) $$\frac{\eta_n + 1}{\eta_x} < \frac{1}{\lambda}.$$

This may be seen by forming the expression:

(11) $$I^* - S^* = \frac{\dfrac{1 - J}{\beta\lambda} - Ja\gamma}{1 - aJ}.$$

This expression is positive when the numerator is positive. Substitute the definitions

$$\beta = -\frac{1}{\eta_x}; \qquad \gamma = \frac{NP_n}{Y_c P_y}(-1 - \eta_n),$$

and then obtain expression (10).

C. The long-run effects of devaluation may also be shown. In the long run, investment grows at the same rate as output and the capital stock. Consequently, we may use the results of Section II-A of this appendix. Recall that we are dealing with devaluation only, so that $w^* = 0$, and $D = \rho^*$.

(1''') $$S^* = Z^* = \rho^*\left[\frac{1}{\beta} + \frac{\gamma aJ}{1 - aJ}\right]$$

(6) $Y_I^* = X^* = \rho^*/\beta$

We may form the equation for $I^* = S^*$

(12) $I^* - S^* = -\dfrac{\gamma aJ}{1 - aJ}.$

This will be positive when γ is negative. This will occur when $\eta_n > -1$.

Notes

1. I wish to thank Peter Kenen and Jerome Stein for their perceptive comments.
2. Fritz Machlup, "Relative Prices and Aggregate Spending in the Analysis of Devaluation," *American Economic Review*, XLV (June, 1955), 255.
3. This approach is suggested by J. L. Ingram in his *Regional Payments Mechanisms—The Case of Puerto Rico* (Chapel Hill: University of North Carolina Press, 1962).
4. S. C. Tsiang, "The Role of Money in Trade Balance Stability," *American Economic Review*, LI (December, 1961). Also contains a good bibliography of earlier articles on this subject. Also see R. R. Rhomberg, "A Model of the Canadian Economy under Fixed and Fluctuating Exchange Rates," *Journal of Political Economy*, LXXII, No. 1 (February, 1964).
5. J. M. Fleming, "Domestic Financial Policies under Fixed and Floating Exchange Rates," International Monetary Fund, *Staff Papers*, November, 1962; R. A. Mundell, "Flexible Exchange Rates and Employment Policy," *Canadian Journal of Economics*, November, 1961.
6. For a proof, see G. H. Borts and J. L. Stein, *Economic Growth in a Free Market* (New York: Columbia University Press, 1964), Ch. VII.

Differential Growth Rates Among Open Economies: Theory and Fact[1]

Jerome L. Stein

THERE is a keen interest in explaining why states or regions experience different rates of economic growth. Many diverse opinions exist on this subject. Gunnar Myrdal, for example, asserts that the free play of market forces aggravates interregional inequalities in income per head. His thesis is as follows:

(i) That there are a small group of countries which are quite well off and a much larger group of extremely poor countries;
(ii) that the countries in the former group are on the whole firmly settled in a pattern of continuing economic development, while in the latter group average progress is slower. . .
(iii) that . . . in recent decades the economic inequalities between the developed and underdeveloped countries have been increasing.[2]

Capital movements among regions are said to aggravate the inequality. "In the centres of expansion increased demand will spur investment which in its turn will increase incomes and demand and cause a second round of investment, and so on. Savings will increase as a result of higher incomes but will tend to lag behind investment . . . Studies in many countries have shown how the banking system, if not regulated to act differently, tends to become an instrument for siphoning off the savings from the poorer regions to the richer and more progressive ones where returns on capital are high and secure."[3]

This view is in striking contrast to the Classical and Marxian views that capital accumulation tends to lower the marginal product of capital. Insofar as capital accumulates more rapidly in countries with high per capita income, the marginal product of capital should decline there relative to that in countries with low per capita income.

Myrdal says, "It is an understatement to say that the theory of international trade does not furnish us with a model or logical mechanism

227

representing a system of rational hypotheses which can be used for explaining why and how the huge economic inequalities between countries have come to exist and why they tend to grow. This theory has, instead, been given a twist, and—mirabile dictu—in very recent years increasingly so, in the direction of suggesting a situation and a development trend quite contrary to the actual ones."[4]

Contemporary interest in growth has been further stimulated by the development of the European Economic Community (EEC). An important economic question is: How will the rates of growth of states be affected as a result of their joining the EEC? Moreover, as the countries of the world liberalize their trade and permit capital to flow internationally, what will happen to their growth rates?

There are two themes to this paper. First, I construct both simple and multisector models of growth among open economies to prove that Myrdal's conclusions can be deduced from a consistent set of economic relationships. There can be permanent differences in the rates of growth of per capita output among countries or regions. Second, I examine the validity of his contention that the rate of growth tends to be higher in the high per capita income countries than in the low per capita income countries. Myrdal bases his conclusions concerning the effects of free capital movements upon the experiences of the developed and the underdeveloped countries. I use the experiences of the states within the United States as my sources of data.

I claim that the U.S. interstate experience is more relevant for a test of the effects of a free market upon growth than are the experiences of countries with different degrees of political stability and restrictions upon private enterprise. I am holding the political factors constant and am examining solely the economic forces at work. Thereby the economic effects of a free market will be clearly perceived. It is shown that the low per capita income regions in the United States tend to have higher growth rates than do the high per capita income regions. Thereby, a convergence tends to occur among state per capita incomes in a free market area. Eventually, interregional differences in the rates of growth of per capita income tend to disappear as the intrastate allocation of resources becomes more efficient.

GROWTH IN AN OPEN ECONOMY[5]

SINGLE SECTOR MODEL[6]

Consider an open economy producing one good with an aggregative production function subject to both technological change and constant returns to scale. Assume that labor is immobile among regions. When the inputs of labor (N) and capital (K) are given, output (Y) is assumed to grow at g per cent per year: the rate of neutral technological change. Let lower-case letters denote percentage rates of change. Then

$$(1) \qquad\qquad y = ak + (1 - a)n + g,$$

where a is the ratio of the marginal to the average product of capital, and $(1 - a)$ is the ratio of the marginal to the average product of labor. (The determinants of the shares a, $(1 - a)$ are discussed below.) Assume that there are both lower and upper bounds on a; $1 > a_1 > a > a_2 > 0$.

The rate of growth of the labor force (n) may be considered as an exogenous variable.[7] But, what determines the rate of growth of capital (k)? Two reasonable functions can be explored to determine k. In a single good model we assume (2.1): that capital grows at such a rate as to bring the marginal product of capital into equality with the world interest rate within a very short period of time. If M is the marginal product of capital and r is the world interest rate, then it is assumed that

$$(2.1) \qquad\qquad M = a(Y/K)$$

and

$$(2.2) \qquad\qquad M = r.$$

For equations (2) to hold, given r, output and capital must grow at the same rate. This means that

$$(3) \qquad\qquad y = k.$$

The rate of growth of output is, using (1) and (3),

$$(4) \qquad\qquad y = k = \frac{g}{1 - a} + n,$$

a linear combination of the rate of growth of the labor supply and the rate of "technological change." Swan obtained the same result, in a closed economy, because his equilibrium condition required that capital and output grow at the same rates.

Per capita output grows at a rate $(y - n)$,

$$(5) \qquad\qquad (y - n) = \frac{g}{1 - a}.$$

(Assume that population and the labor force grow at the same rates.) There will be interregional differences in the rates of growth of per capita output if there are differences in the rates of technological change. Below, we give an economic explanation of why such a phenomenon can occur among open economies.

Logically Myrdal's contention that there can be permanent differences in the rate of growth of per capita output among regions is consistent with this model of economic growth. Regional equality of per capita incomes need not occur.

Will the slowly growing countries export capital to the rapidly growing countries? The answer is: probably yes. Real capital imports occur if investment exceeds savings.[8] Investment, by definition, is kK. Assume that savings (S) are proportional to output:

$$(6) \qquad S = sY.$$

Capital imports occur if kK exceeds S. From equations (2.1) and (2.2) we know that $(Y/K) = (r/a)$. Imports of capital occur if, and only if,

$$(7) \qquad y = k = \left(\frac{g}{1-a} + n\right) > \frac{s}{a} r.$$

If all countries have similar savings-income ratios and similar shares of output going to capital, the rapidly growing countries are the capital importers, and the slowly growing countries are the capital exporters. A numerical example is interesting. Suppose the savings ratio $s = 0.20$, the share of capital $a = 0.33$, and the world interest rate $r = 0.06$. Then countries which are growing faster than 3.6 per cent per annum will be importing capital from those growing at slower rates.

The equilibrium world interest rate will be such as to equate world investment with world savings. Let the i subscripts refer to the ith country. Then, summing investment and savings among countries,

$$(8) \qquad \sum k_i K_i = \sum r \frac{s_i}{a_i} K_i.$$

The equilibrium rate of interest r is

$$(9) \qquad r = \sum k_i K_i / \sum \frac{s_i}{a_i} K_i.$$

If the weighted sum of growth rates, the numerator in (9), is positive, then the world interest rate will also be positive. The world interest rate is a weighted average of rates of growth of capital (or of output).

MYRDAL'S RESULTS IN A MULTISECTOR MODEL

We can extend our analysis to a multisector model and obtain Myrdal's conclusions. Interregional and intraregional labor mobility is permitted in

Variability in Factor Shares

Recent studies have suggested that it is illegitimate to assume that the shares of income accruing to labor and capital are constant.[14] The elasticity of substitution is substantially below unity. This means that the share of the more rapidly growing input will decrease. Our analysis hitherto has assumed factor shares within each industry to be constant. How should our analysis be revised in view of a less-than-unity elasticity of substitution? We may consider a single-sector model, since the results do not differ significantly in a multisector model.

From the definition of the elasticity of substitution (σ), the percentage rate of change of a is:[15]

$$(25) \qquad \frac{1}{a}\frac{da}{dt} = (1 - a)\left(\frac{1}{\sigma} - 1\right)(n - k).$$

Consider an equilibrium situation, for a given value of a, as described by equation (4). Output and capital will grow at the same rate, if the output-capital ratio is to be constant. If $y = k$, then the growth of the capital to labor ratio is given by equation (26).

$$(26) \qquad (k - n) = \frac{g}{1 - a}$$

Substitute (26) into (25) and obtain equation (27) which relates a to g and σ.

$$(27) \qquad \frac{1}{a}\frac{da}{dt} = -g\left(\frac{1}{\sigma} - 1\right)$$

Solve (27) for a and obtain (28). Suppose that there is technological change: g is positive.

$$(28) \qquad a = a_0 \exp\left[-g\left(\frac{1}{\sigma} - 1\right)t\right]; \qquad 1 > a_1 > a > a_2 > 0,$$

where a_0 is the initial value. Since σ is less than unity, the value of a will decline.

The equilibrium growth $y = k$ will decline as the share going to capital declines (i.e., as the share going to labor increases), as can be seen from equation (4). There may be a positive lower bound to the share of output received by capital: a_2. Then $a = a_2$, and the equilibrium conditions are those that were derived from the assumption of a constant share: a_2. In effect σ converges to unity, as a converges to a_2.

If there were no technological change, $g = 0$, then a would be constant.

Again, the equilibrium conditions are those derived from the assumption of a constant share. If we are interested in the very long run, it is legitimate to use a constant share of output going to capital.[16]

AN ECONOMIC INTERPRETATION OF INTERSTATE DIFFERENCES IN THE RATE OF TECHNOLOGICAL CHANGE

The level of technology is simply a term denoting the level of output obtained from a fixed combination of labor and capital inputs. As the level of output increases, for a given combination of labor and capital, we say that technological advance has occurred. Among a set of open economies, why should there be different rates of technological change? Insofar as technological change represents improvements in knowledge, why is not the knowledge disseminated over the entire set of states?

It is useful to distinguish two aspects of knowledge: its dissemination and its application. When new knowledge is *applied* to production, then we could assume that it is embodied in capital goods. The rate of application of new knowledge would then depend upon the rate at which new capital goods are replacing older pieces of equipment. Specifically, the rate of *application* of new knowledge could depend upon the average age of equipment and the rate of gross investment. On the other hand, in a set of open economies the rate of dissemination of new knowledge should be as great as the mobility of capital.

There is another aspect to the rate of technological change in an economy producing more than one good. It will be shown that the rate of technological change is related to the rate at which the misallocation of resources is being corrected.[17] There can be wide differences in the rates of technological change among open economies insofar as there are different degrees of resource misallocation.

Suppose that state employment were divided between the nonagricultural sector N and the agricultural sector A, such that Or_1 per cent of the labor force were in nonagriculture and $(100 - Or_1)$ per cent were in agriculture (Figure 1).

The NN schedule in Figure 1 is a relation between the wage per nonagricultural employee (W_N) and the proportion of total employment in nonagricultural pursuits; the AA schedule is the corresponding function for agriculture. Each schedule is negatively sloped with respect to its own coordinates. As we move from 0 to 100 per cent, nonagricultural employment rises relative to agricultural employment; and the nonagricultural wage declines relative to the agriculture (W_A) wage. For simplicity, we

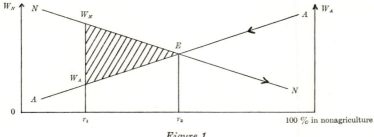

Figure 1

can assume in the graph that the quantity of capital in each sector is fixed. Two reasons exist for the downward-sloping schedules. First, the relative price of a product depends upon the relative supplies of the two outputs. As nonagricultural output rises relative to agricultural output, there will be a decline in the relative price of nonagricultural output. Second, the law of variable proportions leads to a decline in the marginal physical product of labor as employment rises relative to the (fixed) quantity of capital. Both reasons explain why the value of the marginal product of labor in sector N (or A) declines as the volume of employment in sector N (or A) increases.

The potential increase in total income, from a more efficient allocation of a fixed quantity of inputs, depends upon three variables. First, it depends upon the initial wage differential, $W_N - W_A$, in the two sectors. Second, it depends upon the ratio of nonagricultural employment (Or_2) which would equalize wages in the two sectors. Third, it depends upon the extent to which employment in the low wage sector exceeds (100 − Or_2): the efficient allocation.

According to Figure 1 an increase in the ratio of nonagricultural employment from Or_1 to Or_2 would raise total income by the shaded area (W_N E W_A). This rise in income would be called technological improvement, since output increases while the *total* combination of labor and capital in the economy is unchanged. Insofar as there are different degrees of resource misallocation *within* states, or different rates at which the misallocation of resources is being eliminated *within* states, there will be different rates of "technological change" *among* states. In this manner, some economic content can be given to interstate differences in g, the rate of technological change.

Labor migrates from low wage areas, which are usually rural, to higher wage areas, which are usually urban.[18] Thereby the misallocation of resources is reduced. The rate of migration from low to high wage areas could be a linear function of time. Then, the rate at which resource allocation is being corrected (i.e., the rate of technological change) is g (t). This is an economic interpretation of g, the rate of technological change, in equation (1) above.

THE RELATION BETWEEN GROWTH RATES, PER CAPITA INCOME, AND THE DEGREE OF RESOURCE MISALLOCATION

Myrdal's contentions are consistent with the implications of the single-sector and multisector growth models presented above. Permanent differences in the rates of growth of output, and of per capita output, among states are possible. The significant economic questions concern the character of the independent variables g and n. Why are there interstate differences in g and n? Will these differences disappear over time? If these differences are eliminated, then the model claims that states (i.e., regions) will grow at the sames rates.[19]

Myrdal has argued that the states with high rates of growth of per capita income are the states with the initially high levels of per capita income. We indicate that this is contradicted by the United States data. The states with the initially low levels of per capita income have (a) the greatest misallocation of resources in the initial periods and (b) the greatest growth rates of per capita income. In this manner a convergence of per capita income has tended to occur, although at a decreasing rate, in recent years.

EMPIRICAL ANALYSIS

On the basis of Figure 1 above, the misallocation of resources is measured by the initial wage differentials (W_A/W_N) and the ratio of nonagricultural to total employment (N/L). Ideally, we must also know the perfect allocation Or_2. Since this ratio is unknown, it has been dropped from the analysis, at the expense of some predictive accuracy. Assume that the rate at which resource misallocation is being corrected is positively related to the degree of resource misallocation existing at the beginning of the period. The g depends upon (W_A/W_N) and (N/L). According to the results summarized in equation (5) above, the rate of growth of per worker income $(y-n)$ is positively related to g. As a result, we predict the following:

The rate of growth of output per worker $(y-n)$ in a state from period t to period $t+1$ depends (a) negatively upon the ratio of nonagricultural to total employment in period t and (b) negatively upon the ratio W_A/W_N in period t.

Our conditional predictions are summarized by the directions of the arrows in Table 1. Each row refers to the ratio W_A/W_N. States in row 1 have greater ratios than the United States average, and row 2 contains the states with ratios below the United States average. According to the theory developed above, there was a greater misallocation of labor in the bottom row, and hence a higher rate of growth of per worker output should be found among the states in the bottom row.

Columns refer to the ratio of nonagricultural to total state employment (N/L). States in the first column have higher ratios of the labor force in nonagriculture than do states in the second column. There was a smaller concentration of the labor force in the low wage agricultural sector among the states in column 1 than in column 2. A greater rate of growth of income from a reallocation of labor should occur in column 2 than in column 1.

From the valuable study by Richard Easterlin,[20] we have data on service income per worker in agriculture and in nonagriculture, per capita personal income, and the ratio of nonagricultural to total employment by state as far back as 1880. Easterlin defines service income as the sum of wages, salaries, and proprietor's income, with the imputed rents of farm dwellings included in the agricultural component. Insofar as proprietor's income per worker is likely to be greater in agriculture than in nonagriculture, the ratio of service income per worker in agriculture to service income per worker in nonagriculture is higher than W_A/W_N. Bearing this bias in mind, we shall nevertheless use the ratio of service income per worker in agriculture relative to that prevailing in nonagriculture as an estimate of W_A/W_N.

Personal income per capita is income received, whereas the models of growth refer to produced income per worker. There are three differences

TABLE 1
Resource Misallocation and Growth

W_A/W_N	N/L	
	Above average	Below average
Above average	Lowest growth of per capita income $\longrightarrow$	$\downarrow$
Below average	$\downarrow$ $\longrightarrow$	Highest growth of per capita income

between these concepts. First, personal income includes net transfer payments. There is, however, no significant relationship between net transfer payments and the sum of participation (service) income and property income.[21] Hence, we may neglect the role of transfer payments in producing a systematic difference between produced and received income. Second, personal income contains the income earned in one state which is paid to a resident of another state. The main category of income, which is amenable to the criticism that received and produced income differ, is property income. There is good reason to believe that the errors involved in working with per capita personal income rather than with per capita produced income are not serious. Property income is a small part of personal income. And there is a high positive correlation between participation (service) income per capita and property income per capita.[22] Since participation income is a very large fraction of produced income, there should be a positive correlation between produced and received income.

Estimates of produced income by George H. Borts[23] indicate that movements in received income underestimate movements in produced income. It is likely that we would have even more marked results had we used produced rather than personal income.

Third, the theory refers to the growth of output per worker, and the data utilized refer to per capita income. This objection is not serious since (in 1950) the rank order of the states was almost identical for participation income per person employed and personal income per capita.[24]

Tables 2a, 2b, and 2c below summarize the relation between the growth of personal income per capita, in various periods, and the values of W_A/W_N and N/L in the initial period. The top number indicates the average rate of growth of personal income per capita among the states in the cell, and the bottom number (in parenthesis) indicates the per cent of the states in the cell which grew more rapidly than the U.S. average. The arrows are drawn in accordance with the theory developed above; and the rate of growth of personal income per capita is predicted to move in the direction of the arrows. Two cells have only one observation, and this is denoted by the sentence $n = 1$. An analysis of variance was carried out on the four cells in each table. At the foot of each table is the F ratio, i.e., the ratio of the subsample mean square to the individual mean square. The hypothesis tested was that this ratio does not differ from unity. That is, we tested whether the observations in the cells were samples from the same population of growth rates. In each case F was significantly different from unity at the 5 per cent (*) or the 1 per cent

TABLE 2

Growth of Personal Income Per Capita in States Classified
by N/L and W_A/W_N in the Initial Period

TABLE 2a
1880–1900

W_A/W_N	Above U.S.	N/L	Below U.S.
Above U.S.	26% (33%)	$\longrightarrow$	34% (38%)
Below U.S.	21% (33%) $\downarrow$ $n = 6$	$\longrightarrow$	46% (58%) $\downarrow$

$$F = 3.04*$$

TABLE 2b
1900–1920

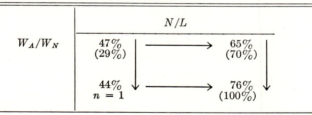

W_A/W_N		N/L	
	27% (10%)	$\longrightarrow$	43% (33%)
	−5% $n = 1$	$\longrightarrow$	57% (83%) $\downarrow$

$$F = 4.69**$$

TABLE 2c
1920–1950

W_A/W_N		N/L	
	47% (29%)	$\longrightarrow$	65% (70%)
	44% $\downarrow$ $n = 1$	$\longrightarrow$	76% (100%) $\downarrow$

$$F = 6.68**$$

N/L = ratio of nonagricultural to total employment at the initial date.
W_A/W_N = ratio of agricultural to nonagricultural service income per worker at the initial date.

(**) level. Hence the four subsamples in each table are probably not drawn from a common population, and whatever population means are involved are estimated in an unbiased manner by the four subsample means.

Except where the number of observations in a cell is very small (as in cell 21), the data are compatible with the theory of growth in an open economy. We must reject the hypothesis that the variables W_A/W_N and N/L have no effect upon a state's rate of growth of per capita personal income. *Hence, the theory that $(y - n)$ depends upon g, and g reflects the rate at which resource misallocation is being corrected, is consistent with United States data.*

We now maintain that states are becoming more similar over time in their ratios of agricultural to total employment and that the intersectoral service income per worker differential has narrowed. The implication is that their rates of growth of per capita income, and output per unit of capital, will converge. Since g in each state will tend to converge to the national rate, $(y-n)$ will tend to converge to the national average.

There can be no doubt concerning the convergence of the ratios of agricultural employment.[25] The average deviation of the ratio of agricultural to total employment fell from nineteen percentage points in 1870 to eight percentage points in 1950. Similarly, there has been a narrowing of the service income differential between sectors over time.[26] During the years 1880 and 1900, the service income differential between the agricultural and nonagricultural sector was quite large in percentage terms. The agricultural service income was always less than 80 per cent of the nonagricultural level; in forty-three out of forty-eight states, it was less than 60 per cent of the nonagricultural figure. However, by 1920, there were only fifteen states where the agricultural service income was less than 60 per cent of the nonagricultural figure. Agriculture was actually the high service income sector in seven states;[27] and in three states[28] incomes were equal in both sectors. With the passage of time, the differential narrowed even more. By 1950 the differential between sectors did not exceed 20 per cent in twenty out of forty-eight states; and in thirteen states agriculture was the high service income sector.

The fact that service income in agriculture exceeds that outside of agriculture is due to the nature of the data. Service income is composed of wages, salaries, and self-employment income. A large fraction of self-employment income is actually a return to the capital invested in the business. It is reasonable to expect this property income component to be a larger fraction of agricultural self-employment income than in such nonagricultural sectors as trade, services, or construction. The reason is the large capital requirements in agriculture compared to these other nonagricultural sectors.

Efficiency would be realized when wages are equalized in the two sectors and when the rates of return on capital are equalized. Due to agriculture's heavy capital requirements, the efficiency condition in fact requires that service income per employee be higher in agriculture.

With the narrowing of the intersectoral income differential, the relationship between the ratio of nonagricultural to total employment and per capita income should be attenuated. A low ratio of nonagricultural to total employment implies a large misallocation of resources only when there is a wide earnings differential between sectors. We have indicated how the percentage differential has narrowed. A reduction has also occurred in the absolute differential between the U.S. average values of W_N and W_A, in 1929 prices.[29] The differential, $W_N - W_A$, was \$680 (1880), \$722 (1900), \$563 (1919–1921) and \$554 (1949–1951). It should follow from the theory developed above that the positive association between per capita personal income and N/L should be weakened over time—since the income differential has narrowed. This, in fact, occurred. Easterlin calculated a coefficient of rank-order correlation (tau) between (1) state personal income per capita, and (2) the state ratio nonagricultural to total labor force N/L. This coefficient was 0.73 for 1880; 0.62 (1900); 0.69 (1920) and 0.45 (1950).

In summary we may say that there is clear evidence that the theory advanced above is not inconsistent with the data. The growth of personal income per capita can be explained by the improved allocation of resources. *Moreover, since g is converging among states, there will be a convergence of growth rates and of output-capital ratios among states.*

The experience of a free capital movement area, such as the United States, fails to produce Myrdal's results. The states with the highest rates of growth of per capita personal income had the lowest levels of per capita income in the initial period. As a result, there has been a tendency for per capita income among states to converge.[30] This convergence has been a slow process; and there has been a more rapid convergence of the high per capita income states downward to the U.S. mean than there has been a convergence of the low per capita income states upward to the U.S. mean. Nevertheless, convergence has tended to occur. The coefficient of variation of personal income per capita among states was the following: 57.9 per cent (1880), 42.5 per cent (1900), 30.4 per cent (1919–1921), and 23.4 per cent (1949–1951). A detailed statistical description of this phenomenon is in Easterlin.[31]

We have neglected the role of interstate differences in n (the growth of the labor supply) in our empirical analysis for a very simple reason. The rates of natural increase are positively correlated with the ratio A/L. Rates of natural increase are highest in rural areas.[32] Since the A/L ratio was included in the analysis, n was also included.

POSSIBLE CRITICISM OF THE EMPIRICAL ANALYSIS

It could be argued that g does not represent the increased income that occurs as a result of a more efficient allocation of resources. Instead, it could reflect the differences in the rates of growth of the prices of output produced by the various states. Since Y is measured in money terms, y is the rate of growth of physical output plus the rate of growth of price. Variable g is then the residual between y and $ak + bn$, which is the rate of growth of the price. It could then be argued that the differences in the rates of growth of per capita income among states simply reflect differences in the demand for state produced products.

There are strong reasons for rejecting this contention. Interstate differences in rates of growth cannot be explained on the basis of interstate differences in the composition of output. Borts and Stein[33] studied interstate differences in the rates of growth of manufacturing employment between business cycle peaks: 1919–1929, 1929–1947, 1948–1953, and 1948–1957. We tested the hypothesis that the growth rate of a state is determined by the composition of the industries it contains. If these industries grow at particular rates nationally, it is assumed that they will grow at the same rate in the region under examination. In order to know how fast a region is to grow, one obtains the national growth rates of the region's industrial components. The national growth rates are then weighted by the proportions in which the components are presently combined in the region; this yields the *projected* growth rate for the region.

We used the national growth rates of twenty groups (mainly two-digit industries) in the Census of Manufactures during each of the four periods mentioned above. The *projected* growth rate of manufacturing employment in each of the forty-eight states was compared with the actual growth rate. Using the Spearman rank correlation coefficient (r_s), we found the following relation between actual and projected growth rates:

Interval Between Business Cycle Peaks	r_s
1919–1929	−0.0334
1929–1947	+0.0601
1948–1953	+0.4348*
1948–1957	+0.1494

*Significant at 5%.

Only during the short period 1948–1953 was there any statistically significant relation between the actual and the projected growth rate. Over a longer period there is no significant relation between the growth rate of a state and its industrial composition. We therefore reject the view that interstate differences in g arise from differences in the composition of output among states.

CONCLUSION

Interregional differences in the rate of growth can occur as a result of differences in the rate of measured technological change. There are two aspects to the rate of technological change: (a) the rate of growth of the maximum output resulting from a given input combination; (b) the rate at which resource misallocation is being eliminated.

Insofar as the lower per capita income regions have had greater rates at which resource misallocation is being eliminated, they have had greater rates of growth per capita output than the richer regions. Over time, the degree of resource misallocation has narrowed among states. Intrastate resource misallocation is being eliminated. Consequently, the growth of per capita output is expected to be more uniform among states. The growth of per capita output would be determined by the first determinant of technological change, which is expected to be similar among states.

Notes

1. This paper is developed from material in G. H. Borts and J. L. Stein, *Economic Growth in a Free Market* (New York: Columbia University Press, 1964). I am indebted to J. Niehans and G. H. Borts for helpful comments on an earlier draft of this paper.

2. Gunnar Myrdal, *Economic Theory and Under-Developed Regions* (London: G. Duckworth, 1957), p. 6.

3. *Ibid.*, p. 28.

4. *Ibid.*, p. 149.

5. Unless otherwise specified, aggregate demand is assumed equal to capacity output through flexible exchange rates and monetary-fiscal policy.

6. See T. W. Swan, "Economic Growth and Capital Accumulation," *The Economic Record*, XXXII (1956), 334–61; R. M. Solow, "A Contribution to the Theory of Economic Growth," *Quarterly Journal of Economics*, LXX (1956).

7. See J. Niehans, "Economic Growth with Two Endogenous Factors," *Quarterly Journal of Economics*, LXXVII (August, 1963) for a paper which does not make this restrictive assumption.

8. This follows from the national income accounting identities:
   (1) Consumption plus savings equal income.
   (2) Consumption plus investment plus exports minus imports equal income.

9. The constancy of "a" and "b" is discussed in Section C.

10. Variations in h will be shown to be a source of the measured rate of technological change.

11. From (11)

$$m_y = y - k_y = 0.$$

From (18)

$$y = bk_y + (1 - b)n_y + g_y.$$

Hence

$$m_y = 0 = (1 - b)(n - k)_y + g_y.$$

Solve for

$$(k - n)_y = g_y/(1 - b).$$

This is the rate of growth of the ratio of capital to labor which will leave the marginal product of capital unchanged.

12. This paper has drawn heavily upon W. F. Stolper and P. A. Samuelson, "Protection and Real Wages," *Review of Economic Studies,* IX (1941).

13. The real wage grows at

$$\frac{a}{(1 - b)} (g_y - r) + g_x.$$

Real produced property income per worker RK_x/N_x grows at a rate

$$r + \frac{(g_y - r)}{1 - b} = \frac{g_y - rb}{1 - b}.$$

14. K. J. Arrow, H. B. Chenery, B. Minhas, and R. M. Solow, "Capital-Labor Substitution and Economic Efficiency," *Review of Economics and Statistics,* XLIII (1961), and J W. Kendrick and R. Sato, "Factor Prices Productivity and Growth," *American Economic Review,* LIII (1963).

15. See Sato, *op. cit.,* p. 900.

16. R. Sato has proven that the stability of the system can only be achieved, with Hicks neutral technical progress, if the elasticity of substitution approaches unity. A constant $a = a_2$ implies a unitary elasticity of substitution.

17. See B. F. Massell, "A Disaggregated View of Technical Change," *Journal of Political Economy,* LXIX (December, 1961).

18. An analysis of the relation between migration and income can be found in H. S. Perloff, E. S. Dunn, Jr., Eric E. Lampard, and Richard F. Muth, *Regions, Resources, and Economic Growth* (Resources for the Future, 1960), Ch. 33.

19. Assume that "a" is roughly similar among the states.

20. Richard A. Easterlin, "Regional Growth of Income: Long-Term Tendencies," in Simon Kuznets, Ann Ratner Miller, and Richard A. Easterlin, *Population Redistribution and Economic Growth, United States, 1870–1950,* II, Analyses of Economic Change (Philadelphia: The American Philosophical Society, 1960).

21. Perloff, Dunn, Lampard, and Muth, *op. cit.,* p. 493.

22. *Ibid.* This is based on 1950 data.

23. "The Estimation of Produced Income by State and Region," *Conference on Research in Income and Wealth* (April, 1961).

24. Perloff, Dunn, Lampard, and Muth, *op. cit.,* p. 495.

25. Ann Ratner Miller, "Labor Force Trends and Differentials," in Kuznets, *et al., op. cit.,* pp. 40, 46.

26. Easterlin, *op. cit.,* Table A4. 3.

27. These states were Connecticut, Idaho, Wyoming, Washington, Oregon, California, and Wisconsin.

28. There were Maine, Vermont, and Nevada.

29. This is the form in which Easterlin presents the data.

30. Easterlin, *op. cit.;* Perloff, Dunn, Lampard, and Muth, *op. cit.,* Part V.

31. *Op. cit.,* especially p. 146.

32. Perloff, *et al., op. cit.,* p. 594 ff.

33. G. H. Borts and J. L. Stein, "Investment Return as a Measure of Comparative Regional Economic Advantage," in W. Hochwald (ed.), *Design of Regional Accounts* (Resources for the Future, 1961) pp. 71–73.

Economic Development and Comparative Advantage

Penelope Hartland

THE resource allocation that results from development planning is frequently evaluated on the basis of the principle of comparative advantage. Resort to comparative advantage is especially common in discussions of appropriate governmental policy toward economic development in national and international groups.[1] These references to comparative advantage continue both despite and because of an analytical discussion in the literature on the subject of investment criteria appropriate to less developed economies.[2]

While this discussion has contributed much to our understanding of the intricacies and interdependencies of growth theories, economists are still very limited in their understanding of the process of economic growth and the nature of its motivating forces, and therefore in their ability to offer advice to policy-makers. It is the burden of this paper that these discussions of investment criteria have given insufficient weight to the influence of development itself on the structure of demand,[3] and therefore have encouraged undue reliance on comparative advantage as an investment criterion in cases of development policy.

THE COMPARATIVE ADVANTAGE MODEL

In its most renowned formulation, the principle of comparative advantage was expounded by David Ricardo (*Principles of Political Economy and Taxation,* Chapter VII) in terms of two economies (England and Portugal) and two industries (wine and woolen cloth). It has been restated many times since, and refined somewhat (especially by J. S. Mill and B. Ohlin), but remains essentially the model expounded by Ricardo. A popular textbook[4] recasts the illustration in terms of America and Europe, each capable of producing food and clothing. The conclusions are stated in four points (p. 640):

247

1. If nature endows two regions or countries unequally with factors of production, the *relative* costs of transforming one commodity into another domestically will probably be different for the two areas.

2. Under free trade, goods will exchange for each other at a price ratio somewhere *intermediate* between the domestic cost ratios of the two countries.

3. Each country will specialize in the commodity in which it has a comparative advantage, exporting its surplus of that product for imports from abroad.

4. Each country is made better off by trade and specialization: if America can get, say, 6 units of clothing for each 10 units of food traded, she is certainly better off than when she domestically transforms 10 units of food into only 3 units of clothing; Europe does better when she trades 6 units of clothing for 10 units of food than when she must domestically transform 8 of clothing into 10 of food. The same would be true if we had picked any other trading ratio than 10:6—just so long as it lies between the limits 10:3 and 10:8.

It is important to make explicit certain of the stability assumptions implicit in the model of comparative advantage. The countries must be assumed to be of equal technological level—to be possessed of the same state of the arts. Either country in the example quoted above is assumed capable of applying the most advanced technology in its production of either food or clothing. The techniques actually applied will be determined, according to the model, by relative factor supplies within the two countries, but the full range of possibilities which the state of knowledge currently offers is known and available to both countries. The difference in relative costs within the two countries reflects only relative factor supplies (supplies of factors of production *in relation to the demand for them*) within each country, not a difference in the state of the arts.

The comparative advantage model also assumes that tastes and incomes—and thus demand schedules—remain constant within each country. The inclusion of the demand-determining factors in the *ceteris paribus* assumption is necessary in order that relative factor supplies be made determinate. The comparative advantage model acknowledges, of course, that changes in taste and therefore in demand can cause a shift in the locus of a country's comparative advantage pattern. The model assumes, however, that the process of specialization and exchange by itself will not affect the structure of demand—that demand is determined outside of this system. It therefore assumes that tastes and incomes, most importantly income distribution, will not be affected by the process of specialization.

If it were admitted that the process of specialization and trade affected a large segment of the economy, then the distribution of income would be influenced by specialization as would relative factor supplies. The shift in relative factor supplies would imply a new pattern of comparative advantage, unless the shift in final demand were to counterbalance the effect of the shift in the demand for the factors wrought by the process of specialization. Such counterbalancing is highly unlikely; the shift in final demand is a function of consumer preferences as well as of income distribution. The parametric characteristics of demand within this conceptual scheme are therefore the result of an essential simplifying assumption. If the assumption of the constancy of demand were to be relaxed, the determinants of demand would have to be defined in a degree of detail which the present state of the art does not permit. The choice is therefore either an arbitrary, probably unrealistic, definition of the determinants of the detailed structure of demand or the assumption that the direction of total demand for various specific commodities and services remains unchanged. The latter course, which is probably most frequently followed, is not necessarily any closer to reality than the former. In order, then, to give the problem a realistic as well as a unique solution, it is necessary to confine foreign trade to a small segment of the economy, and to assume that specialization and trade are so small in relation to total output and input that the process of specialization by itself will not influence the income distribution.

Demand remains the *bête noire* of dynamic as well as static systems. This is true whether "dynamic system" means a formal model of rigorous abstract analysis, or a less rigorous attempt to analyze an actual experience in development. In formal models the definition of demand used is sometimes chosen for convenience in analytic manipulation,[5] and sometimes is simply assumed among the "given."[6] While such assumptions are perfectly proper when the main interest of the author lies in exploring the implications of some other part of the system, the fact that they are little related to reality limits the applicability of comparative advantage to specific cases of economic development. This is not at all to deny that growth theories and theories of international integration are reconcilable or mutually consistent. The point being emphasized is that the structure of demand will be affected by growth in a way that is not at present forecastable and therefore cannot be treated as "given" in actual planning practice. To say that optimum resource allocation policy should allow for unforeseen changes in supply and demand conditions even at the cost of some loss of short-term efficiency[7] goes a long way toward questioning the usefulness of comparative advantage as a guiding principle in actual cases of development planning.

While it can probably be safely assumed that in the short and medium term the extremes of absolute advantage will be unaffected by the changes in relative factor supply induced by development, the margin of comparative advantage can be quite narrow and subject to the influence of much smaller shifts in relative factor supplies. And even in the relatively short run, a five- or ten-year period of rapid economic development can bring massive shifts in the structure of production and distribution of income within the country.[8]

In the long run, not only the structure of demand for goods, but time-preferences are less likely to remain unchanged. Two generations may make quite different choices between savings and consumption. The resource allocation which would yield optimum results, given the preference systems of today's generation, will not necessarily be consistent with the preference systems of future generations. We have not yet found a way to make these interpersonal comparisons meaningful.

The Process of Economic Development

The tremendous differences in per capita income levels which exist today as between the developed, advanced countries and the less developed countries can be described—although by no means explained —in terms of differences in levels of technology, differences in the state of the arts in the two groups of countries. Indeed, when we speak of "advanced" countries, the reference is to the state of the arts including the techniques of production known and in use. The less developed countries lag in technology as well as income. For these countries the process of development is a process of "catching up" technologically. By shifting from traditional ways of satisfying the basic need for food, clothing, and shelter to modern techniques, both the income- and the time-hiatus can be bridged. The shift involves not only new techniques for producing goods already in production, but modern techniques for producing imported goods which have never been produced in this country before. Because the underdeveloped countries have slipped so far behind, the process of catching up, of "developing," will be accompanied by truly revolutionary changes in all aspects of life.

The problem of resource allocation for the developing country is one of answering the question, "In what industries shall we learn and apply modern production techniques?" To this question the principle of comparative advantage can offer solutions which are likely to be only transitory, because the very process of modernizing implies a change in the state of the arts, a revision of production functions, preference systems, and relative factor scarcities in this economy.

As a country learns that there are other ways of producing the goods which it produces—as, for example, the production of textiles is moved from the household or craft shop to modern, highspeed factories—a number of changes will occur. The new technique of production will mean new factor proportions and larger absolute quantities of input and output. The shift to modern techniques will be accompanied by an enlargement of the market area served by one producing unit. The larger volume of output will require larger quantities of inputs, but probably not larger in proportion to the increase in output.

The original shift from traditional to modern techniques of production is likely to imply a more rapid increase in inputs of capital than in inputs of labor or output of the product. Modern techniques are "capitalistic"; while there may be a choice among the more modern techniques available in certain industries, with some methods being more capital-intensive and some more labor-intensive, the shift away from the traditional technology will in most cases involve a larger expansion of the capital stock, both per unit of labor and per unit of output—average and incremental—than was previously the case.[9]

The process of modernization, which is the essence of economic development, will therefore mean an increase in the relative scarcity of capital[10] because of technological requirements, but also for additional reasons. Because modernization is likely to involve an expansion of the market area served by the producing unit, inventory requirements will be enlarged as well as technological requirements. The greater relative scarcity of capital is likely to cause a shift in relative prices, with capital becoming more expensive relative to labor and land. Thus, from the viewpoint of the firm or the industries shifting to the modern sector, capital requirements increase more rapidly than labor requirements or output both for real reasons—those to do with technology and inventory —and for price reasons too. This implies, of course, an immediate decline in the marginal productivity of capital in the modern as opposed to the traditional techniques. For modernization (i.e., economic development) to occur despite the decline in the productivity of capital that would accompany the process at its outset, expectations about the future returns to capital in the modern variant of the industry must have been increased to the point where the divergence between the productivity of capital today and its anticipated productivity in the future is equal to the cost of attracting additional capital.

The developing country can also bring into the modern sector of its economy industries which have not previously existed within the country, but whose product is being imported. Such industries are likely to be characterized by capital-intensive techniques of production and a relatively low elasticity of substitution between labor and capital. The industries already in existence, by contrast, are more likely to be characterized by production functions in which, at least over some range of output, the elasticity of substitution between labor and capital is relatively high. In both cases the capital-output ratios of the modernized variant of the industry would initially be high and the marginal productivity of capital low. In both cases expectations about the future return to capital would have to be considerably higher than its current marginal productivity for capital to be directed into these industries.

As the modern sector of the economy gains experience with its new form of operation and as existing technology is adapted to the specific requirements of the country, it is likely that the capital required for an expansion of output will decline. The adaptations of modern technology to its present uses are likely to be labor-using and capital-saving, and the fact of experience is likely to make both labor and capital more productive.[11]

Over the long run, as modernized and import-replacing industries gain maturity, capital is likely to become less scarce relative to labor.[12] The supply of capital is likely to accumulate as the income of the country grows while incremental capital-output ratios in the modernized sector are likely to decline. Only where the rate of growth of the labor force is equal to or greater than the rate of growth of the capital stock would the relative factor scarcities not shift in this direction. Such seems to be the case in the stagnant or slowly growing underdeveloped economies. In these cases the failure of capital to become less scarce and therefore cheaper relative to labor impedes the further modernization of the economy, for a decline in the relative price of capital will make profitable the modernization of those industries in which the marginal efficiency of capital remains relatively low. The marginal efficiency of capital in most uses will probably be higher if the original spark which motivated modernization and growth (and, through growth, the fact of development planning) was the result of spontaneous combustion. In contrast, the marginal efficiency of capital in all uses is likely to be lower if development planning is originally undertaken in the hope of igniting a chain of modernization and growth. The problem in this case is to raise the marginal efficiency of capital and/or to increase the supply of capital sufficiently to cause the process to become self-generating.

Thus, in an underdeveloped country which achieves sustained growth and shifts, industry by industry, from traditional to modern techniques of production while at the same time initiating the production of goods to replace imports, the relative scarcities of labor and capital will be affected, with capital at first becoming significantly more scarce, but then decreasing in relative scarcity. If the shifting of relative scarcity ceases, the impetus to further modernization—i.e., sustained growth—will tend to evaporate.

The Problem of Investment Criteria

The shifting of relative scarcities, of course, implies shifting relative prices and therefore shifting factor and personal incomes. Where growth is sustained, a large segment of the economy is likely to be concerned and the distribution of income affected. *Ex ante,* therefore, the direction of the comparative advantage of a developing country indicated by existing factor scarcities may be quite different from that implied by the revisions in production functions and preference systems that will probably be wrought by development. Even *ex post* it will be impossible to say that a country has misallocated its resources (except in cases of flagrant violation of absolute advantage) because the distribution of income and preference systems that would have resulted from an alternative path of development cannot be compared with the system of relative scarcities in existence. This is not to deny that a country could be more efficient in producing what it is producing. The point to be stressed is that comparative advantage is in large part what a country makes it; there is no basis for judging *a priori* whether or not a country would be at a relative disadvantage in world trade ten or twenty years hence if it now commences the production of commodity X.[13]

The pattern of resource allocation of the Soviet Union since the 1930's is a case in point. Before World War II, if the average well-trained economist had attempted to determine the direction in which the comparative advantage of the U.S.S.R. lay, the chances are very *small* that he would have cited machine tools in his list of probably-efficient Soviet industries. And yet, according to the evidence available today, the U.S.S.R. is more efficient in the production of metalworking machinery than in most other fields of output.

Assuming a fixed relation between prices and costs in the U.S.S.R. and the U.S., then the Soviet Union could be said to be relatively efficient in the production of those commodities for which the ratios of ruble to dollar prices are lowest; it would be least efficient in the production of those goods for which ruble-dollar ratios are highest. In 1955, when the official exchange rate claimed, in essence, that the purchasing power of four rubles was the equivalent of the purchasing power of one dollar, ruble-dollar price ratios for metal-working machinery were 3.3:1 (with a median of 2.5:1). Between 1950 and 1955, moreover, the ruble-dollar ratios for producers' durables had been cut in half.[14] While the 1955 ratios for consumer services were low (roughly 3:1 using Soviet weights, over 5:1 using U.S. weights), other consumer goods ratios were considerably higher, ranging between 12 and 18:1 depending on the weights used.[15] The data obviously leave much to be desired; the differences, however, are extreme enough to suggest that today the U.S.S.R., as a result of four decades of emphasis on machine-building in its resource allocation, has achieved a comparative advantage in the production of machine tools.

What guidelines then can be offered in the problem of resource allocation during rapid economic growth? The question can be reformulated thus: How should a country about to embark on a development plan allocate its resources between the two classes of modern industry —that already in existence but using traditional techniques, and that not in existence and probably requiring large doses of scarce capital? Given the country's time preference, the productivity of the country's resources from the viewpoint of today's generation would probably be maximized by directing a large segment of new investment into non-existent import-replacing industries, at least in the short run. The opportunity cost of allocating resources to the production of goods already being produced domestically in many cases is likely to be higher than its opportunity cost in totally new industries. Capital in the traditional industries is fixed and illiquid. It may be obsolete according to the relative scarcities prevailing in developed countries, but it can continue to be productive given the relative scarcities of the developing country. And in the short run the marginal productivity of capital in the modern sector of these industries would be lower than its productivity in the traditional sector, as pointed out above.

In addition, the marginal efficiency of capital in the new import-replacing industries will probably be higher than its marginal efficiency in the modernized sector of the traditional industries. Because they are associated with the more advanced stage of development toward which this economy is moving, it seems likely that the demand for their product will be highly responsive to growing income and more so than the demand for the product of traditional industries. The stream of future earnings to be expected from investment in these industries is likely to be relatively large.

This, however, is only an amendment to the obvious: A country about to embark on a comprehensive development plan should attempt to economize on the most scarce factors of production, and to maximize its productivity according to the structure of demand of today's generation. Investment should flow into those industries where the opportunity costs are least. Today's preferences and scarcities may be revolutionized by today's investment decisions; planning for the succeeding time-period will have to cope with a new set of scarcities.

Such a planning process developed as a series of quantum jumps appears very makeshift. That this is so follows from the fundamental inconsistency between planning and freedom of choice involved in consumer sovereignty. Any attempt to define an index of social welfare or the social marginal product of an investment in terms which ignore individual preferences and income distribution implicitly assumes an authoritarian planning body responsible for all economic decisions including those involved in personal consumption. The planning of economic development in a free society can thus only attempt to maximize a stream of income over the short-run period during which scarcities will hopefully not change much. Then, on the basis of the new relative scarcities in the next time period, planning goals can be adjusted to the revised consumer preferences. The development path that results may not be an optimum from the viewpoint of any one generation, but it will allow each succeeding generation's preferences to be felt.

Summary and Conclusions

The process of economic development by its nature changes the structure of the country's economy, changes relative supplies of its factors of production, changes its income level and distribution, and very probably is accompanied by fundamental shifts in consumer preferences among goods and between income and leisure. It is likely also to be accompanied by more or less fundamental shifts in the state of the arts. Because it is a dynamic process, economic development causes or is accompanied by changes in all of the variables which are treated as parameters in the concept of comparative advantage. In fact the goal of rapid economic development can be described as a more or less conscious effort to transform the "comparative advantage" of the underdeveloped economy from one set of industrial specialties to another, dynamic set which will change through time in a way which can be planned, but not otherwise predicted.

Notes

1. Examples are legion: e.g., Report by Secretary General of the United Nations Conference on Trade and Development, 12 February 1964 (Prebisch Report), p. 93; Annual Report of the Council of Economic Advisers, January, 1964, p. 155.

2. A. E. Kahn, "Investment Criteria in Development Programs," *Quarterly Journal of Economics,* LXV (February, 1951); H. B. Chenery, "Application of Investment Criteria," *Quarterly Journal of Economics,* LXVII (February, 1953); W. Galenson and H. Liebenstein, "Investment Criteria, Productivity and Economic Development," *Quarterly Journal of Economics,* LXIX (August, 1955); O. Eckstein, "Investment Criteria for Economic Development and the Theory of Intertemporal Welfare Economies," *Quarterly Journal of Economics,* LXXI (February, 1957); H. B. Chenery, "Comparative Advantage and Development Policy," *American Economic Review,* LI (March, 1961); papers by W. Malenbaum, W. A. Chudson, W. Baer, and I. Kerstenetsky, and discussion by A. O. Hirschman, W. F. Stolper, and R. Vernon in Papers and Proceedings of 67th Annual Meeting of American Economic Association, *American Economic Review,* (May, 1964), pp. 390–436.

3. Cf. R. W. Jones, "Factor Proportions and the Heckscher-Ohlin Theorem," *Review of Economic Studies,* XXIV (1) No. 63 (1956–1957). And H. B. Chenery, "Patterns of Industrial Growth," *American Economic Review,* L (September, 1960).

4. P. A. Samuelson, *Economics: An Introductory Analysis* (3rd ed.; New York: McGraw-Hill, 1955), pp. 633–651.

5. E.g. Md. U Rahman, "Regional Allocation of Investment," *Quarterly Journal of Economics,* LXXVII (February, 1963), where the assumption is a linear and homogeneous consumption function. One of the most imaginative attempts to date to trace the influence of both demand and supply on the growth of individual industrial sectors is contained in Chenery, *op. cit.* (1960), where the assumption that demand is determined by per capita income implies that tastes and preferences everywhere at the same level of income are the same. While this assumption is not too far from reality when the analysis is confined to fifteen broad commodity categories, it does not provide much help in explaining why a particular country imports some forms of, say, machinery but exports others.

6. Chenery, *op. cit.* (1961), pp. 32, 35.

7. Chenery, *op. cit.* (1961), p. 25.

8. Historical examples include Canada (1900–1913), Argentina (1880–1892), Australia (1875–1888), U.S. (1830–1839); in each case massive inflows of foreign capital and labor resulted in the expansion of new industries for export. P. Hartland, "Private Enterprise and International Capital," *Canadian Journal of Economics and Political Science,* (Febuary, 1953); R. Nurkse, "International Investment Today in the Light of Nineteenth-Century Experience," *Economic Journal* (December, 1954). A current international comparison of size distributions of income is found in S. Kuznets, "Quantitative Aspects of the Economic Growth of Nations: VIII. Distribution of Income by Size," *Economic Development and Cultural Change,* Vol. XI, No. 2, Pt. II (January, 1963).

9. Data relating to the pre-modernization phase of the economy are scarce; suggestive, however, are the cases of China, Japan, and India. G. Ranis, "Factor Proportions in Japanese Development." *American Economic Review,* XLVII (September, 1957), p. 601; W. Malenbaum, "India and China: Contrasts in Development," *American Economic Review,* XLIX (June, 1959), p. 298.

10. The relative scarcity of capital in the underdeveloped countries has probably been considerably over-emphasized in comparison with the abundance of "labor." The relevant kind of labor is industrial labor. The relative availability of reliable, disciplined factory labor is not likely to be all that much greater than capital. Cf. A. Gerschenkron, "Economic Backwardness in Historical Perspective," in *Progress of Underdeveloped Areas,* B. F. Hoselitz, ed. (Chicago: University of Chicago Press, 1952).

11. For examples of such adaptations historically, see G. Ranis, *op. cit.,* or D. Granick, "Economic Development and Productivity Analysis: the Case of Soviet Metal-Working," *Quarterly Journal of Economics,* LXXI (May, 1957), pp. 205–233.

12. Cf. Malenbaum, *op. cit.,* (1964), p. 393.

13. Cf. R. G. Lipsey and R. K. Lancaster, "General Theory of Second Best," *Review of Economic Studies,* XXIV (1), No. 63 (1956–1957).

14. Becker, A. S., *Prices of Producers' Durables in US and USSR in 1955,* RM 2432, (Santa Monica: The RAND Corporation, Aug. 15, 1959), *passim.*

15. *Comparison of Consumption in USSR and US,* U.S. Central Intelligence Agency, ER 64–1 (January, 1964), *passim.*

BIBLIOGRAPHY OF THE WRITINGS
OF PHILIP TAFT

BOOKS

Organized Labor in American History. New York: Harper and Row, 1964.

American Federation of Labor from the Death of Gompers to the Merger. New York: Harper & Brothers, 1959.

American Federation of Labor in the Time of Gompers. New York: Harper & Brothers, 1957.

The Structure and Government of Labor Unions. Cambridge: Harvard University Press, 1954.

Movements for Economic Reform. New York: Rinehart and Co., Inc., 1950.

How Collective Bargaining Works (co-author). New York: The Twentieth Century Fund, 1942.

An Introduction to War Economics (co-author). Chicago: Richard D. Irwin, 1942.

Economics and Problems of Labor. Harrisburg: Stackpole and Heck, Inc., 1942. (Revised ed. 1954.)

History of Labor in the United States, 1896–1932, with Selig Perlman. New York: The Macmillan Co., 1935.

SELECTED ARTICLES

"Stretching the Line on Wages," *Challenge* (May, 1964).

"Differences in the Executive Council of the American Federation of Labor," *Labor History* (Winter, 1964).

"Is There A Crisis in the Labor Movement? No," *The Annals of the American Academy of Political and Social Science* (November, 1963).

"On the Origins of Business Unionism," *Industrial and Labor Relations Review* (October, 1963).

"Interplant Transfers in the Automobile Industry," *Monthly Labor Review* (March, 1963).

"A Backward and Forward Look at the Labor Movement," *Industrial Relations Center, University of Hawaii* (August, 1962).

"Labor History and the Labor Issues of Today," *Proceedings of the American Philosophical Society* (August, 1962).

"The Federal Trials of the IWW," *Labor History* (Winter, 1962).

"Erosion of an Ideal," *Challenge* (July, 1961).

"The Impact of Landrum-Griffin on Union Government," *The Annals of the American Academy of Political and Social Science* (January, 1961).

"The Responses of the Bakers, Longshoremen and Teamsters to Public Exposure," *Quarterly Journal of Economics* (August, 1960).

"The IWW in the Grain Belt," *Labor History* (Winter, 1960).

"Internal Affairs of Unions and the Taft-Hartley Act," *Industrial and Labor Relations Review* (April, 1958).

"Independent Unions and the Merger," *Industrial and Labor Relations Review* (April, 1956).

"The March of the American Labour Movement," *Free Labour World* (November, 1955).

"Ideologies and Industrial Conflict," *Industrial Conflict* (1954).

"Theories of the Labor Movement," *Interpreting the Labor Movement* (December, 1952).

"Germany," *Comparative Labor Movements* (1952).

"Internal Characteristics of American Unionism," *The Annals of the American Academy of Political and Social Science* (March, 1951).

"A Rereading of Selig Perlman's A Theory of the Labor Movement," *Industrial and Labor Relations Review* (October, 1950).

"The Unlicensed Seafaring Unions," *Industrial and Labor Relations Review* (January, 1950).

"Labor and the Nation," *Patterns for Modern Living* (1949).

"The Association of Catholic Trade Unionists," *Industrial and Labor Relations Review* (January, 1949).

"Status of Members in Unions During Appeal from a Penalty Imposed by the Local Union," *Quarterly Journal of Economics* (August, 1948).

"Attempts to 'Radicalize' the Labor Movement," *Industrial and Labor Relations Review* (July, 1948).

"The Constitutional Power of the Chief Officer in American Labor Unions," *Quarterly Journal of Economics* (May, 1948).

"European Trade Unionism," *European Ideologies* (1946).

"Understanding Union Administration," *Harvard Business Review* (May, 1946).

"Jurisdictional Disputes," *The Annals of the American Academy of Political and Social Science* (November, 1946).

"Democracy in Trade Unions," *American Economic Review* (May, 1946).

"Dues and Initiation Fees in Labor Unions," *Quarterly Journal of Economics* (February, 1946).

"Judicial Procedure in Labor Unions," *Quarterly Journal of Economics* (May, 1945).

"Opposition to Union Officers in Elections," *Quarterly Journal of Economics* (February, 1944).

"The Problem of Labor Relations in the Maritime Industry," *The American Seaman* (February, 1940).

"Strife in the Maritime Industry," *Political Science Quarterly* (June, 1939).

"New Unionism in the United States," *American Economic Review* (June, 1939).

"Labor's Changing Political Line," *Journal of Political Economy* (October, 1937).

"Problem of Structure in American Labor," *American Economic Review* (March, 1937).